D1142201

CENTRE OF EXCELLENCE

The Jim Renwick Story

Centre of Excellence

The Jim Renwick Story

By David Barnes
with Jim Renwick

BIRLINN

This edition first published in Great Britain in 2006 by

Birlinn Ltd
West Newington House
10 Newington Road
Edinburgh
EH9 1QS
www.birlinn.co.uk

ISBN 10: 1 84158 421 5
EAN: 978-1-84158-421-8

British Library Cataloguing-in-Publication Data
A catalogue record for this book is available on request from the British Library

Typeset by HewerText UK, Edinburgh

Printed and bound by Cromwell Press, Trowbridge, Wiltshire

Contents

Acknowledgements

I've had a lot of help and support during the creation of this book and I am grateful for it all.

Thanks to all those people who made the time to speak to me about Jim, including Robin Charters, Jeff Connor, Jonathon Else, Terence Froud, Derrick Grant, Brian Hegarty, Andy Irvine, Roy Laidlaw, Ian Landels, Norman Mair, Kenny McCartney, Bill McLaren, Ian McLean, Syd Millar, Gary Murdie, Ronnie Murphy, Peter Peacock, Addie Renwick, Marion Renwick, Scott Renwick, John Rutherford, Fergus Slattery, Tony Stanger, Norman Suddon, Colin Telfer, Alan Tomes and Harry Whitaker. Not all are directly quoted in the book, but their insight and guidance was still invaluable. Thanks also anyone else I may have inadvertently forgotten to mention.

Thanks to Mike O'Reilly at the SRU Library for allowing me to kidnap a substantial portion of his books. On the subject of books, I was helped greatly by 'Green Machine – 125 Years of Hawick Rugby' by Ken Bogle.

Thanks to Stan for setting this up, my editor Donald Reid for sorting it out, and Birlinn for letting it happen.

Thanks to Jane, Neil, Stuart and Alex, who allowed me to take over their living room on countless occasions so that Jim and I could chat about rugby.

Thanks to my father, Barney, for all his advice and words of wisdom – most of it was very helpful.

And special thanks to Johanne, for putting up with me when it all seemed like getting too much.

David Barnes
Glasgow, September 2006

Author's Note

The reason why there has not been a Jim Renwick biography before now is that this is the first time he has been persuaded that it would be a good idea.

When I first suggested to Jim that somebody should write his biography – and that I should be that person – we were exiting The Hut at St Leonards on the Thursday of Hawick Common Riding. It was nine o'clock in the morning.

Initially he dismissed the idea, stating in his broad Hawick accent that: "Naeb'dy wid be interestit."

I was unperturbed, partly because I knew that for the previous three hours he had sat with 400 fellow Hawick men, drinking rum and milk, toasting Cornet Greg McLeod (the principal figure in that year's festival) and singing songs about the town which has played a central role in creating the man he is today. He was well lubricated and feeling nostalgic. That made him vulnerable – so I persisted, and eventually he relented.

This episode is typical of the way that Jim leads his life. With everything he does he is at first reluctant, often for no other reason than the sheer bloody mindedness of it, but once he is committed to something he will pursue that end with singular determination and enthusiasm. True to form, this is the way he has approached this project. He has, at all times, been readily available to me, even offering to drive from Hawick to Edinburgh for our interviews, seemingly oblivious to the fact that he is the star of the show. I thank him for that.

The only proviso Jim made when he agreed to work with me on this book was that it wasn't to be a ghosted autobiography. "That's no ma style, I dinnae want to sound bumptious," he explained. For that reason the book has been written in close association with Jim, but also draws heavily on the testimonies of various individuals who have crossed paths with him over the years. I also made extensive use of newspaper cuttings which hopefully give an accurate representation of how the most important moments in Jim's rugby career were perceived at the point when they happened.

Anyone who has ever spoken to Jim Renwick will be aware of his distinctive Hawick brogue. I have to confess that it's almost impossible to replicate his accent effectively in print, so I haven't tried. I trust not too much of Jim's character has been lost in translation.

DB

The Moat

Ocht worth tippence gaun on i' the toon
Aye comes there, sune or later –
Cornets and Callants and mairchin bairns –
It's a local law of natur'!
Golfers and sledgers and dydie-eggs,
Or auld folk seekin a sate
O'a simmers nicht, the hill's aye there
And his welcome never blate

from 'The Vertish' by David Hill

James Menzies Renwick was born and bred in Hawick Loan, which stretches steeply uphill from Drumlanrig School to Thorterdykes Roadhouse, and is the epicentre of the West End – a garrulous pocket of fun, song and serious native pride for young men growing up in that part of the town.

Hawick gravitates up the Loan, through the West End, to the Vertish – the hill that dominates the West End, with its panoramic views over Hawick, and down the Teviot valley to the sweeping vista of Ruberslaw, the Minto Hills and the distant Eildons. It's perhaps the finest view in the Borders.

The vista, along with the annual Vertish Hill Sports for the local primary schools, the Common Riding, the golf course, and some fine walking, contrives to pull the people of Hawick towards the West End. A day out of Hawick might not necessarily be a day wasted but the *guitter bluids,* as the dyed-in-the-wool West Enders are known, need a pretty good reason to take their socialising away from the Spartan conviviality of bars such as the High Level, Jock Reid's or the Stags. "The West End is the best end," say the natives. Not everyone in Hawick agrees, but the vast majority understand and respect the sentiment.

Moat Park lies half way up the Loan. The Moat itself is a man-made earthen mound, 60 feet high and 60 feet wide. Its origins are lost in antiquity. There is romantic talk about druids and King Arthur, but in all probability it is the impressive remains of a motte and bailey castle built by the Anglo-Norman Lovell family in the twelfth century.

And as far as Jim Renwick is concerned, the Moat is where his story begins.

To me it was a leisure centre before its time. We would race up and down or around and around the Moat hill, and we could climb every tree in the park. There were swings, and round the back there was a sand pit that we played in. There was plenty of room to play football. We used to have drop-goal competitions over the swings, and we used to play shooting-in at the bottom of the hill so that you didn't have to run and get the ball if it went by you. We even had a four-hole golf course set up that we had built ourselves.

I was brought up in one of the pre-fabs which used to back onto the Moat Park and as soon as I was old enough to climb over the dyke to get into the park I was playing in there all the time. At that time there just happened to be a lot of young boys living in the West End, and we were well organised – we'd have games against other parts of the town and every one of those matches was like a cup final.

We just played with the ball all the time and although we played a lot of different games it was always really about rugby – because that was what Hawick was about. There is no doubt that the Moat was where I picked up the basics of the game.

Some of the older boys like Chuck Muir and Keith Thomson, who were already getting rugby at the school, would show us things. So by the time we started playing at the school, in primary five, I maybe didn't know all the laws but I knew the fundamentals.

Kenny McCartney has been a close friend of Renwick's since their child-hood days in the late 1950s and early 60s. Between 1971 and 1980 he played 163 games for Hawick at wing, full back and occasionally stand-off. During that time he scored 130 tries for the club. He later became a top-grade referee and officiated in ten international matches. Having retired from the fire service in 2002, McCartney became actively involved in local politics and was elected Provost of Hawick in 2005.

As soon as your tea was finished you were over the Moat with a football or rugby ball. I suppose you played more football because it was easier to organise, but it was just whatever ball came out first really, and off you'd go and you'd play until it got dark.

All you had to do was bounce a ball and every door in the street would open and there would be kids running out to play. You made your own fun in those days, and you would never, ever have seen signs saying 'No Ball Games'. I think every sign like that should be ripped down – we should be encouraging kids to play ball games, not stopping them!

We used to run along the High Street on a Saturday morning when it was busy, side-stepping off both feet past all the old folk. I can mind that like it was yesterday. We used to think this was great.

We used to play outside all the time – every night of the week. We would be kicking a football or rugby ball, we would be playing tig, we would play what we used to call *beds* (which is basically hop-scotch), dodge-the-ball, cock-a-rossie and British bulldogs – you could write a book about the games we played in those days. We used to race round Longcroft Crescent, diving over the top of the hedges between the gardens – we called that the Grand National. There'd be six or seven of us going hell for leather.

I remember on Guy Fawkes night we used to build a huge bonfire in the Moat Park. We would go up to the Dick's Wood to cut down a tree for it – you'd get jailed for that now. We'd go for the biggest tree in the wood and there'd be ten of us walking down the road with this muckle tree on our shoulders.

Sometimes Renwick and his gang would spread their wings and venture away from the Moat and even out of the West End – especially in the summer when the better weather broadened their horizons. They might go to Wilton Park for a game of tennis or a swim in the Dunk – a deep pool in the nearby Teviot. Or to Buccleuch Park to play cricket, at the picturesque and characterful home of Hawick and Wilton Cricket Club, where Renwick's father and his Uncle Jock played for years. Often they would sneak onto the Vertish Hill golf course, and sharing an old golf bag and a handful of ancient clubs, they would play as many holes as they could before being spotted by the green-keeper and sent packing. Some days they would jump on their second-hand bikes and head for the hills, climbing Ruberslaw or Skelfhill or Cauldcleuch. These were great days and a pleasant break from the norm, but each night they would be glad to get back home to the West End and their old friend the Moat.

Renwick has seen a fair bit of the world on rugby tours and family holidays, but, apart from an enforced sabbatical in Galashiels soon after he was married, he has never had any inclination to move away from Hawick's West End and the Moat.

In 1980 Renwick was named in the British and Irish Lions Test team for the first of their four-match series against South Africa. The game was being played on the Saturday before Hawick Common Riding. Before the match, under the grandstand at Newlands Rugby Stadium in Cape Town, he sat quietly in the corner and opened some of the telegrams and letters he had received from well wishers back home. One in particular caught his eye. It was from two of his oldest friends, the brothers Bobby and Terence Froud. Its message was simple and to the point.

ALL THE BEST IT'S A LONG WAY FROM THE MOAT

Jim Senior and Teenie

Jim Renwick senior and his brother Jock joined the Salvation Army as teenagers in the early 1930s. The local corps was conveniently located opposite the family home on Allars Crescent in Hawick, but they had also noticed that Teenie Hogg and Maimie Cavers were members.

It was a great way of getting to know the young ladies, but it was not an undertaking they took lightly, and they remained committed members of the organisation throughout their lives.

In 1936 Jim married Teenie and together they had four children – Addie (born in 1936), Charlie (1940), Marion (1947) and Jim (12 February 1952). Jock and Maimie also married and had three children – Elliot, Francis and Katherine. Both families were brought up within the Salvation Army community.

JMR:
We had to go to the Salvation Army every Sunday and I enjoyed it. Some days you didn't want to go if your pals were out playing, but most of the time it was good fun. In the morning you went to Sunday school and in the afternoon there was a sort of meeting for kids – they got their message across but we also played games and you learned to play an instrument. At night there was a more serious meeting which wasn't so great for the kids, but it wasn't bad. All in all it was a pretty good way of life, and I think people generally had a good time there. They were serious about their religion but they enjoyed themselves too. There's no reason that you can't do both.

They had open air meetings, so every Sunday night they would stand in the Tower Knowe and have a service. And on Sunday mornings they would go out to somewhere in the town and have a service. They would pick a different street in Hawick each week, so one Sunday it would be Trinity Street, the next Sunday it would be Duke Street and the week after that it would be Dixon Street. Now that maybe didn't please some folk at nine o'clock on a Sunday morning, but the attitude was that if

[5]

folk won't come to the church then we'll take the church to the folk. At Christmas they would go round all the parts and up to the old folks' home singing carols.

And as well as the religious stuff you would have plenty to do during the week – sport and music and things like that. It was like a youth club and a lot of kids got into the Army after getting involved in that side of things.

I remember one of the officers we had was keen on the Scouts and he set up a troop at the Salvation Army. It was good. We had a trip down to London, which was a big thing in those days. We went and saw Buckingham Palace, the Tower of London and all those sorts of places.

My father used to run football games over the Miller's Knowes, and he was also the Young People's Bandmaster for a while. I played in the band – I played the cornet, other boys played the horn or the euphonium.

The Renwicks and a few other families kept the Salvation Army going for years but it's falling away a bit now which is a shame because it was a good way of life and it taught you what was right and what was wrong. It taught you what was fair in life. Having said that I think a lot of people still go to listen to the services and sing songs, but they don't actually join.

I kept on going until I was sixteen or seventeen, but when you get to that age it's time to start thinking about joining off your own bat. They have fairly strict laws which they call Articles of War, and you have to sign a pledge saying that you're not going to gamble and drink and things like that. And if you're honest with yourself . . . well . . . I knew I wasn't going to be able to stick to that, so that's when I backed out. I've been back along a few times. I don't want to go every night but I still think that what they do is pretty good.

I think my mother and father were disappointed when I dropped out, but I think they understood. My father was the strong one on it – he was there hell or high water – but he was a fair man and he let us do what we wanted to do. My brother Addie had done the same as me, but Charlie kept in, and Marion is a Salvation Army officer now.

As a committed member of the Salvation Army, Jim Renwick senior was a strict teetotaller. But that didn't stop him using his skills as a joiner to build a bar in the Hawick and Wilton Cricket Club pavilion. He had been asked to help out by his friends at the club, and although he was at first reluctant to get involved, he was soon talked around and ended up doing the whole job more or less single-handedly.

On another occasion it was decided to grow a hedge around the perimeter of the cricket oval, but on the day in which the shrubbery was to be planted only one other club member turned up. The pair spent several hours doing the job themselves.

"If he'd got paid for half the work he did he'd have been millionaire," says Renwick. "But that was just his style. He was some man."

Jim Senior spent most of his working life as a labourer and laterally a joiner for British Rail. When the Waverley line, which ran through the Borders linking Hawick to Edinburgh and Carlisle, closed in 1969, he took a job as a caretaker at Hawick police station. The final few years of his working life were spent as a gateman at the Braemar Mill on Victoria Road in Hawick – where Teenie had been a bar filler for years.

He was a keen sportsman and had been a handy wing forward for Hawick Linden before injury curtailed his rugby career in the mid 1940s. Addie recalls being taken by his mother to watch his father play at Wilton Lodge Park.

> I was three maybe four years old and I'll always remember it. We were five minutes late and I said to my Mum, 'I can't see him.'
>
> She said: 'That's because he's no there.'
>
> He'd been carted – he was in the cottage hospital. He'd done something to his leg and he never played again.

As Jim Senior came off the pitch he handed over his boots to Jock Edgar – a real West End character who now claims to have come on and kicked the winning conversion from the touchline, wearing footwear two sizes too small.

In those days a player injured playing sport could not expect any sort of sick pay or compensation if they were unable to work as a consequence, and with a young family to support Jim Senior could ill-afford to risk his income for the sake of rugby. So from then on he restricted his role in the game to that of spectator, and in the years that followed he, along with Teenie, would be their youngest son's most committed fans – travelling all over Scotland and beyond to watch him play.

Marion remembers going with her father to watch Jim play an international at Murrayfield.

> As we walked to the match we passed a group of supporters with a huge banner which had written on it the words: 'Jim'll fix it.' And you know, my Dad just stopped in his tracks and the tears just

drove down his face. My Dad was just so proud, he was terribly proud.

Injury might have forced Jim Senior to give up playing rugby, but the competitive spirit still burned strong. Along with his brother Jock, he was a long-serving stalwart of Hawick and Wilton Cricket Club.

Every summer a six-a-side cricket tournament is played at Buccleuch Park and for a number of years from the mid-fifties onwards the Renwick family entered a team selected from Jim Senior, his five brothers and various offspring. They managed to win the tournament one year and always put up a good show.

JMR:
During the summer I would be down at the cricket club every Saturday with my father. He'd be down early to mark the pitch, then in the afternoon he'd be playing while my mother was making the teas, and I'd just be running about the side, playing with a ball, trying to climb trees and just having a good time.

Then, when I was a wee bit older, I started playing myself. I used to bat right handed but bowl with my left. I got a few games for the first team but I was only fourteen maybe fifteen years old and the guys I was playing with were much older, so it wasn't much fun. The final straw was when I got knocked out. The boy I was batting with skelped the ball and I looked round to see where it had gone. It hit me right on the back of the head and ran for four. I was out cold and I had to take a couple of days off the school. I didn't play much cricket after that, although I still turned out for them a few times over the years, when they were short of players.

Jim Senior was also a member of Hawick and Wilton Bowling Club and was President in 1982, while Teenie was President of the women's section in 1972. Later on they were both made life members. In the mid-sixties Jim Senior entered a Renwick team consisting of himself and his three sons – Addie, Charlie and Jim – in the club's annual four-man bowling competition played on the Thursday of Hawick Common Riding, though his youngest son complained of being bored and the team was disbanded. Jock was President of the Scottish Bowling Association in 1999.

But the light which shone brightest for Jim Senior was that of the Salvation Army. It was the ethos of this organisation which informed his approach to life and guided the way he interacted with others.

JMR:

They made me captain of my class for the first year cricket competition that they had every summer. I didn't know didn't know anything about cricket, so I asked my father for some advice.

'What are you going to do about field placings?' he says.

'I dinnae ken,' I say.

'Well,' he says. 'You put somebody there, somebody there and somebody there. Now, how are you going to choose your bowlers?'

'I dinnae ken,' I say.

'Right, gie everybody in the team a bowl.'

So everybody got two overs and we got humped because some of the boys couldn't bowl at all. Afterwards he says: 'Now, go back to the players and explain what you want to do.'

So the next week I spoke to the boys that weren't so good and said: 'Is it alright if you don't bowl the night because if you do we aren't going win this game? Would you rather just field away and try and let the good bowlers bowl and then we can maybe win the game?'

He was right, as some of them said they hadn't wanted to bowl anyway because they had got cuffed all over the place the week before, and others said they still wanted to bowl and that they'd been practicing a bit. So that's the way it was, and we did alright in the end.

My father wasn't a ram it down your throat man, so that was his way of saying that you should give everybody a chance and then, once you've found out what's best for your team, you can explain what you want to do and everybody is happy. It's not all about winning – it's about everybody having a bit of fun and enjoying the game.

When you play a sport you should do everything in your power to win otherwise there's no point taking part, but the other side of that is that there is no point taking part if you haven't won it doing things right. When he was bowling he wasn't keen on firing because if you fire you ruin the end, so he was always drawing rather than driving his shots, that was his style. Looking back, I think that's what the Salvation Army gave us – it gave us that sort of fair-mindedness, rather than just me, me, me. It made us more team minded.

Don't get me wrong, he liked to win as well. He had that competitive edge, but when the final whistle went he'd just shake the boy's hand and that was it – there's nothing you can do about it then. I think I picked some of that up from him. I hope I did.

Alexandrina Renwick (née Hogg), universally known as Teenie, was a matriarchal figure of almost comic book proportions.

Addie Renwick:

Jim thinks that my father was the strong member of the family, but he wasn't. Our mother was the rock – nobody could take a lend of the Renwicks as long as she was around. She was the forceful one in the house and she was very protective of her family – she looked after us alright. She was my mother, but I wouldn't have liked to be on the wrong side of her because she could handle herself.

My mate Ronnie Murphy was the bath master at the old baths and he ran the steam as well, and he used to have a hell of a time with her. She would complain if folk got too much time in the tub or too much time with the dryer, but she would take as long as she wanted for herself. Ronnie was absolutely terrified of her, and there wasn't many folk that Ronnie Murphy was frightened of. When he used to see her coming he'd turn around and run away and hide – he didn't want anything to do with it. He christened her 'The Queen of the Steam'.

Ian Landels was a contemporary of Renwick's at Drumlanrig Primary School. He is now principal teacher of History at Hawick High School and one of the town's most prominent citizens as a result of his ceaseless dedication to all things Hawick.

Jim Knox, who lived up a close at 17 The Loan, was emigrating to New Zealand, and he had a strive – which is usually associated with a wedding but he had one for moving away. And I remember scrabbling round for the coins and all of a sudden I saw this shiny half crown sitting there, so I went for it. But there was Teenie Renwick and her foot came down on it – hard. She was keeping it for Jim – it was for her boy. She was a strong woman with a heart of gold.

JMR:

My mother used to embarrass us. She was pretty loud and she used to open her mouth before she thought about what she was going to say. She would just jump in and call a spade a spade. That's just the way she was.

When my son Neil was born there was another couple had had a bairn at the same time, so when my mother went in to visit she looked at both of babies and then said as loud as you like: 'Well, their one's nice, but he's no as nice as oors.'

I remember when I was a kid we were asked to look after the neighbours' budgie while they were on holiday and on the morning of the day that they were due back my mother decided to clean the cage out. So she put it in the big old-fashioned sink we had and started to run the hot water tap, but she must have forgotten to take the budgie out and then the doorbell rang so she went and answered it. The water level kept rising and the budgie had nowhere to escape from this piping hot water. She realised just in time and got it out, but all the feathers were out, and when the neighbours came to pick it up it was like a plucked turkey – sitting on its perch shivering with fright. How it survived, I'll never know.

Of course, my father once shot her in the head. I must have been seven or eight years old and my Dad came over the Moat to get me in for my tea. While he was there he found this ancient air rifle that some of the older kids must have been playing with. So he picked it up and came into the house like John Wayne. He points it at me and says: 'I'm going to shoot you,' and he fires it – and I just pretended I was dead. Then he pointed it at Charlie's wife Irene, and does the same again. Then he swings round, and my mother is sitting there watching the telly, and he says: 'Right, your getting it next.' But when he fires it this time . . . well . . . there must have been a slug left in it, because next thing there''s blood pouring down my mother's face. I remember Irene running up to the phone box at the end of the street and phoning the police.

'What's happened?'

'Jim Renwick has shot Teenie.'

So the ambulance came and took her away and when they were taking her out the house and putting her in the back of the wagon she kept saying 'Jim shot us'.

The police were there, and all the neighbours were out, and my father was in an awful state. He never lived that down.

'Remember the night you shot Mum?' we'd say to him.

'Aye, I should have aimed lower,' he'd reply.

My mother died in the summer of 1994. She was in the Borders General Hospital and my father was up in Edinburgh getting a bypass operation on his heart. Going in to tell him what had happened was the toughest thing I ever had to do. I think he knew when he saw me, but he was still a bit woozy from the operation and I had to sit and wait until he came round properly. That was tough, I was sitting there thinking about how I was going to handle it, and to be honest I didn't have a clue what I was going to say. She'd been in and out of hospital a lot and my father used to go over and sit with her the whole day. I think it hurt him that he wasn't there at the end.

It was a pretty bad time for the Renwicks. Six weeks earlier, on 24 April 1994, we had lost Charlie to cancer. He was ill for a while but we hadn't known how bad it was because he had kept it quiet. Charlie was a big influence on me when I was growing up. He took me to buy my first suit, taught me how to knot a tie and all that sort of thing. It was a tough one to take.

Jim Senior died in August 2003 at the age of 89.

The Golden Boy

Teenie's father, Charlie Hogg, who was universally known as 'The Mumper', had been a stalwart Hawick forward during his youth. Her brother Jock, who was deaf and dumb and with typical Hawick bluntness was universally known as 'Dummy', also played for Hawick and had trials for Scotland as a full back. Her nephew Graham Hogg, the son of her other brother George, was capped twice in 1978.

On the Renwick side of the family, both Jim Senior and his brother Jock were enthusiastic sportsmen, while both Addie and Charlie played rugby for Hawick.

From an early age it was clear that the youngest Renwick had inherited the family's sporting gene.

Addie Renwick:
He's just a natural at sport. Everything he's taken up he's been above average at without trying – he's just good at everything. Mind you, I say that but there is nothing Jim doesn't try at, he can't help himself. If he's playing any sort of game he has to win. From a young age, he had to be first, he had to be the best – he just loves to win.

There used to be an Italian chip shop down the road from our house in the Howgate that sold the best ice-cream in the Borders, and I remember in the summer, when my Mum and Dad were out and me and Charlie were keeping an eye on Jim, I'd say to him: 'Fancy an ice-cream?'

Jim would say: 'Aye.'

'Well away get one for us all then.'

'Nah, I'm no goin' all the way doon there by myself.'

So we used to say: 'The last time you went we timed you, and it took you five minutes. Charlie and I used to be able to do it in four-and-a-half minutes and that's the world record.'

'Alright,' he'd say. 'I'll away and get it.'

We'd no bother timing him, and when he came back we'd say: 'You

[13]

missed the world record by five seconds.' And we'd do it again the next night and he would fall for it again and again because he was that desperate to beat that world record. He was such a desperate boy to win, and he's still the same now. He's never been any fun if he isn't winning – you just can't have a friendly game with Jim.

I remember years later, when Jim was nearing the end of his rugby career, a group of us put in a team for the cricket sixes in the park. I played cricket a bit, Jim could play and Jim Gray, an old Hawick full back, was a good wicket keeper – he hadn't ever played cricket properly but he had a good eye for the ball. It was a shower of toffee-legs that played, it was a joke, but somehow we got to the final against a Hawick Select VI. When we entered this team it was just for a bit of fun with everybody getting a bat and everybody getting a bowl, and we hadn't bothered appointing a captain or anything like that. But when we got to the final Jim said: 'Right – I'm captain. Now the fun stops. We're no here for a laugh now boys, we're here to win.'
He had everybody keyed up, and we won it in the end. But I'll always remember Jim saying: 'Right – the mucking about stops now boys.'

Everybody was saying: 'What's going on here?'

And Jim just looked them straight in the eye and said: 'We're here to win.'

This was at the end of his rugby career. He'd already won 52 caps for Scotland, played for the British Lions in South Africa and was maybe the best player Hawick had ever produced. But that didn't matter. He wanted to win that tournament.

As far as the dynamics of the Renwick family were concerned there seems to be little doubt that the youngest of the children was the apple of their parents' eye.

Marion Wright (née Renwick):
We didn't have a lot but because he was the youngest and he was a bit of a moaner he got what he wanted a lot of the time. It was usually silly things like he would only eat beans and chips, the rest of us would be having something else but Jim would have to have beans and chips. And it had to be Heinz baked beans. If my Mum tried to fob him off with anything else he'd refuse to eat it.

As a child he whined all the time – it was just the sort of child he was. And he used to get excited about stuff and he'd get a little bit of a stutter and he wouldn't be able to get things out, but that disappeared when he went to school.

He was quite a nervous boy. He would be wary of things – he wouldn't just charge in. And he wasn't a child that smiled a lot – now he's quite happy-go-lucky, but he wasn't as a youngster. He was a nice looking baby and a nice looking boy, but he was dour. In photographs of him he's never smiling.

This shyness is something Renwick has managed to conquer over the years, and as both a player and coach he has tended never to be too far away from the fun and games during rugby tours or on team buses. However he would never seek the limelight or enjoy the attention if it was heaped disproportionately upon him. He is well known for his quick wit and playful character, but that has always been tempered by an essentially taciturn and self-effacing nature. Even now, as a widely sought-after speaker at rugby dinners, Renwick is prone to self-doubt and is racked with nerves before making his speech.

Marion Wright:
He's still easily embarrassed – if you said to him: 'You were a great rugby player,' he'd be awful embarrassed. Having said that, right from the very beginning he always seemed to steal the thunder. He didn't do it on purpose, but it often worked out that way. I remember I was having my seventh birthday party and it was a big thing to have a party – you didn't get one every year. Well, Jim made himself a pest the whole day and right at the end of the party, just as my school friends were leaving, he was bothering my mum by crawling about at her feet, so she turned to him and she said: 'For goodness sake Jim, will you get away.' And he got up and walked for the very first time. The most important thing that day wasn't the fact that I'd had a birthday party, it was that Jim had walked – I was so angry. When Addie came home from work it was: 'Jim walked today.' When Charlie came home: 'Jim walked today.' That's just the way Jim was always going to be – the centre of attention.

No matter what he was doing he was good at it. When he played tennis and cricket in the summer, or when he was swimming, or if he was doing athletics at the school, you could see there was that ability there, and I thoroughly believe to this day that it wouldn't have mattered what sport he had chosen he would have succeeded in it because he had that sort of natural talent.

When he played tennis, he played tennis well. Everybody else was just hitting the ball about but you could see that Jim had that natural aptitude and he was thinking about what he was trying to do. It was the same when he started to swim – he just had that natural capacity for it.

So I suppose if we had been looking for a sign of what was to come we might have seen it then, but of course he was just Jim – our little brother who spends all his day over the Moat – and we thought it was going to stay that way forever.

Looking back, I don't think he was all that keen on growing up, and I think that is still true today – you can see it in his sense of humour and his character. I remember one Common Riding when he was fifteen or maybe even sixteen years old but still in short trousers, and my Mum bought him a new pair of long trousers and a jacket but he refused to wear either. He stayed in and wouldn't go out because he wasn't allowed to wear short trousers, and I think that was sort of something he wanted to hold onto.

Then, when he did grow up, it all happened so quickly for him. He'd had quite an uneventful life until he started playing rugby and then everything just took off, but give him his due he took it all in his stride. He was a nice boy who became a nice man, and of all his achievements I think that is the thing about him that makes me most proud.

Terence

Terence and Jim for a long time were inseparable. In fact they still are. There's that boyishness about them. It's good that their friendship has lasted so long, but what a nightmare they can be.

Marion Wright (née Renwick)

If you need to get hold of Jim Renwick on a Sunday afternoon, and you know he is in the country, then there is only one place worth looking. At the top of Green Terrace is the High Level – an old-style, no-frills watering hole which is home to some of the West End's best-known worthies.

Turn left after you enter the building, through a stained glass panelled door and into the public bar. This is a wood-panelled room dominated by a half-crescent bar surrounded by regulars. The walls are adorned with pictures of local racehorses and Hawick rugby players. The furnishings are basic. The clientele eclectic yet parochial.

In the far corner at one of only two tables in the bar sits Jim Renwick, a pair of rimless spectacles perched precariously on the end of his nose. In front of him you will find a newspaper opened at the racing pages. Alongside him, shouting instructions, opinions and insults at the bar staff, other patrons and anyone else who comes within range, is the unmistakable figure of Terence Froud.

The pair have been friends since their earliest days when they played over the Moat together. When the pre-fabs in which the Renwicks lived were demolished in 1962, and the family moved across the road to number 32 The Loan, the pair became neighbours.

Terence Froud:
The Renwicks moved in up the stairs from us, and I suppose that's when Jim and I got really friendly. I was two years younger than Jim, my brother Bobby was a year older, and the three of us used to live our lives between the Moat and the back green.

When Bobby went to the High School he started going about more with the boys in his class, and me and Jim started getting friendly with Alan Reid (who lived further up The Loan at number 36 and used to get called Pei). Then when we got a wee bit older still, Pei started drifting away. He just had other things going on in his life, but Jim and I have stayed close.

We didn't go to school together because I was at St Margarets, the town's Catholic primary school, while he was at Drumlanrig, and by the time I got to the High School he was about finished, but we did everything else together. I used to go to the Salvation Army picnics and he used to come to the Catholic ones. We used to train together at the baths, play together over the Moat and then, when we got older, we used to go out drinking together.

I was his best man when he got married to Shelagh. It was about a month after he got his B cap in Oyannax in 1971 when he asked me if I'd do it. He just came downstairs to our flat one Sunday night, where I was lying on the couch, and he says: 'You want to go out for a pint?'

I didn't fancy it, so he says: 'Do you want to be my best man?' As blunt as that.

So I said: 'We better go for a pint.'

The only period of our lives when Jim and I haven't seen that much of each other was when he first moved to Gala, just after he got married. He would have been in the town three times a week to train and play for Hawick, but I was still playing for the YM at that point, and because he couldn't drive he was getting lifts off Barney [Ian Barnes] and Colin Telfer, who were based in Edinburgh and used to head straight back up the road after training. And with having a young family he wasn't really around that much. But then when he moved back to Hawick it was like he had never been away. We play golf together, we go drinking together, and we've been away on holiday together.

Cecil Froud – Terence and Bobby's father – had played for Hawick during the post-war years, and had captained the club during the 1947–48 season. Like Terence he was a forthright and entertaining character, but unlike his son he was rather small for a forward, even by the standards of the time.

Cecil won immortality in Hawick for his antics during the 1949 New Year's Day game against Heriots FP, which came to be known as 'Cecil's match'. The game had originally been cancelled due to the weather conditions, which meant Cecil was able to make an early start to his day of celebrating the New Year. However, a mix-up in communication meant that Heriots arrived at Mansfield ready to play and it was decided to go ahead with the match after all. Cecil had to be pulled out of the Wilton Bar in Dixon Street and chased down to Mansfield by his mother. As he ran onto the pitch from the old pavilion, at the top end of the ground where the club house now stands, Cecil was so busy exchanging seasonal greetings with spectators that he ran into one of the posts.

Amazingly he made it through to half-time in one piece and then, recognising the need for a pick-me-up before another gruelling 40 minutes of rugby, he nipped off for a glass of brandy – commenting to a team-mate as he returned to the fray: 'Ah'm gaun tae try that mair often.' Despite, or more likely because, of his condition, Cecil scored a brilliant opportunist try in the second half, when he nipped in to collect a quick drop-out and darted over the line.

Having started his rugby career as a full back, Terence's ever-expanding frame made it only a matter of time before he joined the front-row union, and in 1973 he followed his father into the Hawick team, making his debut against Musselburgh on the morning of Scotland's match against Wales – and so nervous was the tyro prop that he was up knocking on the Renwick family's door at 8am ready to catch the 10.30am bus.

It wasn't until the 1979–80 season that Terence became a regular in the Hawick side, the two propping berths being hogged during most of the seventies by the three Normans – Pender, Suddon and Webb. He made a total of 123 appearances for the club before playing his last match against Ballymena early in the 1984–85 season. He played one more season for Hawick YM before hanging up his boots altogether.

Since then Terence has been coach or team manager with several clubs – Hawick, Hawick YM, Hawick PSA, Langholm and Edinburgh Academicals – and is now President of Hawick RFC.

Bill McLaren

As a ten-year-old schoolboy Jim Renwick played like a 25-year-old. I used to ogle in disbelief at what he could do in terms of a pleasant deceit with a dummy or a clever little kick. He was a very advanced type of player.
Bill McLaren

From an early age Renwick had been playing a lot of rugby in scratch games over the Moat, which had given him a grounding in the basic skills of the game and by the time he started to be coached in primary six at St Cuthberts-Drumlanrig Primary School he was already showing a level of ability and maturity that marked him out from the rest.

His first official coach was none other than Bill McLaren, the legendary rugby commentator who was in those days first and foremost a PE teacher in Hawick. During his time McLaren played a key role in the early rugby development of great players such as Colin Deans, Alister Campbell and Tony Stanger, so he is no stranger to raw ability.

I first came across James Renwick as a ten-year-old schoolboy, and without knowing much about him I was impressed right away because he seemed so advanced with his skill levels. He just seemed a natural to me.

He played stand-off and inside centre for Drumlanrig, but you could have stuck him in any position in the back division – you could have played him at scrum-half and he would have done well, because he was that kind of boy. However it was at stand-off that he could really run the show.

He was quick and he had a terrific change of pace, he could come off a standing start in a blink and he could go right or left and leave his opponent stranded. He had great command of the ball so far as punting was concerned – he could punt the ball onto a sixpence if he had to. He did little things instinctively which made him special – be it a little dummy, coming off either foot for a side-step, or that kind of hitch-kick that he had. These deceptions were just natural to him. So right from the early days he hinted at quality.

And he was lucky because he had a delightful temperament, he took everything on board and nothing seemed to faze him much. Of course the way Jim was brought up was important. His family were very much into the Salvation Army and that approach to life – and that was great for him. It gave him that ability to take the rough with the smooth, and that made him very popular in every team he played in.

At that time McLaren coached rugby at four primary schools in Hawick – Drumlanrig, Burnfoot, Trinity and Wilton. During the course of a school year the primary seven classes at each school played two fifteen-a-side matches against their counterparts from each of the other schools. They also played against Blanerne Preparatory, a private school which was located approximately five miles north-east of Hawick near Denholm, and against Melrose Primary School.

These matches were played under exactly the same rules as adult rugby, meaning that there was always a danger of major mismatches. But McLaren made a conscious effort to guide his players towards playing in a manner which would ensure that all participants enjoyed the experience. "I always insisted on achieving the right feel," he explains. "I didn't want primary pupils to be playing the game like international players. I wanted them to just have fun, and enjoy running and handling. That was the most important thing from my point of view and Jim fitted into that so beautifully because he was naturally gifted."

In Renwick's opinion, this policy of using a bit of common sense when coaching and refereeing the games, rather than introducing artificial rules, was the sensible way to do things.

Bill was good at getting everyone involved. He was good at encouraging and helping the guys that were not so good. Even if you weren't good at rugby you were pretty pleased to have Bill McLaren as a teacher. We played fifteen-a-side and it was just rugby – we played exactly the same rules as the seniors played, so you copied the guys you had seen playing at Mansfield. It was very much if your father was a prop then you were a prop. But Bill wasn't daft – he had a feel for it and he could see the boys who were quick and the boys who were better in the forwards.

The highlight of the primary school's rugby calendar was the Border Primary School Sevens, which was played annually at Mansfield Park. In the 1964 final Burnfoot drew 3–3 with a Drumlanrig VII captained by Renwick. Instead of playing extra time a coin was tossed and Renwick called wrong. His recollections of losing that toss more than forty years ago reveal a great deal about his attitude towards winning and losing.

> Bill shouted Burnfoot up first because they had won the toss and they got the winners' medals while we got the silver ones. Bill said afterwards: 'I maybe made a mistake there Jim, I should have shouted you both up at the same time because you did draw, but it'll no matter.' It maybe didn't matter to him, but it meant a wee bit to me.

In the autumn of 1964 Renwick left Drumlanrig for Hawick High School, where Bill McLaren continued to coach the first year team and young Renwick continued to improve as a rugby player. In second year overall responsibility for the team on Saturdays was taken over by Ian McLean – an English teacher at the school who also played wing forward for Hawick YM.

Addie Renwick believes that it was McLean who first recognised just how much potential his little brother had.

> I remember one Saturday night Ian McLean says to me: 'You see that young brother of yours, he's got the best kick I've ever seen for a thirteen-year-old boy – he's got a real natural talent. I bet he'll play for Scotland one day.'
>
> I said: 'Get away and chase your Granny.'
>
> But there you are, he went on and did it, so Ian must have seen the potential.

> Ian McLean:
> It was obvious that the talent was there – he could do anything really. Okay, there was a degree of coaching but you can't take any of the credit – how do you take credit for a player who you can throw a ball to and he can do anything he likes with it? You could just depend on Jim – at thirteen years old he could kick an old-fashioned rugby ball 50 yards. All the skills were there – all the movements. He could dummy, he could side-step, he could kick and he could pass – he had it all.
>
> Like Bill McLaren, I had him playing stand-off because he was just so good at running the game. He was such a complete player that there was no-one else you could consider for that key position. You just had

to stand back, watch it, and marvel. I was slightly surprised that he didn't continue in that position.

The rugby wasn't very structured. There were no in-depth game-plans or anything like that. It was more a case of saying: 'That is where you stand, get the ball and show us what you can do.' We taught them things like scissors, and you would find that the kids would devise little moves of their own, but we were really only in the business of drilling the core skills into them. But, as I say, there wasn't a hell of a lot you could teach Jim Renwick. He was a natural and fortunately for me he was available to pick for the team.

Talented youngsters such as Renwick might not need much coaching, but McLean insists that McLaren had a crucial role in the number of players produced in Hawick during the sixties, seventies and eighties who were capable of playing at the highest level. It is a sentiment shared by practically every person involved in Hawick rugby at that time. He is a man with an infectious enthusiasm for the game and the feeling in Hawick is that McLaren was ahead of his time in the way he introduced the game to the town's youngsters.

Ian McLean
I wasn't a PE man, I taught English, but because I was young and played rugby I took the second year team on Saturdays, and I was out there three days a week helping Bill with training the first to third years. He had a very structured coaching system that benefited the boys enormously. He'd have little groups – a tackling group, a passing group, a kicking group – and the boys would spend an hour going round these groups developing their ball skills, then they would have a half-hour game at the end. Bill was giving them a terrific grounding. I taught at quite a few schools before and after being at Hawick High School, and I'm pretty sure that what we were doing there was way ahead of the times.

Peter Peacock, who is now a Labour MSP and at the time of writing is the Scottish Parliament's Minister for Education and Young People, grew up in Hawick and was another one of the several promising young players in Renwick's year group at both Drumlanrig primary school and Hawick High School. He also recalls Bill McLaren as the key figure in the rugby development of Hawick's youngsters.

The great thing for us when we were growing up was having Bill McLaren around because he really could get the best out of us. When you were playing you would suddenly hear Bill shout: 'Stop. Everybody freeze' – and he would then start to point out what was right and what was wrong. 'There was a space out there as big as the Gobi Desert,' that was a typical phrase of his. And he'd say: 'Look at you all. Now, you should be there, and you should be there, and you should be there.' And he'd restructure you before he let you get on with the game, then a wee while later he would stop you again and point out something else.

He used to do a lot of skills work. He would teach you how to pass and tackle properly and he'd show the forwards how to ruck properly. He didn't do much in terms of moves and tactics, but there would be things like looping round in support, and suggesting what angles you might want to run in different situations.

And I remember that he would come round the school on the days before he was going to commentate at an away international and he would collect a shilling from you and he would bring you back a programme. In those days, that was as exciting a present as you could ever hope to get. I've still got a raft of programmes from the 1960s that Bill brought back – from Paris, London, Cardiff and Dublin, places which seemed very glamorous to a boy growing up in Hawick.

I also have quite a vivid memory of being around the Moat listening to Bill telling us about Hughie McLeod, who was playing for Hawick and Scotland in the early sixties, and how he used to practise his scrummaging against the kitchen sink and it broke – we'd all be listening wide eyed in amazement.

He would also talk about the big stars of the day, he would say: 'Pierre Albaledejo the French stand-off wouldn't do that, he would do this.' So he was a role model but he was also bringing that whole international perspective to these wee boys in Hawick which is quite remarkable, and I think that would have had a huge impact on us and on the strength of Hawick rugby in the years that followed.

Of course it helped that this international influence was not as remote to the kids growing up in Hawick as it is today.

Ian McLean:
When Jim was growing up the kids at school had role models, something to aspire to, and to play for the Greens was a goal to aim for. You would hear them on a Monday morning talking about a try Stevie [George Stevenson] had scored against Heriots at the weekend, or Oliver Grant's tackle on Christie Elliot, or something Hugh McLeod had done.

I think that still is the case, but in those days you could go to Mansfield

Park and see seven or eight internationals on the field – you don't get that now and that has inevitably had an effect. When Jim was growing up he would go down to Mansfield and there would be 4000 to 5000 down there for a Hawick–Gala game, now you're lucky if you get 1000.

Swimming

Given the promise and enthusiasm that Renwick was already exhibiting as a rugby player, it is astonishing that after his second year at Hawick High School he chose to turn his back on his town's principal sport to concentrate on swimming instead. He was thirteen years old.

"I can't believe he did that without somebody saying: 'What the Hell are you doing?' If I'd known about it, I'd have been at his door," says Ian McLean, who had left Hawick by this point. "Mind you, Bob Elliot was in charge of the third year team at Hawick High School, he was a Maths teacher and primarily a tennis player, but he was also a huge influence in school's rugby at that stage – so if he couldn't talk Jim around then I don't think anyone could have."

The thoughts of Roy Laidlaw on this subject are pertinent. "It says a couple of things – it says a lot about Jim being quite single-minded; and it gives you an indication of the strength in depth that Hawick had in their feeder system that losing a player like that wasn't a major crisis," says the scrum-half, who played 47 times for Scotland and in four Tests for the British and Irish Lions during their tour of New Zealand in 1983.

As a player who came through the ranks and played all of his club rugby for Jed-Forest – a club from one of the smaller Border towns – Laidlaw is ideally positioned to reflect on the relative embarrassment of riches in terms of playing resources available to Hawick at that time.

Jim Renwick has his own explanation.

I got into swimming through Terence and Bobby [Froud], who had gone to St Margaret's where the headmaster was a guy called Jock Love. He had been an international swimmer and he thought swimming was more important – which was maybe right – so they had done swimming at primary school instead of rugby. In fact I think there had been a fall-out between Bill McLaren and Jock Love because Bill had wanted the kids at St Margaret's to play rugby, but there wasn't enough time in the day for them to do both.

Anyway, because we were all in the same gang I used to go along to the swimming club with them and I enjoyed it. At primary school I had a bit of success – in primary five and six I won the 25-yard freestyle competition in the primary school swimming gala, and then in primary seven I went up against the McConnell brothers, who were really good swimmers, and I did alright. So I must have thought: 'I can do this. I'm going to have a go at it.'

I started swimming seriously during my first year at the High School and over the next two years I started training more and more for swimming, and if I'm being honest I was getting less and less interested in rugby. Eventually it just reached a stage when I couldn't see the point of going to rugby training when I could be at the baths practising in the pool, so I decided to give rugby up. I went to Bob Elliot, who was in charge of the third year team, and I told him that I wanted to concentrate on my swimming. He tried to talk me out of it, but I'd made up my mind.

We had a good swimming squad at Hawick at the time. Ronnie Murphy was the coach and he kept the thing going. He trained us hard and we had trips away to Aberdeen, Edinburgh and places like that. There was a bit of interest in water-polo in those days so we played a bit of that too, I remember playing against Leith, Warrender, Dunfermline and I think Gala had a good side as well.

I enjoyed the swimming, but it was hard. We used to do a hell of a training. We used to swim across the pool, pull ourselves out, touch the cubicle, back into the pool, across the pool again and pull ourselves out at the other side. The circuit training we got was mainly press-ups, sit-ups, burpies and things like that – all hard stuff, but all very good for you. None of it ever did me any harm. You got into the way of doing the hard graft and I suppose you built yourself up a wee bit.

Once swimming had become his sole preoccupation, Renwick began to enjoy even more success in the pool. He won the Scottish 100-yard freestyle title in the under-fourteen age group in 1966, and many believed that he was on the way to achieving great things in the sport. "If he hadn't gone back to rugby I think he could have gone to the very top as a swimmer. There's a very good chance he would have made the Commonwealth Games in Edinburgh in 1970," says Ronnie Murphy.

However it was tough going – and the time, energy and money required to compete against the best began to take its toll.

Addie Renwick:
Nearly every Sunday he was having to travel up to Edinburgh, Perth or Aberdeen and back to train, which is a long haul, especially when you're that young. He was absolutely knackered when he came home on Sunday night. He just used to lie along the settee, worn out by all the training and travelling.

And you didn't get any money for all that travel. My Mum and Dad had to pay out their own pocket, and it got to the stage where they couldn't afford to send Jim on all these trips. We were brought up in a council house – we weren't poor, but we weren't rich either – and it was costing pounds and pounds and pounds to send Jim away swimming every weekend, and sometimes it was through the week too. It got to the stage where my Mum had to say: 'You're going to have to cut it back because we can't afford it. We don't want to stop you swimming, but we really can't afford to send you all these places.'

But I think the big problem was that it was all beginning to get on top of him, and he was finding he was getting less and less time to himself.

The final nail in the coffin of young Renwick's aspirations as a swimmer was hammered home when he left school in the summer of 1967 and moved into a flat in Edinburgh for a year while he completed the college section of his apprenticeship as an electrician.

JMR:
I was staying in digs on Lorne Street in Leith with Kenny Lawrie, the Gala hooker who got a few caps in 1980. Even then I was still swimming fairly seriously – I used to go along to Victoria Baths off Junction Street and Warrender Baths in Marchmont – but I was beginning to realise that I'd gone as far as I was going to go as a swimmer.

You know when your not going to be good enough at something – and wee, stocky, fat guys like me are always going to struggle in that game. For starters I wasn't any good with my legs – when they did exercises with legs only I hardly moved. But it wasn't just that. To be the best in swimming you have to be totally dedicated all of the time. You have to eat, breathe and dream swimming, and I don't think it was that important to me.

During his time in Edinburgh, Renwick had spent every possible weekend back in Hawick, travelling home by train on Friday evenings and returning early on Monday morning. At the end of his college placement he couldn't wait to move back home on a full-time basis.

By this time a lot of friends, including Bobby Froud, Brian Hegarty and Kenny McCartney, had started training with Hawick PSA (the initials stand for 'Pleasant Sunday Afternoon', an organisation formed in Hawick in the 1890s), one of the town's two semi-junior (under-eighteen) rugby teams. Renwick decided it was time to give the sport another go.

A Working Man

Having never shown any real interest or particular aptitude for academic studies there was no reason for Renwick to stay on at school any longer than necessary.

> JMR:
> If you were like me, and most kids in Hawick were, then you just wanted to get out and get into the mills and make some money as soon as you could. So when I left school after my third year I got a job as an apprentice frame-worker at Pringles, but on my first morning I got shown round by the foreman and the noise was that bad that I knew I couldn't work there the rest of my days – so I turned the job down.

On the surface he might appear to be a laid-back and easy-going individual, but that disguises the single-mindedness that adds steel to his character. On the issues that are important to him he knows what he wants and he is prepared to take a hard line in order to get his own way. In this instance he was a boy with no experience and no qualifications being offered the same job as most of his friends were being offered, but Renwick decided he wanted something different and his natural reticence quickly evaporated when it came to making that tough call.

His boldness would, however, have been bolstered by the healthy state of the Hawick economy at that time. The people of Hawick were able to boast that the town's hosiery trade made them the biggest dollar earners per head of population in the UK and they revelled in their relative prosperity. Bailie John Hardie had introduced the first stocking making frames to the town in 1771, and in 1844 half the worsted frames in Scotland were to be found in Hawick. In the 1960s unemployment did not exist and the Hawick women were a critical and well-paid constituent of the local workforce, meaning that families tended to have two good wages coming in. Access to the mill sales meant that on a

Saturday morning the well-dressed shoppers on Hawick High Street could stand comparison with their counterparts on Princes Street in Edinburgh or Oxford Street in London, with Hawick even winning the accolade of 'best dressed town in Britain' in 1962. Life was good and civic pride was sky high.

Renwick could be confident that a more suitable job would come along fairly quickly – which it did. Within a matter of days he had applied for, and been given, a job as an apprentice electrician with the South of Scotland Electricity Board.

JMR:
All of my friends went and worked in the mills and they were all making far better money than me. They were on good money for their age. It was quite hard at first because I was only making a fraction of what these boys were making. But you started getting a little bit more the further into your apprenticeship you got – and I was doing what I wanted to do, so I was happy.

I know I was lucky. I wasn't bright and I didn't try much at school – how many boys in that situation can pick and chose between good jobs? Not many – especially not nowadays.

It was just as Renwick left school that Hawick's fortunes began to wane. The world was shrinking and globalisation punished the town severely for its over-dependence upon the dollar market. Conglomeration and rationalisation took their toll. Joseph Dawson Ltd of Bradford (or Dawson International as they were to become) exercised their stranglehold over the cashmere supply to pick off Pringle of Scotland, Barrie Knitwear and Braemar, while Lyle & Scott fell to Courtaulds – meaning that Peter Scott's was the only one of the five major hosiery manufacturers in the town to stay in local hands.

In 1972, around 5000 Hawick textile workers went on strike, along with their colleagues in the satellite mills in Berwick, Arbroath and Cumbernauld. Ostensibly they were protesting against wage levels which were out of kilter with what was being paid in Bradford and elsewhere in England, but the underlying issue was concern about the future of the industry.

After four weeks of industrial action the Hawick strikers eventually decided to go back to work at a summit attended by 2000 knitwear workers at Mansfield Park. At the beginning of that meeting a broadcast was made to all present by loudspeaker. "I have been asked to make an announcement on behalf of Hawick Rugby Club," the voice said. "Saturday's game will be at home against Selkirk." The new pay deal which was about to be approved gave the workers substantially less than they had originally hoped for, and it was evident that hard times were around the corner, but priorities are priorities and in Hawick rugby was never too far away from the top of the agenda.

The emergence of access to cheap labour and mass output in the Far East, which tempted away major retailers, has been a crucial factor in the loss of 35,000 textile industry jobs in the Borders since the mid-sixties. Some terrible business decisions have also been significant – the nadir being Pringle's degeneration in the eighties to become the garment of choice for fat, middle-aged golfers and drunken football hooligans. In recent years the company has managed to stage a minor recovery, but much of the damage inflicted during this period was irreparable.

Hundreds of jobs went when the Waverley railway line closed in 1969 and Hawick was left the largest town in mainland Britain more than ten miles away from a railway station. Hawick auction mart, in its day the oldest-established livestock market in the United Kingdom, went not long after.

On the week Renwick left school in 1967 there were 41 different companies advertising more than 50 full-time jobs in the situations vacant page of the *Hawick News* – the vast majority of which could be described as career posts. In the corresponding week in 2006 there were only nine full-time employment opportunities advertised.

Hawick has endured a tough time over the last 30 years and the economic problems have impacted on the rugby scene in the town. The migration of youngsters out of the town in search of work has reduced player numbers, and the erosion of local pride has perhaps diminished the allure of the green jersey.

JMR:
When I left school you could go job hunting in Hawick in the morning and have an apprenticeship or a job in one of the mills by lunchtime – and it was a job for life so you could relax and concentrate on other things, like rugby. I don't think many boys these days can do that, they've got more important things to worry about – like where the next rent cheque is coming from.

It may seem like a pretty bleak scenario, but the reality of the situation in Hawick is not all bad. The hosiery trade appears to have bottomed out and several of the local mills have managed to re-establish themselves as up-market, niche suppliers. Meanwhile construction skills and expertise are highly developed in the town – with a veritable army of workers heading up the A7 every morning and heading back each evening. Unemployment is above the average for the Scottish Borders region but it is no worse than the Scottish average.

However the fact remains that the proud working class culture which underpinned Hawick rugby for 100 years has taken a few major knocks during the last three decades and that has had an impact.

After finishing his apprenticeship in the early seventies Renwick had a choice between moving to Bathgate to work as an electrician and taking a job as a linesman helping install and maintain the many power cables in the South of Scotland. Because he was reluctant to leave the Scottish Borders he chose the latter, and continued to do that job until taking early retirement in 2003.

Renwick was fortunate that his chosen career was not linked with the textile industry, which meant that he was not directly affected by its problems; the job security he enjoyed throughout his working life enabled him to take full advantage of the many opportunities to travel that his rugby ability brought him.

PSA

If Bill McLaren can take much of the credit for the conveyor-belt of talented young rugby players that Hawick has produced over the years, then the way in which club rugby in the town is organised has been instrumental in ensuring that Hawick was able to maintain a strength in depth which no other club in Scotland could match.

The work of McLaren at Hawick's primary schools, and with first to third year pupils at Hawick High School, provided the base upon which the Hawick rugby pyramid was built. From there youngsters would graduate to either the Hawick High School 1st XV or one of the town's two under-eighteen club sides (Hawick PSA and Hawick Wanderers) which play in the Scottish Border Semi-Junior League. Thereafter they would fan out to play for one of Hawick's four junior sides (Hawick Harlequins, YM, Linden and Trades), which all played in the Border Junior League until fairly recently. It is these clubs which have provided the backbone of Hawick's excellence over the years.

From the four junior clubs the best players would graduate to the Hawick team, while a Hawick regular making his comeback from injury would play for his junior club until he was ready to return to the senior team. It was a system which worked remarkably well for a long time. However, changes in the game and the way it is organised during the last twenty years or so have altered the balance of the relationship between Hawick RFC and the junior clubs, meaning that the system is no longer as smoothly efficient and mutually beneficial to all parties as it once was.

JMR:
The junior clubs used to be the strength of Hawick, because it meant that there were effectively four reserve teams in the town. They were happy for their players to move up into the Hawick side because it was an achievement – in fact they would be disappointed if a boy from another team got in and they thought their guy was better.

That was until 1986 when the rules changed to allow replacements for every league match, and you found that the junior clubs weren't so pleased about their best players going to sit on the bench – especially because the replacements were unlikely to get on because they could only be used when there was an injury. So they set up a rota which meant each junior club took their turn to give Hawick a guy to sit on the bench, and that worked for a bit – until it became four subs for each match, meaning that Hawick started taking the best players from every junior team every week. So the junior clubs started sending their weaker players and it ended up that Hawick were getting guys to sit on the bench who were second team players at junior level, and you were getting the situation that a Hawick player would be getting injured in a tight match against Jed and the guy who was coming on wasn't up to the job. Then, when the junior clubs started playing the Scottish Cup the situation became impossible because guys were getting cup-tied for junior clubs and Hawick had nowhere to go if they were short. So, in 1997 they had to introduce a second team, but I don't think that has ever worked because the older guys want to go back and play for their junior clubs when they can't get in the Hawick side, which means that the young guys in the second team don't have the experience alongside them that they need if they are going to learn.

Declining player numbers have not helped the situation. Up until the mid eighties all four junior clubs in Hawick would field a first and a second team on a regular basis, meaning that once the semi-junior clubs and the High School had been taken into account there could be as many as twelve competitive teams from Hawick playing the game on any given Saturday. However, economic pressures, changes in lifestyle and a shift in the way the game is perceived and organised have taken their toll, and in September 2004 the Trades were forced to pull out of the Border District League due to a lack of player numbers. They had hoped to start afresh the following season but so far the club has failed to resurrect itself. The other junior clubs are also finding it a lot harder to field competitive sides.

Back in the summer of 1968, when Renwick decided to give rugby another go, these problems were not yet on the radar.

By opting to dedicate his early teenage years to swimming Renwick had stepped off Hawick's conveyor-belt to rugby excellence, but when he decided to hop back on two years later he was still young enough to catch up with his contempories without too many problems. Besides, even though swimming had been his primary pre-occupation in recent years, he had not turned his back on rugby completely – growing up in Hawick during the sixties it was virtually impossible to escape the game altogether.

JMR:
Even when I was swimming I would be playing with the ball during my spare time. And because we played on the Moat up until we were about fifteen or sixteen, I had a bit of an idea about what I was trying to do. There's no doubt in my mind that a lot of youngsters have maybe picked up skills in the past that kids can't pick up now. We just used to just play all day and you learn more playing the game than when you're being coached. That was certainly the case with me.

And of course it helps if you are blessed with an innate understanding and feel for the game, and the natural ability to transfer those instincts into actions.

It's in you when you're born. When you coach kids you see some boys who can step and some boys who can't. Now, I'm not saying it can't be learned – of course you can learn how and why to do it – but what you can't teach is when to do it. All players are different – some do it early, some leave it late – and only they can tell what suits them best. That's the kind of skill you pick up from playing, but you also have to have this thing that your born with that makes you able to work out instinctively when is the right time to go.

With all this in mind, it is safe to say that it wasn't a huge leap into the dark when he decided to return to rugby with Hawick PSA. In fact, those who watched Renwick grow up believe that rather than hinder his development as a rugby player, his time as a swimmer actually helped him come through the ranks as quickly as he did during the next two years.

Addie Renwick:
He had good upper body strength – in fact he still does – and the swimming gave him that. I think his job was good for it too, but that training he did as a young boy gave him the strength he had in his shoulders. He had skinny legs and a skinny bum but his upper body strength was always good, and I think that was important to his game – especially in the early days before he had filled out properly.

"In some ways the swimming might have done him quite a bit of good because when he was growing and developing he wasn't taking the knocks," Addie points out, before adding that a relatively slight figure such as Renwick, whose game is based on out-witting bigger, more powerful players, would inevitably have been the target of some heavy-handed treatment in the notoriously tough school of Borders rugby. The longevity of Renwick's career, which was blighted by only one serious injury at the very end of his time as a player, may well owe a lot to the fact that his body was not being bumped and bruised during this important stage in his development.

While swimming might have helped his upper body strength, Renwick was quick to discover that rugby fitness is very different to swimming fitness.

JMR:
The rugby was easy enough, I didn't feel out of my depth in terms of skills and reading the game, but I found the training hard because it was different from the swimming. The first game I played for the PSA was against Hawick Wanderers at Melrose Colts Sevens – we beat them and then got beat in the next round – but what I remember most about that day is saying to myself afterwards: 'If I'm going to play this game I'm going to have to get fitter.'

And I suppose the PSA did get you fit in those days because you did a lot of road runs, a lot of exercises like press-ups, hold your arms out until they drop, and all that sort of stuff. It was good for you. We did a lot of sprinting on the cinder track and to me that was very important because it gave you pace. Duncan Paterson used to say: 'I've seen rugby players who are too fat, too skinny, too tall, too short; I've seen players who are too clever and others who are not clever enough; and I've seen players too slow, but I've never seen one who is too fast.' He was right.

Billy Hunter, who won seven caps for Scotland during the mid sixties and was just finishing his career at Hawick, coached the PSA in those days. He wasn't there all the time but he helped out, and when he wasn't there the captain, Tucker Robson, took training. You were encouraged to play off the cuff – basically if you had time you moved it, if you didn't you kicked it. The handling and other skills came from playing on the Moat and I just had to brush that side of things up a bit.

Following his debut at Melrose, Renwick quickly found his feet the following week when he scored two of his team's four tries in a 16–6 victory over the hosts in the final of Gala Red Triangle's tournament.

During the course of the 1968–69 season Renwick played stand-off with ever increasing proficiency and composure as Hawick PSA marched to the Semi-Junior League title. They lost only one league match against Hawick Wanderers at the start of the season, and the key victory was their 23–9 defeat of Selkirk Youth Club in March. Renwick side-stepped the opposition's full back to score one of his team's three tries in that match, and he set up another score for Jake Murray with a clever chip ahead. In the spring the PSA won their own sevens tournament.

At the end of the season Renwick had to decide where he was going to play his rugby the following year. He was young enough to have another season with the PSA but in those days the maxim that 'if you're good enough then you're old enough' was more keenly applied than it is today, and Renwick felt it was time to test himself at the next level.

At that time the YM, Trades and Linden all had well-established number tens in the shape of Alec Jackson, Cameron Thomson and Graham Hogg respectively; if this wasn't enough to persuade Renwick that Hawick Harlequins ('The Quins') was the right club for him to join, then the deal was sealed by the fact that both his brothers were actively involved with the club – Addie as coach and Charlie in his final years as a player.

During his season with the PSA Brian Lauder had been Renwick's half-back partner, and he was another player of whom big things were expected. The pair had been keen to keep the partnership going and had decided to join the Quins together, but at the last moment Lauder opted to join the Trades instead. Renwick was reluctant to go back on his word so the partnership was split up. As it turns out it was only a temporary parting of the ways – the pair were destined to reunite in spectacular fashion in the not too distant future.

The Mighty Quins

*Everybody wanted Jim to go to the YM or the Linden – the sort of glamour
sides in the town – but he decided to come to the Quins. And I remember
seeing the potential then, but I didn't think he would be playing for Scotland a few years later – never in a million years.*

Addie Renwick

Renwick had played a handful of games for Hawick Harlequins during
the 1968–69 season on weekends when the PSA did not have a game,
so he did not find adapting to adult rugby too arduous. In fact, such was
the ease with which he made the step that after only a few games for the
Quins he was selected to play in a Hawick Junior Select XV against the
senior side at the end of September 1969.

Even though it was not a full-strength side, the senior Hawick team
should have had enough firepower to win this game comfortably, however
the junior team, containing several stars of the future – including Renwick,
Alistair Cranston and Bruce Elliot – won the match by a point.

Afterwards the rugby correspondent of the *Hawick Express* noted that:
"One player who really did catch the eye was seventeen-year-old Jim
Renwick, a natural ball player [who] showed exceptional promise."

The Quins pride themselves on being the Cinderella club of Hawick
junior rugby. They have always had a lot going for them but are usually
overshadowed by their older sisters – the YM, the Linden and until recently
the Trades. They had enjoyed a brief flirtation with glory in the mid sixties
when they won the Border Junior League for the first time in their history
in 1967, but by the time Renwick joined the club many of their key players
were well past their best and others had moved onto the full Hawick side.

There were, however, still a number of experienced players such as Norrie
Leadbetter, Tony Elliot, Jock Graham and Jim Aitken in the side, all of
whom played an important role in encouraging Renwick's development.

[39]

Most significantly of all as far as Renwick was concerned was the presence of his brother, Charlie, who had recently moved to the Quins from the YM, where he spent most of his time as a player. "I was stand-off and Charlie was at full back. I think he kept me right a lot of the time. He was getting older but he was still a useful player," says the younger brother.

That may well have been the case, but already there were signs that the pupil was overtaking the master – as Addie recalls.

> Charlie was a very hard critic . . . a real hard critic . . . and I remember we were speaking in the house, and Charlie was telling Jim that he should be doing this and he shouldn't be doing that. But during the game . . . well . . . Charlie was long in the tooth by then, he was past his best, and I remember he dropped the ball and Jim covered round for him. And I remember Jim says: 'Giving me all this shite about doing this and doing that, and I'm having to look after you.' Charlie didn't like that.

The Quins won about as many games as they lost during the 1969–70 season and finished about mid table in the League. For Renwick the highlight of that first season playing for the Quins was the international weekend in February, when the team travelled down to Wales for their annual fixture against Bargoed. It was Renwick's first taste of rugby touring and he had a great time – even if the experience was a bit of an eye-opener for the sixteen-year-old.

> JMR:
> The bus left Hawick on Wednesday night and we stopped at Langholm for a couple of beers. We were going to Wales and we stopped at Langholm!
>
> We had a carry out on the bus but there was no such thing as on-board toilets in these days so we just had to use a big pail at the front of the bus. It was terrible. I remember it was snowing and at some points we were out pushing the bus. When we arrived down in Wales it was eight in the morning – we'd left at six so it had taken us all night and some.
>
> We went to the rugby club and they gave us our breakfast, then we booked into the hotel. We stayed in a place called the Old Mill and let's just say it wasn't the Ritz. The carpet must have been too short for the last three stairs so it was just pulled straight across – it was that kind of hotel.
>
> There was eight to a room – in four double beds. And while I had my pyjamas on nobody else was bothering. I didn't know know what to

do. They weren't bothered at all about about it, but I was a wee bit shy, and I didn't fancy getting into a bed with somebody I didn't know with just their underpants on.

I remember one of the boys wet the bed. I woke up in the middle of the night and Ross Gordon had climbed into our bed as well. He'd just been lying there and he felt this warm wet sensation on his back. I couldn't get him out so we had to sleep with three of us in the bed. When they went down in the morning they told the landlady that one of the young boys had wet the bed – she thought it was me and didn't give us any breakfast.

We went to the Conservative Club in Bargoed and I won the jackpot on the fruit machine. I was sixteen so I shouldn't have been there at all. I was drunk and shouting for Labour so we got flung out, but only after I dropped the bandit and took the cash.

We played our game against Bargoed on the Friday, and then we were off to Cardiff on the Saturday. I mind going into Cardiff was good, and going to the game was great. Scotland were leading at half-time but they got beat (18–9) in the end. Ian Robertson of Watsonians was playing stand-off and little did I think I'd be playing there in two years time. Never in my wildest dreams did I think I'd be playing. I was just happy to be playing for the Quins – enjoying myself. No ambitions to go anywhere in rugby – I wanted to play for Hawick but even that was a long way away then.

Sevens

During the early months of 1883 Melrose Rugby Football Club were staring down the barrel of a cash-flow crisis. They had recently lost most of the proceeds from what they had hoped would be a bumper gate for a match against local rivals Gala, when the visiting supporters had refused to pay the entry fee for the match which had been raised from threepence to sixpence in a shameless piece of profiteering by the home committee. With a typical piece of Border intransigence the visiting supporters had decided to take matters into their own hands by rushing the gates and barging their way into the ground without paying at all.

In order to overcome the financial shortfall brought about by this incident Adam 'Ned' Haig, an apprentice butcher in the town and a keen rugby player, came up with a novel fundraising idea. He suggested hosting a knock-out rugby tournament to be worked into an afternoon of athletics. In order to fit all of this into one day he suggested shortened games of rugby which would last fifteen minutes and be played by teams reduced to seven men.

The day was a huge success with special trains bringing several hundred supporters to the tournament from Galashiels and Hawick. The other Border towns quickly recognised the potential of this enterprise and began hosting tournaments of their own. It wasn't long before the Borders sevens circuit became an integral part of the area's strong rugby culture, and a colourful constituent in the rugby calendar throughout Scotland and the rest of the world.

A regular routine was soon established which has lasted, more or less intact, to the present day, with Gala (first played in 1884), Melrose, Hawick (1885), Jed-Forest (1894) and Langholm (1908) each hosting a tournament on consecutive Saturdays through April and into May.

By the time Selkirk (1919), Kelso (1920) and Earlston (1923) had joined the roster with their autumn tournaments, which were played throughout

September, a number of other clubs in Scotland – including the now defunct Edinburgh Institution, Edinburgh Borderers and the Royal High School – had also established their own tournaments.

The game continued to spread throughout Scotland and beyond, with the Middlesex Sevens being held at Twickenham for the first time in 1926. By the time Hawick reached the final there in 1963 the tournament was being played in front of more than 40,000 spectators.

Such was the appeal of the Borders Sevens that in their heyday Melrose routinely attracted crowds in excess of 12,000, while Hawick would expect crowds of around 7000 for their tournaments.

As far back as 1886 there had been an English winner at Melrose when Tynedale defeated their hosts 6–0 in the final. Rosslyn Park triumphed at the Greenyards in 1951, but the now common practice of inviting guest sides from other countries was not yet established, and it wasn't until the 1960s that English guest teams really became a force to be reckoned with at Melrose. In that decade Cambridge University, London Scottish and then Loughborough Colleges ensured that the honours would be evenly split between sides from north and south of the border, with five winning teams each during that ten year spell.

The 1970s and early 1980s witnessed a return to the traditional hegemony of Scottish sides. However, from the mid-1980s onwards the organisers at Melrose became increasingly aware of the pull that their tournament could have if graced with big enough names, so they cast their net beyond the British Isles and caught some big fish as a result.

Serge Blanco, Jean-Pierre Elissalde, David Campese and Mark Ella all won medals at Melrose as the tournament's international profile blossomed. And although the other tournaments did not quite attain the same international profile, they continued to prosper at a time when you could still expect international players to run out for their club on a spring afternoon and risk being shown-up by a youngster with a point to prove.

With the advent of professionalism the profile of these essentially amateur tournaments has suffered as much as the rest of Scottish club rugby. Those who play and organise the game at the highest level have neither the time nor the inclination to encourage the sevens circuit, and the autumn tournaments in particular have suffered as a result of clubs becoming increasingly focussed at that time of the year on the fifteen-a-side season (although it should be noted that this is a process that started well before professionalism became a reality, with Hawick controversially deciding not to send a team to Earlston in 1971, instead giving precedence to a fifteen-a-side match against Heriots).

Nowadays Kelso and Selkirk hold their tournaments on a Sunday to avoid clashes with the ever-expanding fifteen-a-side fixture schedule, while the Earlston tournament has been moved to the spring where it is also played on a Sunday.

While they might not be able to attract the big name players, the media coverage or even the crowd sizes that they once did, the Borders Sevens tournaments are still as important as ever at ground level. The prestige attached to success in these competitions might, to the uninitiated, appear to be disproportionate to the reality of what is at stake, but the Borders Sevens have always been about much more than spending a pleasant afternoon playing a quaint alternative to fifteen-a-side rugby. For the winners there is the pride of knowing that you have taken on all-comers in a single day and walked away the better team, while the host clubs still regard these events as important fundraisers in an increasingly fraught financial climate.

As far as the actual playing of the game is concerned, Renwick insists that the abbreviated game continues to offer a great deal in terms of developing the key rugby skills which any good player should have in his armoury.

I like sevens because you have to learn how to spot a three-on-two, how to pass out the tackle, how to take guys on. And you have to learn how to defend because if you miss a tackle then he's away and they score.

Any weaknesses in your game will be shown up. In fifteens you can sometimes get away with not being able to do things because you maybe won't be asked to do something for five or six games, but in sevens you are continually getting different questions asked of you in both defence and attack. In fifteens you might not do much all game, then you do a couple of good things and you've had a good match – that doesn't happen in sevens because there's no hiding place.

If you can't tackle you get found out pretty quickly; if you're not fit then you'll soon be in trouble; and if you can't beat a man then you're not much use to the team. Basically, if you are going to play sevens then your weaknesses will be shown up pretty quickly, and if you want to be any good at sevens then you are going to have to work on improving the things that you're not so good at.

My first game for the PSA was in the sevens, my first game for the Quins was in the sevens, and then my first game for Hawick was in the sevens – so that was maybe a strength of mine. Some folk thought it was too much like a hard-work but I didn't – I liked it. It was a nice change, lots of space and it gives you the chance to play some off-the-cuff stuff when you can just play what you see in front of you.

I'd like to see some of the boys in the Scottish team at the moment playing sevens. I think most of them would be playing in the pack, but you wouldn't put Shane Williams in the forwards, and that's the difference between the Welsh team which won the Grand Slam in 2005 and our team which has been struggling to score tries in the last couple of years. That Welsh team had boys who could really ask you questions, not just run at you and make them tackle you, but run at you and make you think about what they're going to do next.

I remember Mossy [Chris Paterson] playing for Gala at Melrose in 1999. He'd had a good season so I don't think he got his contract just because of that one performance – but that day he showed he was a special player. But then he went professional and since then he has only played one sevens tournament [for Scotland in Dubai later that year] and that's it. To me that's a shame.

The Border Sevens was a great learning environment when I was coming through, and I'd like to think it can still help to develop our best young players. We've got something there that no other country in the world has – a ready-made set of tournaments which folk are interested in and teams really want to win. But there's a danger that it's going to become just another kick about at the end of the season – maybe not Melrose, but tournaments like Langholm. I'd hate to see that happen because Langholm's always been a great tournament.

I don't know what the answer is because the professional boys are still playing in April, but I hope we can keep the sevens going strong because for me it's an important part of the game.

The seed of Renwick's love affair with the shortened game was planted when, as a child, his Uncle Wat, the only member of the family to own a car, used to take Jim and his father to all the spring and autumn tournaments – except for Gala and Melrose because special train services were laid on for those trips which provided even more fun and excitement than travelling by car.

JMR:
Each tournament had a different character. There was never much going on at Gala – it was always cold. At Melrose we used to always juke in and stand at the road end and if the ball went over the top then we used

to go and get it and throw it back. In fact I think we stole a ball from Melrose once. It was the most exciting of the tournaments, probably because of the big crowds. Hawick was our own sports and we would spend all day running up and down the hill and mucking about, and I remember waiting for autographs outside the tent that the players used to change in. You used to get soaked at Jed-hart because you were playing in the bridge and the river. And Langholm was more of a picnic because the weather was starting to get better – you'd be hunting for pheasants' eggs on the banking and down playing in the water.

It was good stuff. Your heroes were playing rugby and you got to go and watch them. And it was always in the back of your mind that you wanted to be out there doing what they were doing, but at that age you didn't really think it was possible. These guys were from a different world than us.

Success in the Borders Sevens circuit tends to come in waves with one club dominating for a prolonged spell before they are eventually toppled by a team of younger and hungrier upstarts.

During the mid to late sixties Hawick were the dominant force – winning an unprecedented ten tournaments on the trot during 1966 and 1967, including a 'Grand Slam' in 1966 when they won all eight Border tournaments.

However, at the end of the sixties it was Gala who emerged as the force to be reckoned with. In 1969 they had won at their own tournament as well as the Jed and Langholm competitions, they had reached the final at Melrose and the semi-finals at Hawick. In the course of these five tournaments Hawick had managed only two semi-final appearances, although they faired slightly better after the summer when they beat Gala in the final at both Earlston and Selkirk and lost to Melrose in the semi-final at Kelso.

Injury and international commitments (Scotland were touring Argentina) meant that at various points during that autumn Gala had been deprived of key players such as Duncan Paterson, John Frame, Jock Turner, Johnie Gray and PC Brown – but they were all back and firing on all cylinders by the time the spring series kicked off on the first Saturday in April 1970. At their own tournament Gala hammered Hawick 15–0 in the second round, before defeating Llanelli 23–11 in the final. A week later they were victorious at Melrose with a 28–3 victory over Loughborough Colleges in the final. And so it was with high expectations that Gala entered the same seven that had won at Melrose to compete in the Hawick tournament for the Paterson Cup.

"If Gala maintain their sparkling form, they will have good reason to think that by the end of this circuit they will have emulated Hawick's feat of winning all the Borders trophies in the spring of 1966," wrote Jack Dunn in *The Scotsman* on the morning of the tournament.

Meanwhile, the Hawick committee had been stung into action. Losing was bad enough, but to add salt to the wound it was Hawick's arch-rivals who were profiting at their expense. Such a situation was unacceptable to everybody in Hawick and it was clear that desperate times called for desperate measures.

Renwick had been the star of the show for the Quins in their victories at the Langholm and the Dumfries junior sevens tournaments during the previous two weeks and he was rewarded with a call-up to the full Greens team in place of his cousin Graham Hogg. Brian Lauder, Renwick's old half-back partner from his days at the PSA, was selected at scrum-half. Another youngster in the form of Ian Chalmers was given his first senior sevens start on the wing – although he had already played 23 games for Hawick during the recently finished fifteen-a-side season. And the other new face in the side was in the forwards where Wat Davies, a buzz-bomb in the back-row for Hawick during the regular season, was selected.

The three survivors from the seven that lost to Loughborough Colleges in the semi-finals at Melrose the previous week were the brothers John and Brian Hegarty, who were selected at centre and hooker respectively; and Norman Suddon, who had been capped thirteen times for Scotland at prop and was a survivor from the famous 1966–67 ten-in-a-row team.

On the Tuesday before the tournament a Hawick select team containing Renwick, Lauder and Brian Hegarty crashed out of the St Boswells junior sevens in the second round – prompting the *Hawick News* to state that: "No member won much support for inclusion in the senior seven." So when the seven to play at Hawick was announced later that week, and all three of these players were in the side, it is little wonder that the same rugby correspondent was less than optimistic.

"The necessity of the changes will not be disputed but the replacements do not inspire confidence that the side will show much improvement on recent displays," he wrote. "Young Jim Renwick is thrown into the Greens seven without ever having made an appearance in the full fifteen and his undoubted ability and promise will be tested to the full."

Such was the confidence that Hawick would not prevail that the book-makers were giving any punter willing to back the home team odds of 33–1 on the morning of the tournament, and although those odds were cut to 25–1 just before kick-off it is clear that nobody was really giving this experimental team with four teenagers a chance.

The *Hawick News* takes up the story:

> The Greens, with only N Suddon surviving from the 1968 seven who won at Mansfield, had their uneasy moments. These came mainly in earlier ties when inexperienced bunching in defence and occasional jittery handling were exploited by their opponents. But, even after an uncertain start in the final, they displayed all the traditional determination of the wearers of the green jersey. Grit and guts and a refusal to accept defeat were the main essentials. But, given the chance, they also showed that they had all the skills of the sevens rugby as understood and played by Border sides, and Hawick in particular. This was nowhere more apparent than in the old-fashioned blind-side ploy worked so neatly in the semi-final [against Watsonians] by B Lauder and J Renwick which gave the Greens that vital first try which led to victory.
>
> [The] young Hawick side completely upset all predictions by a triumphant win in the final over the more fancied Glasgow Academicals. After being down 8–0 within four minutes and still behind 8–5 at half-time, the young Hawick side systematically destroyed and demoralised the Accies to score 24 points in ten minutes.
>
> The last but not the least word of praise must go to as clever a pair of half-backs as ever made a first appearance for the Greens. Those who can recollect the debut of George Reid and Ally Fiddes, Glen Turnbull and Drew Broatch, and Harry Whitaker and Colin Telfer, must have appreciated the potentialities of Brian Lauder and Jim Renwick. They, too, very understandably, had moments of uncertainty but they had the temperament to refuse to be unsettled, as their play in the final proved.
>
> Renwick lived up to the reputation he had already acquired in semi-junior and junior rugby circles. Like the rest he was not free from fault in occasional mishandling but he more than compensated for that in his quickness in creating his own openings and in exploiting any gaps. Not only did he go through the gaps but he varied his running so effortlessly that he caught more than one defender on the hop. The most outstanding of his five tries was the one in the final where, getting possession on his own 25 he set off on a zig-zag run that frustrated all would-be tacklers and scored under the posts.

He maybe hadn't yet arrived, but it was the clearest indication so far that Renwick had the potential to achieve great things as a rugby player. Many of those closest to him, not least the man himself, confess to being taken aback by the chain of events which saw him become the toast of Hawick that April evening in 1970.

JMR:

That was big time. I wasn't even old enough to drink and there I was playing in front of 7000 folk against Ian Robertson, who I'd watched playing for Scotland when I went down to Cardiff with the Quins earlier that year. We played Watsonians in the semis and I think I scored a couple of tries against him.

A seventeen-year-old boy playing a full-blooded sevens match against current Scotland internationalists – that would never happen in rugby now, but in those days that would happen fairly regularly.

Beforehand we didn't know what to expect at all – we had no idea how fast it was going to be, how we were going to handle them size wise, or anything like that. We had Suddon in the team – he'd played for Scotland and he had a bit of experience, and John Hegarty was the guy in the middle that did all the hard tackling, but the rest of us were just young guys.

But Chalmers could beat a man on a sixpence and we all had a bit of rugby ability, and most importantly we were fit and if you're fit then you've got a chance. Mind you, we were all knackered afterwards: I could hardly walk along Mansfield Road to get home.

We made a lot of mistakes too, don't get me wrong, but we weren't feared and we had a go. I remember seeing the French Baa Baas play at Melrose in 1983. Their stand-off got hurt so they moved their hooker out to take his place, they played their smallest man on the touchline, they kicked down the middle of the park, they didn't chase, they did everything wrong – but they had that much ability with the ball in hand that they could get away with it. I suppose that was the same as us in 1970 – we had ability and we could run all day.

All this was achieved despite Renwick having to spend his time between ties in a cold bath, trying to cool off his burning limbs after mistaking hot muscle rub for Vaseline.

When the pitches were hard we used to put Vaseline on our knees and one of the boys in the changing room must have had capsalene, which was brown in colour but came in the same kind of tub. I must have thought it was Vaseline and I rubbed it up and down my legs until it was caked on. At first it was alright but after two minutes of the first tie, once I started sweating, my legs felt like they were on fire – I didn't know what was going on. It burnt you alright and I got a gliff, a right gliff, but my legs never got tired and I never felt any knocks, so I suppose it worked out for the best in the end.

Having started the day as red-hot favourites Gala only managed to make it to the second round at Hawick, where they were beaten 11–10 by Watsonians. They were back to their best, however, the following week when the same Hawick seven lost 23–10 to their arch-rivals in the final at Jed-Forest.

At that tournament Renwick gave yet another good account of himself, although he did not shine to the same degree as he had done the week before. This was partly because the opposition had quickly learned that he was a player to be wary of, but mainly because Lauder had to play with injuries to both his back and his hand, which meant that his service to Renwick at stand-off wasn't quite as efficient as it had been: "[Renwick] had to expend a great deal of his energy in the final in tackling and covering," the *Hawick News* pointed out afterwards, adding that ". . . his fine running still succeeded in troubling the Gala defence [and] he was more closely watched by all the defences, a tribute to the respect he has already earned in a short time."

Renwick had done more than enough to retain his place in the side for the last of the spring tournaments at Langholm on 2 May. However, Colin Telfer, Hawick's international stand-off, who had been unavailable since the Gala Sevens due to a flu virus, was available again, and having helped Hawick Harlequins win the Penicuik Sevens the previous week, he initially got the nod ahead of Renwick. It was only when Telfer was ruled out at the last moment with a leg injury that Renwick was given his third consecutive start. Meanwhile Graham Hogg had replaced John Hegarty, who was about to sign for Wakefield Trinity Rugby League side, in the centre.

If everything had seemed to be going too smoothly for Renwick up until this point then it was at Langholm that the hand of fate ensured that things were evened up a little bit.

I remember walking next to Heg on the way out to play Watsonians in the first round at Langholm and the medics carried this boy off in a stretcher. Heg looked round and said: 'That could be you next time, Renwick.'

I said: 'Aye, nae chance.'

Two minutes into the game and BANG – I didn't know where I was. They carried me into the changing rooms and I remember Derrick Grant saying: 'Aye, that's just the stairt of it son, that's the way it is. Dinnae have any drink, go and have a cup of tea.' The tea lady at Langholm, Peg Houston, gave me a cup of tea and and the next thing I spewed up.

Heg said nothing, but that gave him a gliff. The things you say, eh?

Reduced to six men, and with no replacements allowed in those days, Watsonians won the tie 8–3. The absurdity of not allowing replacements in sevens was highlighted at Gala in 1973, when three West of Scotland players were forced to retire injured from a tie against Hawick, leaving the scrum-half with no-one to pass to after receiving the ball from the back of a scrum. Hawick, not surprisingly, won that tie 38–0.

Watsonians went on to reach the Langholm final before losing 27–10 to Gala, meaning that Gala managed to win four of the five Sevens tournaments that spring. It was an impressive enough achievement, but a bittersweet one for the Netherdale men given their high hopes of a clean-sweep.

It is worth noting that Murrayfield Wanderers reached the final of the Middlesex Sevens in both 1969 and 1970 but did not enjoy the same success in Scotland, which might be regarded as a demonstration of the strength of the abbreviated game in the country at that time.

Typically of Renwick he realised that while raw ability and enthusiasm were enough to upset the apple-cart once in a while, it would not pay off indefinitely. So he quietly set about improving his understanding of the abbreviated game.

I liked playing sevens, and if you like something you think about it, so between ties I used to go and watch players. We'd all be sitting having a bit of chat and keeping an eye on what was going on, but I made a special effort to watch the games closely and try to learn something from each tie. I'd always look for the best players to see what they do – see what foot they came off, see what their strength was, see how they kicked. I just liked to sit and watch them, I never took notes but I had an idea in my head about how to beat them.

It was a little bit of homework that paid off in the long run. During the fifteen years in which he played senior rugby, Renwick derived great pleasure from the abbreviated game. He played in 76 Border Sevens tournaments – during which time he picked up fifteen winners medals, thirteen runners-up medals and reached the semi-finals on seventeen other occasions. The biggest prize, however, always alluded him – he was never a winner at Melrose.

He has also played in countless sevens tournaments in destinations across the globe – including Amsterdam, Madrid, Hong Kong, Dubai and Oman – for Hawick and for various invitation sides.

Hawick RFC

According to the commemorative stone at Rugby School, the game of rugby union owes its existence to former pupil William Webb Ellis, who, in 1823, "with a fine disregard for the rules of football as played in his time, first took the ball in his arms and ran with it, thus originating the distinctive feature of the rugby game".

It was almost fifty years later before the seed was planted from which Hawick Rugby Football Club would grow. That was at a meeting of members of Hawick and Wilton Cricket Club in October 1872, where it was decided to buy an inflatable ball so that they could try out this game which they had read about in the national press, and heard about from their friends and associates at other cricket clubs.

By this time rugby union was fairly well spread throughout England and there were already twenty senior clubs in Scotland. However the lines of communication were not as sophisticated as they are today, which meant early rugby contests in Hawick were wild, disorganised affairs between sets of players playing in their shirt sleeves who had very little idea about tactics or the basic skills of the game. The playing field was defined by the boundaries of the cricket pitch and the only generally agreed rule was that the two teams should play in opposite directions. That was until Robert Michie, the club's first ever captain, obtained a copy of the rugby union rules, and several meetings were held to interpret their possible meanings.

However some players were not convinced by the merits of rugby union ahead of association football, so on 22 November 1873 a special game was played to decide which path the club should go down. The first half of this match was played under the rules of association football and the second half was played under rugby union rules. An article in the *Hawick Express* soon after stated: "As far as can be judged at present, the afternoon's play will probably result in the club adopting the rugby union rules as

[53]

being the manlier and more congenial to the Border nature than the tame association game."

Hawick and Wilton Football Club was instituted on 8 December 1873 and on 7 February 1874 the club played its first official game against Langholm – where the game had already been popular for some time thanks to the influence of several sons of local tweed manufacturers who had been educated at fee-paying schools in England. That match, which was played on the Hawick and Wilton Cricket Club's ground, finished scoreless, as did the return fixture in Langholm six weeks later.

The popularity of the game in Hawick led to a second club in the town being formed towards the end of 1875. St Cuthbert's was associated to the Episcopal Church of the same name, and played its home games at Brewery Haugh, a narrow field on the banks of the River Slitrig. On the occasions when the ball ended up in the water play would often continue midstream. On 25 March 1875 St Cuthbert's lost their first ever match, against Hawick, by one goal and two tries to nil.

By now clubs were being set up in other Border towns. Hawick's first game against Gala, on 16 December 1876, finished as a 0–0 draw. And on 20 October 1877 they lost their first ever match against Melrose by one goal to one try.

During the winter of 1877–78 Hawick played a total of ten matches, one of which was a one try to nil loss to Merchiston FP. It was Hawick's first fixture against an Edinburgh side and an indication that they were beginning to be taken seriously by the rugby establishment.

The popularity of the game in Hawick by this point, and the ambitious nature of those running the club at this time, was demonstrated when, inspired by a football match which was played under electric lights in Sheffield in autumn 1878, it was decided to do the same against Melrose at Hawick Cricket Ground on 24 February 1879.

It was an audacious undertaking given that electricity at this time was still regarded as a modern marvel. Two dynamo machines supplying a total of 3200 candle power were hired and despite a snowstorm the day before the match, and a treacherous frost on the day itself, the game went ahead.

The event ended up being a bit of a farce. Despite extensive advertising throughout the Borders only one gatekeeper had been appointed. He sat at a kitchen table with a small lamp and a bowl to collect the admission fee. He was ill-equipped to deal with the huge crowd which turned up, and on several occasions the gate was rushed by frustrated spectators. Inside the ground the spectators stood in front of the lighting equipment, casting shadows across the pitch and plunging large sections of the field into darkness. Players were left tackling thin air, falling over each other, and hacking at balls which did not exist. Despite all this the evening was considered a success, with the large crowd highly impressed by the technology being used.

In 1885 it was decided by the rugby players that the club should no longer be a subsidiary of the cricket club, and Hawick Football Club (as opposed to Hawick and Wilton Football Club) came into existence. This event caused considerable ill feeling and the cricket club barred the new football club from using the cricket field. Fortunately Volunteer Park, which was right next door to the cricket field, was made available by the Duke of Buccleuch. At some point in the 1870s the football club had acquired blue and white strips, but at this point the now familiar dark green colours were adopted as a symbol for this new era of rugby in Hawick.

The Hawick and Wilton Football Club carried on for five more years, and actually won Hawick Sports in 1887, but it was becoming increasingly clear that the town could only support one senior team and it was discontinued in 1890. St Cuthbert's lasted two years more before disappearing in 1892.

Meanwhile the new club went from strength to strength. In 1886–87 they played fifteen matches including one against the exotically named Edinburgh Australians, and more significantly also against Edinburgh Academicals – who were, and remain, Scotland's oldest club, having been formed in 1857. A permanent grandstand at Volunteer Park seating 200 spectators was constructed during the winter of 1887–88, and the fixture list continued to expand, with Hawick playing 25 games (winning fifteen, drawing four and losing six) that season. During this campaign they managed a notable victory over Royal High School, and the following week they lost only narrowly to Edinburgh Academicals, the reigning Scottish champions.

There were, however, a few inevitable hiccups. During this period Hawick's supporters developed a reputation for their rowdy behaviour and hostility towards the opposition. They frequently booed the other side and were known to run onto the field of play to argue with the referee. On one occasion a group of Hawick spectators invaded the pitch and removed the goal posts to prevent the opposition from taking a kick at goal. In 1890 the Hawick club were compelled to apologise to the referee of their match against Edinburgh Academicals after he complained about being "subjected to a great deal of abuse both during the game and upon leaving the field."

In 1888 the club moved their home ground to Mansfield Park, where they had managed to secure a long-term lease (before buying the ground outright from the Duke of Buccleuch in 1920 for the princely sum of £500). And Hawick might well have been crowned Scottish champions for the 1889–90 season, had they defeated Edinburgh Academicals in front of 4000 spectators at Mansfield, but in the event they lost by one try to nil.

That same year three Hawick players, Bob Burnet, William Burnet and Alex Laing, went on Messrs Shaw and Shrewsbury's tour to Australia and New Zealand. They were away for nine months, three of which were spent travelling. The playing squad contained only twenty players, and early in the tour their captain, Bob Seddon, was drowned in a boating accident on the Hunter River. But they still managed to play 35 games (no Tests), winning 27, losing six and drawing two. On their return the Hawick contingent were interviewed by the SFU (later to become the SRU) about the terms, management and conduct of the tour. They were able to give satisfactory assurances and any suggestions of professionalism were dropped. Sandy Thorburn notes in *The History of Scottish Rugby* that at a dinner given by the Hawke's Bay FC, Alex Laing sang something in "untranslatable Scottish dialect".

The 1888–89 Maori tour of Britain had only one game in Scotland – at Mansfield Park, were they were beaten 5–3 by Hawick.

Hawick won their first championship in season 1895–96 under the captaincy of Davie Patterson, who along with Matthew Elliot formed a legendary half-back pairing known locally as 'Mattha and Davie'. It was a triumph of great import in the town, and at a celebratory dinner in the Tower Hotel in Hawick one enthusiastic speaker made the impressive boast that Hawick "were now a team without an equal from Carlisle to the North Pole."

There followed a thirteen-year barren spell before Hawick shared the championship with Watsonians in 1908–09. However during that time the club did enjoy the kudos of winning the first ever Border League competition for the 1901–02 season. In later years they would mirror this feat by winning the first official league championship in 1974 and the first Scottish Cup in 1996.

When the club's fortunes did begin to change it was largely thanks to the half-back pairing of Tom Neil and Sandy Burns, Bill Kyle in the pack, and a youthful three-quarter called Walter Sutherland, or Wattie Suddy, who would go on to establish himself as one of the all-time greats of Hawick rugby. Suddy won thirteen caps for Scotland before he lost his life in the First World War, along with another 36 club members.

Hawick continued to be a major force but did not manage to win the title again until after the War, when lost time was well and truly made up for, with Hawick claiming nine Border Leagues and their second outright Scottish championship in season 1926–27. The club also dominated the Border Sevens circuit and managed a Grand Slam of spring tournaments in 1927 – a feat which would not be repeated by any club until Hawick did it again in 1966. In 1932–33 Hawick shared the championship again, this time with Dunfermline.

After the Second World War it took some time before a full and comprehensive fixture list could be reinstated but when that did happen Hawick were quick to assert their place near the top of Scottish rugby's pecking order. They won the 1948–49 championship, and then during the 1950s – which was a time of prosperity and optimism in the town – the popularity of the game as a participation and spectator sport flourished.

Surprisingly the club failed to win the championship in that decade, although they were runners-up on several occasions and won the Border League three times. But more significantly it was during this period that the foundation of the extraordinary success of the sixties and seventies were laid, with the likes of Robin Charters, Norman Davidson, Adam Robson, George Stevenson, Jack Hegarty and Hugh McLeod earning their spurs.

It was McLeod who was the catalyst to Hawick becoming the pre-eminent rugby club in Scotland over the next 30 years. As a prop forward he won 40 caps for Scotland between 1954 and 1962, and he went on two British Lions tours to South Africa in 1955 and New Zealand in 1959. A profound thinker about the game, he used these experiences to transform his beloved Hawick into a ruthlessly efficient rugby machine. Rugby would remain a strictly amateur sport until the mid 1990s, but at Hawick McLeod introduced a professional attitude in terms of the way the game should be approached which no club in Scotland could match. It was a template which was adjusted and added to during the sixties and seventies by Charters, Hegarty, Wattie Scott and Derrick Grant when they became committee men after their playing careers were over.

In the 1960s Hawick took full advantage of the solid foundations which had been laid during the previous decade. Apart from one hiccup, against Glasgow High School at Mansfield Park on the holiday Monday game at the end of September, Hawick captained by Jack Hegarty swept all before them on the way to the 1959–60 Scottish championship. Having missed most of the first half of the season, Addie Renwick played twenty games for Hawick in that campaign and finished as top try scorer with eighteen touch-downs. Charlie also featured for Hawick although he managed only six games. The following year Hegarty was again captain as Hawick made it two championships in a row. It is generally accepted that this was one of the greatest Hawick teams of all time. The club were outright Scottish champions five times during the sixties – in 1959–60, 1960–61, 1963–64, 1965–66 and 1967–68, and they also shared the title with West of Scotland in 1964–65. During this period eleven Hawick players were selected to play for Scotland.

However, by the time Jim Renwick was making his fifteen-a-side debut for Hawick against Melrose on 7 November 1970, many of the stalwarts of the previous decade had either retired or moved on. Fortunately a new generation of highly capable Hawick players were emerging and they were more than willing to pick up where their predecessors had left off.

JMR:
When you got into the Hawick side you knew that you were carrying on the tradition. At that age I maybe didn't know about Wattie Suddy and guys like that, but I knew that getting to wear the green jersey was a privilege and that you had a lot to live up to. I had grown up watching Stevie [George Stevenson] and Robbie Welsh wearing the number thirteen jersey for Hawick, and now it was my turn, and I didn't want to let that tradition down.

That might sound a bit over the top, but it's true: everybody wanted to play for Hawick. I'm not sure that it's the same now, Hawick is not the cause anymore – it's just a stepping stone into professional rugby. I'm not saying that my boy doesn't want to play for Hawick, but in my day, if you were in the Hawick side, you didn't have to think about playing anywhere else if you were ambitious. You could go from the Hawick side into the Scotland team and onto Lions tours – now you have to be at the Border Reivers.

I'm not saying it should be clubs instead of districts, because I don't know what the answer is. All I'm saying is that I'm not sure that anyone grows up wanting to play for the Border Reivers, and I'm not sure that anyone is that bothered if the Reivers get beat at the weekend. But when I was playing I was feared to go down the High Street on Monday morning if Hawick got beat at the weekend because that result had ruined the week for a lot of folk, and they would let you know all about it.

I know you shouldn't take rugby too seriously because it's only a game, but it has got to mean something – otherwise what's the point? If everything is geared towards the fifteen guys that play for Scotland . . . well . . . then you're never going to make it work at any level underneath that.

Going Green

In the summer of 1970 Renwick, along with Terence and Pei Reid, set off to visit their old friend and former swimming mentor, Ronnie Murphy, who was by this time based in Sunderland. The initial plan had been to hitch-hike the whole way, but by the time the trio had reached Jedburgh without managing to tempt anyone into giving them a lift, it was clear that they were going to have to fork out the cost of a bus ticket.

Meanwhile Colin Telfer, Norman Suddon, and Derek Deans were enjoying a rather more exotic adventure in Australia touring with Scotland. After returning from that trip Telfer took a family holiday, so he was unavailable for the Earlston and Kelso sevens tournaments that autumn, which meant Renwick was given another opportunity to wear Hawick's green jersey. Hawick reached the final in both competitions, defeating Gala 18—14 in the first then losing 21–5 to the same opposition a week later.

There had been rumours at the end of the previous season that Telfer would be leaving Hawick to play in Edinburgh, but these proved to be unfounded, and following his return from his holiday he was immediately re-installed in the Hawick seven which was eliminated in the second round at Selkirk, before taking his place in the full Hawick side for the visit of Queen's University, Belfast. Renwick was back playing for Hawick Harlequins.

And so things stayed until the last day of October when Hawick visited Old Anniesland to play Glasgow HSFP. The visitors won 3–13 but Telfer broke his arm. Having done so well in the both the spring and autumn sevens, and because he was continuing to shine with the Quins, Renwick was the obvious choice as his replacement.

His first start for Hawick in fifteen-a-side rugby looked certain to be a baptism of fire against Melrose at Mansfield. Injuries meant that the home side were missing five first-choice players plus two of their most obvious replacements, and with Jim Telfer, Alistair Wilson and Jerry Bird forming a formidable back-row for Melrose, the debutant was going to have to be on his toes. Sure enough, after only a few minutes of play, Renwick was on the receiving end of a late tackle from Wilson. First on the scene was the powerful lock Robbie Brydon, who picked up the youngster, dusted him down and demanded the name of the culprit. After the next ruck Wilson was left flat-out on the turf and had to be carried off on a stretcher. Hawick won the match 11-3.

Renwick played the remainder of the season whilst Telfer's broken arm kept him on the sidelines. He also played in all five spring sevens tournaments that year, during the course of which Hawick were beaten 25-3 by Gala in the final at Melrose, before retaining their own trophy with a 14-11 victory in the final over the same opposition.

Hawick's unbeaten record in fifteen-a-side rugby, which stretched back to 18 October 1969, was relinquished against Edinburgh Wanderers on 21 November 1970, when they were comprehensively defeated 14-0 at home, having been forced to field a team without seven first-choice players who were all playing for the South against the North and Midlands. It was a bad-tempered encounter which saw the referee, a Mr JWA Ireland, booed by the Mansfield crowd and pushed by one irate spectator. Hawick lost a further six times that year and drew once having played a total of 34 matches. By their own high standards it was a fairly average record for the season. West of Scotland finished as the top club in Scotland while Hawick only managed to finish fourth in the unofficial table behind Melrose and Edinburgh Wanderers. This was enough to ensure that the Hawick selectors had some tough decisions to make when it came to getting the right personnel in the right places for the 1971-72 season.

Having missed most of the previous campaign Colin Telfer was at last fit again to play and was asked to captain the side. He was the axle around which the team would revolve, and as such he was the automatic choice at stand-off. Renwick had played in 24 matches during the previous season, scoring five tries, three conversions and three drop-goals. He was still very raw, but the potential he was exhibiting could not be overlooked.

Robin Charters played eleven seasons for Hawick between 1957 and 1958, and in 1955 earned three caps for Scotland in the centre. After hanging up his boots he became an enthusiastic and knowledgeable administrator, first of all for Hawick, then the South, and finally for Scotland. In 1992 his service to the game was recognised by his election as

President of the SRU. When Renwick broke into the Hawick team Charters was coaching the side and was also a selector.

> Jim would always be the youngster in every team he moved into, so he was always having to pick up fast. All we could do was give him the opportunity to get some experience under his belt because he wasn't the type of player that needed a lot of coaching. He needed to be fit, so it was important that he worked hard on that side of things. But his game was based on instinct and natural ability so there wasn't that much coaching that needed to be done. You didn't like to take his individualism away, you wanted it brought into the team. Jim, Colin Telfer, Alistair Cranston, Ian Chalmers, there was a lot of talented boys there, and they all had different ways of playing – what we had to do was use their styles to suit the team. With Jim we just needed to give him as much rugby as we could because he had a good enough rugby brain to learn from experience.

John Hegarty, who had been the rock in midfield during Hawick's success in their own sevens tournament in 1970, had gone to rugby league the previous May, but Hawick still enjoyed an embarrassment of riches at centre. They could call on the services of Robbie Welsh, who had been capped twice for Scotland against Ireland and England in 1967, as well as Alistair Cranston and Graham Hogg who would both be capped in years to come, not to mention a handful of junior players such as Davie Lyall and John Auchinleck, who would have commanded a place in the first team of almost any other club in Scotland. Despite this it was decided that the new kid on the block should be given a run in that position.

For the next eight seasons Hawick boasted perhaps the most accomplished and well-balanced midfield in the history of Scottish club rugby – with Telfer the master swordsman, using Cranston as his cutlass and Renwick as his rapier. "Colin Telfer was as crafty as a bag of weasels and used to run the show, while Alistair Cranston had the physical ability to knock doors out of windows, and of course Jim Renwick was the perfect amalgam of speed and skill," says Bill McLaren. "Hawick were very lucky that those three came together when they did and with the Hawick forwards providing the ammunition those three played some marvellous rugby together."

Eventually, in 1979, Telfer had to call it a day after the various injury problems which had meant he missed most of the 1978–79 season finally became too much of a burden. Cranston and Renwick would continue to play together until the end of the 1983–84 season, when Cranston eventually dropped out of the Hawick set-up after a record 415 games for the club, his career stretching back to 9 November 1968, when he made his debut for the club in an 18–9 defeat away to Royal High School FP.

Despite their success at club level, the three players would never appear together in international rugby. Telfer made his Scotland debut against Australia in 1968 and went on to play in seventeen internationals. His last match was against France in 1976 and in Scotland's next game Cranston made the first of his eleven appearances at that level against Wales. Renwick's international career straddled those of his two clubmates.

JMR:
They always seemed to stick with Geech [Ian McGeechan], and it was me, Cranny or Telfer who missed out. I suppose that's fair enough because Geech was a good player. Hawick used to play Headingley every year so we always came up against him and he was a talented player who worked hard on his game – he tackled well for his size and he had an okay left peg which got better with time. But they quite often played Geech at ten ahead of Telfer and to me Telfer was a better stand-off. Maybe Geech was better at inside centre than at stand-off.

Back in 1971, Renwick still had long-term aspirations to play stand-off but he also appreciated the need to be pragmatic at this stage in his career.

It was quite obvious that with Colin there I wasn't going to get in at ten. At that age you don't really know how good you are so you say to yourself: 'Aye, alright, I'll play for Hawick anywhere.'

Throughout the remainder of his career Renwick would step back into the stand-off slot when required to do so by Hawick, but fairly quickly it became apparent that he was going to come to be regarded primarily as a centre.

I think starting off playing number ten was quite useful because it gives you a different perspective. When you're playing stand-off you tend to be the playmaker – the pivotal guy. You call the shots and you have to know how everybody else on the field is doing. You need to be able to weigh up whether the centres are getting the better of their opponents, or if it would be better to get the forwards back involved. You're trying to bring everybody into the game at the right time. Rugby is a momentum game, it's easy if you're going forward, but how you get moving forward is the important bit – and that's the stand-off's responsibility. So if you have been in the stand-off's shoes then it helps, because you understand where he's coming from.

And I think it's easier to move out in rugby, from ten to twelve or thirteen, than it is to move in. Every time somebody was injured I'd get moved back into stand-off, but the more you play outside the harder it is to go back to thinking like a number ten. You still have a feel for what they are trying to do, but you're not in the mindset of making those decisions on the spot.

When you're playing stand-off regularly, you're doing the kicking and you're thinking like a stand-off. Then when you move out to centre somebody else is doing that and you're chasing the kicks, and before long you start thinking differently. I used to take all the touch kicks for the Quins and the PSA, but as soon as you stop doing it you don't practice as much, and you don't think about it as much, and you lose that wee bit skill.

If I'd been born in Jed or Gala or somewhere else I might have ended up playing stand-off all my days, but the other side of that is that I was lucky to have come though the Hawick system because I had guys with a lot of experience around me – especially Colin who probably taught me more about rugby than anyone else.

I still fancied myself as a stand-off but I was also enjoying my rugby in the centre. If I hadn't been enjoying it, or I couldn't handle it, then I would have had to do something about it. Nowadays I'd have to play stand-off because I wouldn't be big enough to play in the centre. But back then it wasn't a major problem. I wasn't a big centre but I was big enough, and I had pace, which was the most important thing.

Robin Charters watched Renwick develop from a fresh-faced youngster into a senior player for both Hawick and Scotland. He says that although Renwick had the ability to play anywhere in the backs, centre was the position that suited him best. "Jim was a scorer – he liked to score points," he says. "You had some guys who made tries, the likes of Colin Telfer was a maker – a setter-upper, a tactician. Jim was more of an individual scorer and that was why he was more effective in the centre. And he was a goalkicker, and they are worth their weight in gold."

In fact Renwick had done very little goalkicking before he became a Hawick player – as he explains: "Davie Cranston was an old-fashioned toe basher and when he got injured Hawick didn't have anyone to take over, so Robin organised a goalkicking competition at training. I hadn't been a front-line kicker before, as Lauder had done it at the PSA and somebody else had done it at the Quins, but I won the competition, so I got the job."

Scotland B

Jim Renwick, whose Hawick accent made the French think he was a neutral observer, had a super first appearance. He said himself he was only asked to tackle – but did so to devastating effect.
Brian Meek in *The Express*, 14 November 1971

On 13 November 1971, Scotland B played their first ever fixture against France B in the town of Oyannax, high in the French Alps, near the Swiss border. Renwick was selected in the centre in the team, for which only uncapped players were considered. There were four Boroughmuir players in the side, reflecting the healthy state of the club in the aftermath of their decision to go 'open' the previous year.

The team was:

W.B.N. Ross (Kilmarnock/Ayrshire); L.G. Dick (Loughborough Colleges), M.D. Hunter (Glasgow HSFP), J.M. Renwick (Hawick), D. Shedden (West of Scotland); A.A. Black (Boroughmuir), D.W. Morgan (Melville FP); R.D.H. Bryce (Bristol), R.L. Clark, J. Steven (both Edinburgh Wanderers), J.S. Wilkinson (Boroughmuir), I.A. Barnes (Hawick), S.G. Fowler (Dunfermline), W.S. Watson (Boroughmuir), W.H. Howie (London Scottish).

A young full back from Heriots called Andy Irvine had initially been selected, but had been forced to withdraw from the squad after injuring his leg playing for Scottish Universities a few weeks earlier.

Renwick had neither flown nor been out of the country before and his trepidation showed. He wanted to sit nearest the door on the plane and as it gained altitude he became extremely concerned that his "lugs" were "popping". On the bus to the game everyone sang but him.

His anxiety would not have been helped by the 40-mile bus journey from Geneva, where the team's flight had landed, to their hotel in St

Claudien. It certainly did not impress Norman Mair, a seasoned rugby traveller, initially as a player who earned four Scottish caps as a hooker in 1951, and then as a highly respected rugby writer. He reported in *The Scotsman* that: "The way up through the snow-dappled Alps lay along a road which is itself a cross between a spiral staircase and the Big Dipper – the most poignant moment coming when after the bus had twisted and turned tortuously for over an hour with, almost always, a mountainous fall on one or other side of the narrow road, our guide blithely announced that we were 'now leaving the main road . . .'"

The party had departed from Edinburgh on the Thursday before the match at 4pm GMT, and arrived at St Claudien on Friday at 1.10am French time, meaning that they had spent a full eight hours in transit. Writing in *Scottish Rugby* magazine a few years later Brian Meek described it as "a journey that would have done credit to Marco Polo".

On the Friday morning the squad trained at 10am on a training pitch near the hotel in St Claudien and enjoyed an afternoon off. The following day they set off for the match, and embarked upon what proved to be another unexpectedly long journey. Just as the Federation Francais de Rugby had "estimated" that it was a ten-mile trip from the airport to the hotel, when in reality it was 40 miles, so they had told the SRU that the hotel was "just up the road from Oyannax", when in fact it was twenty miles away. As a result the team arrived at the ground only half an hour before kick-off.

The French had played a well fancied Wales B side three weeks earlier in the first ever B international and had won at a canter (30–9), prompting a mood of uncontainable optimism amongst the French media. One local reporter stated that: "I would sleep well after naming this fifteen to play Scotland at Murrayfield on 15 January."

JMR:
Hamish Bryce was the captain. He was a prop from Bristol and I remember him coming across to Barney and me in the changing room before that match and saying: 'You Hawick boys, you think you're the bee's knees. Well, you're useless.' He was doing that line: 'You're no good, you shouldn't be here. Go out and prove you should be here.' That was him trying to get us worked up, but he wasn't that good himself. If somebody is going to say that to you then they've got to have a bit power, a bit fire – and he didn't have it.

The star of the show for the French that day was their scrum-half, Jean-Michel Aguirre, who would win his first cap against Australia later that month and go on to play 41 times for the senior French side at both scrum-half and full back. The other future French internationalists were all in the pack. Jean-Louis Martin, Jean-Pierre Hortoland, Jean-Claude Rossignol, Olivier Saisset and Yvan Buonomo would all be capped before the end of the year, against either Australia or Romania.

The French registered an emphatic 23–9 victory. Scotland's points came from three Dougie Morgan penalties. In truth this outcome was as much as the Scots could have hoped for. The French were much bigger and more experienced, and as a result the Scots spent the vast majority of the game on the back foot. The shambolic build-up to the match had not helped. However, the expedition was far from being a complete disaster, as Norman Mair pointed out on the Monday after the match:

> The day a country starts treating a defeat by 23–9 as other than a bad result, that country is finished. Yet not all the evidence gained by the selectors at Oyannax was negative – not by a long chalk – while the players had the opportunity to learn in an afternoon things about the game they might not learn for a decade back home.
>
> Both centres tackled heroically, the nineteen-year-old Jim Renwick – much more strongly built than a stranger seeing him in mufti would ever guess – covering himself in glory and giving more than one encouraging glimpse of attacking promise.

Renwick had once again been thrown in at the deep-end and had more than managed to keep his head above water. The Scottish selectors had taken note.

The party had travelled with 21 players only to discover upon arrival that they were restricted to four replacements, so on Friday morning coach Bill Dickinson told the Heriots pair of Jim Craig and Norman McLeod that they were surplus to requirements. The two therefore set off to sample the local hospitality, staggering back into the hotel noisily in the early hours of Saturday morning.

Having had hardly any time to sober up the dynamic duo enjoyed the committee hospitality on the Saturday, and were well oiled by the time they rejoined the players after the game. Back in St Claudien, a real one horse town, they led the way to the local nightspot. Upon arrival Craig surveyed the scene – two old boys drinking Pernod – and grandly announced: "Tout la monde boire avec Jeemee Craig." He then approached the bar, ordering "trois mille bieres".

The barman raised his eyebrows and asked: "Trois bieres?"

Craig answered emphatically: "Non, trois milles bieres."

So the barman shrugged and started opening every bottle he could lay his hands on.

Trial

National trial matches were a staple ingredient in the Scottish rugby calendar up until the mid 1990s when congested fixture lists, improvements in player analysis techniques, a narrowing of the elite player base and the need for any team playing at the sharp end of professional rugby to have extensive preparation times, all contrived to render the idea of such matches obsolete.

JMR:

The question is: do you need a trial to find out who's the best player, or can you prove it during the normal course of a season? I would have thought that if its eeksie-peeksie between two players then going head-to-head in a one-off match can answer a few important questions about a player's mental toughness and whether he has the ability to operate in a difficult environment.

If you've got two guys going against each other, and neither of them are playing in a team that they are used to, then surely you are going to get a clearer picture of who works better under pressure – who has the ability to keep it going when things really start to go wrong. Rugby maybe has changed a lot in the last fifteen years, but the bottom line is that it is still a simple game. And if you understand what's going on then I think you can learn a lot from watching guys thrown into a situation like a trial match.

That's especially the case when it's a young guy coming up against a guy with a reputation, because you can see who wants it more and who is working harder, and I would rather find that out in a trial than in the big match. Some guys maybe didn't like playing in trials because they were always hard games to play in, but I always quite liked them for that same reason. At Hawick I think it was maybe too easy for us sometimes but in a trial match everybody was under the microscope. It was a good way of testing yourself and keeping yourself sharp.

Some folk might say that trial matches don't fit into modern-day rugby and that I'm stuck in the past, but in New Zealand they still have an All Blacks trial and it doesn't seem to have done them any harm.

Renwick's first experience of playing in an international trial match came four weeks after he returned form his Scotland B adventure in the French Alps. He was selected at outside centre for the senior Blues team for the first National Trial at Murrayfield on Saturday 18 December 1971. He was stepping into the space opened up by the retiral from international rugby of Jock Turner and Chris Rea at the end of the previous season.

The teams had been named eleven days before the actual game, but neither side had the opportunity to meet up before the morning of the match.

JMR:
There would usually be a few boys from the Borders coming up for the trial so you would get a lift with them. We would meet at the North British Hotel where we had our dinner and then got sorted out for the trial. The two captains would take the teams and you would just sort out a few things before the game. It was never anything much, just the line-out codes and maybe a few basic moves in the backs.

I was shocked to be picked in the Blues, but once you've played in the trial you hope you've done enough. I remember being worried that they thought I was too young. To be honest I didn't really know what they were thinking because I didn't really know what I was thinking myself.

The Blues team won the match fairly convincingly by 31 points to 16, with Lewis Dick from Loughborough Colleges grabbing a hat trick of tries. Bobby Clark, the Edinburgh Wanderers hooker, also had a good match, taking seven strikes against the head, which thrust him into poll position for a starting spot in the absence of Frank Laidlaw from Melrose, who was Scotland's most capped hooker at that time and had toured New Zealand with John Dawes's Lions in 1971, but whose season had yet to take off because of a knee injury which would not go away. In fact Laidlaw never played for Scotland again.

While Renwick had a tidy, if unspectacular, match, Norman Mair felt that Colin Telfer at stand off had "kicked not only too much but somewhat vaguely." Mair then went on to speculate that: "The selectors may toy with the idea of having a look at Jim Renwick at stand-off but, particularly as he is so inexperienced, I expect them to decide instead to retain him as the other centre to John Frame."

Andy Irvine, who had been drafted into the Whites team after Dave Shedden was promoted to the Blues in place of the injured Alastair Biggar, had an unhappy afternoon on the left wing. "For all that he twice misfielded punts I remain convinced that this entertaining, if unevenly gifted, young player's greatest potential lies as an attacking full back," surmised Mair. And so it would prove, but not quite yet.

Renwick kept his place on the Blues team for the second Trial, which was played on 8 January 1972. The teams that day were:

Blues: A.R. Brown (Gala); W.C.C. Steele (Bedford), J.N.M. Frame (Gala), J.M. Renwick (Hawick), D. Shedden (West of Scotland); C.M. Telfer (Hawick), I.G. MacCrae (Gordonians); J. MacLauchlan (Jordanhill College), R.L. Clark (Edinburgh Wanderers), A.B. Carmichael (West of Scotland), A.F. McHarg (London Scottish), G.L. Brown (West of Scotland), N.A. McEwan (Gala), P.C. Brown (Gala, captain), R.J. Arneill (Northampton).

Whites: A.S. Turk (Langholm); L.G. Dick (Loughborough Colleges), M.D. Hunter (Glasgow HSFP), G. Turnbull (Jed-Forest), A.R. Irvine (Heriots FP); I. Robertson (Watsonians), A.J.M. Lawson (Edinburgh Wanderers); R.D.H. Bryce (Bristol, captain), Q. Dunlop (West of Scotland), J Steven (Edinburgh Wanderers), I.A. Barnes (Hawick), R.W.J. Wright (Edinburgh Wanderers), W. Lauder (Neath), W.S. Watson (Boroughmuir), S.G. Fowler (Dunfermline).

The Blues won the match by a convincing margin of 35 points to 3, with John Frame (2), Nairn McEwan, Alastair Biggar (who replaced the injured Billy Steele on the wing soon after half-time), PC Brown and Arthur Brown all touching down. Colin Telfor played much better; he kicked a drop-goal, while there were two conversions apiece for the name-sakes PC and Arthur Brown. The Whites could only manage a solitary Wilson Lauder penalty.

JMR:
I remember a headline in one of the papers the next day was: 'Cap Cert'. It was for me so I must have done alright. But to be honest I think I made the most of the good pack we had. I knew I had done okay, but folk were still telling me that I was too young, and that I hadn't worked

hard enough to justify a cap. I suppose it was a risk by Scotland but to
be fair I think I justified their faith.

On the Monday morning after the trial the Scotland team was announced
for their match against France the following weekend. Renwick would
make his international debut at the tender age of nineteen, with the selectors deciding to go with the same fifteen that had played so well for the
Blues two days earlier.

Norman Mair gave his thoughts in *The Scotsman* on the day the team
was announced:

> From one of those rugby-playing families in which the Scottish Border
> country abounds, Jim Renwick will, I think, reckon that he has come by
> his first cap with almost discomforting ease. However the point is that
> there is a vacancy created by Chris Rea's departure to [a new career in]
> sound radio and that Jim Renwick has so far done everything asked of
> him: and though there are those who argue that that has turned out not
> to be all that much, that is hardly Jim Renwick's fault.
>
> Moreover, those of us who were at Oyannax for the B international
> with France will not readily forget the way he raised his tackling to emerge
> as the hero of a plucky Scottish defence. A neat exponent of the basic
> skills, Renwick – smallish but solidly built – is one of those players who
> fits easily into a team: and as befits a son of Hawick, the game matters
> desperately to this young apprentice electrician. Which is a very important
> point when you are maybe a point behind, time fleeting, lungs bursting
> and would give much just to be free to lie down and die.

Renwick had come a long way during a very short period of time and
there was plenty of doubters who feared he had been elevated too quickly.
In five days time everyone would find out if this was the case.

Capped

Jim Renwick won his first cap for Scotland against France at Murrayfield on 15 January 1972. Also in the side that day was his Hawick team-mate Colin Telfer, who was winning only his sixth cap but was already well established as Scotland's leading stand-off. Bobby Clark, the 28-year-old hooker from Edinburgh Wanderers, was the other debutant.

In the professional era, when international teams prepare for matches at training camps in Polish resorts, where players recuperate from training sessions in cryotherapy chambers and undertake intensive nutrition education programmes, Renwick's recollections of the build-up to his first cap help highlight just how much things have changed in a relatively short period of time.

You were meant to get rested before your first cap but it didn't always happen like that. Toomba [Alan Tomes] had to play against West of Scotland the week before his first cap because it was a big game, and he was rused about that. As far as Derrick [Grant, Hawick coach] was concerned Hawick was the most important thing – so he might tell you that you were playing and it was hard to say no if Derrick told you. It was the same all the way through with Derrick, he never mellowed. If you went away to play for the Baa Baas, he would say: 'Ah, yir always away to play for the Baa Baas – you. There's nae need to play for the Baa Baas, you've played for them once.'

I remember right at the end of my career, at the tail end of 1981–82 season, Hawick were playing Gala in the Border League, and I was asked to go to the Hong Kong Sevens with the Scottish Borderers. The league was already won but Derrick says: 'We're playing Gala and you're going to Hong Kong?' He couldn't understand why I'd want to go to Hong Kong instead of Netherdale.

In the year I was capped the trial was the week before the first international so I had to play in that, but it wasn't so bad because I was in the same boat as all the other boys in the side, and I knew that I had to do it if I was going to get in the team. I wouldn't have been so happy if the Scotland side had already been picked and I'd had to play for Hawick. I never used to worry much about getting injured but I think I would have been pretty nervous if that had been the case.

The next year they moved the final trial forward and picked the team earlier, which meant we could go up to Murrayfield for a squad session on the Sunday before the match. Bill Dickinson was behind that, he was a lecturer at Jordanhill College who had been appointed adviser to the captain in 1972, and he started bringing in a few ideas to make us a bit more professional. At first these sessions were just a runabout really, but by the mid seventies they started getting more and more intense.

All the way through my career I would go down to Mansfield and train with the boys on the Tuesday night before a cap – I'd do a bit of sprinting, have a hot bath, and just try to get myself right.

I did that before my first cap and I remember afterwards I was doing a bit of work on the clubhouse, putting in a couple of heaters as frost protection for the water pipes, and Robin and Derrick were in the bar having a bit of chat. They didn't know I was there, and they were talking about me. They said that they thought I was a bit young and that I was a lucky boy to be getting capped as soon, and that I was maybe not ready yet. They were just saying what they thought, and they weren't saying anything they wouldn't have said to my face, but I remember I was a wee bit unhappy with that at the time. It maybe did me some good though – it would have stopped me getting carried away with all the hype.

The week at work before an international is tough. You're just kidding yourself on, but you only have to make it through three days because you're back up the road on Thursday morning – which was the earliest the IRB would let you meet up. In the early days I had to take the Thursday and Friday as holidays, but later on they started giving me them as days off. It would be a harder session on Thursday morning, but by now we'd done our bit on France so it was mainly thinking about what we were going to do ourselves – how we were going to play it, where we were going to attack them, that sort of stuff. After training we watched a film of Scotland's game against France the year before.

We'd meet at ten o'clock in the morning and it would be about two in the afternoon before we got our lunch, and the stuff you got at Murrayfield in those days was pretty different to what I was used to –

they got outside caterers in and it was stuff like game pie and pigeon pie, which wasn't for me.

Then it was up to the Braids Hill Hotel to find your room, and you needed an O-grade in map reading to do that because it's an old rickety place with winding corridors. I liked the Braids, it wasn't a flash hotel – it was old style with creaking floorboards, squeaky beds and rattling windows – but it was a good hotel for getting out the road and getting the team together, and it was good food, and they looked after us well. They used to spoil us a wee bit with cocoa and biscuits whenever you wanted it, that sort of stuff.

Thursday night we used to go to the pantomime. Can you believe it? Grown men getting ready to play for their country and we went to the pantomime. Before my first cap we went to see 'Aladdin' at the Kings. We were sitting there shouting: 'Look out behind you!' and all that. Then at half-time we had to stand up and wave to the audience. It had aye been that way, and I suppose it was something to do to pass the time.

Friday was basically a wasted day. We got up and went to Murrayfield but we didn't do anything apart from pose for photographers. That was when the press came along and started building up the hype for the game. I used to think that it was a wee bit too much, but that's just the way it was I suppose.

The only guys that got anything meaningful out of it were the goalkickers because they were the only ones allowed on the pitch. I was never a front line goalkicker, it would be Arthur Brown or PC, but because I was a back-up goalkicker I used to go out and kick the ball back to them. I quite liked that, it was something to do. Mind you, that only started happening later on after I'd been in the side a couple of seasons – in the early days not even the kickers got on the pitch before the match.

We'd get a shower at about one o'clock and then head back to the Braids for lunch. We'd get the works – prawn cocktail, fillet steak – the whole lot. Friday afternoon was free. Laterally we would tend to stick together as a squad, but in the early days if you wanted to go somewhere you would just go. There was quite often a game on in Edinburgh – Heriots or Edinburgh Accies might be playing a team from Wales or Ireland depending on who Scotland were playing – so we'd go and watch that. Or we might just go for a walk along Princes Street and have a look in the shops. Later on we used to go and play snooker, or go tenpin bowling. There'd usually be a team meeting at five o'clock so you would have to be back for that – but there was still a lot of spare time to just get on and do what you wanted.

There'd be two or three committee boys at the Braids on the Thursday, and then on the Friday they'd all be there because that night they had their dinner before the international – and some of them would be looking rough on the Saturday. For the players it was a long night, you were just kicking your heels – thinking about the next day and getting yourself ready.

I've seen myself have a couple of pints on the night before an international. You're in the Braids, you're in a strange bed, the windows are rattling in the wind and you can't get to sleep because you're playing the game in your mind. Its murder, there's nothing worse, so you'd nip out for a couple of pints at the bar next door. It maybe wasn't encouraged, but it wasn't a secret, you were just going for a couple of pints before bed. Changed days when you think of it. They wouldn't get away with that now.

On Saturday morning some folk liked to lie long but I tended to get up, get down the stairs, get my breakfast and that would be me – I wouldn't eat any more until after the match. In between times the coach might come round your room and speak to you, talk about the game and what you were going to do. The kickers would go down to Murrayfield to get a feel for it – which was important because Murrayfield was a hard place to kick goals in those days with its open ends which meant the wind used to swirl around you – but most of the time you were just trying to relax.

At eleven o'clock we would meet in the players' room and that was the coach's big pitch, he would go over the conditions, what we'd planned and what we'd practised. He would say his major bit at that meeting. After that some of the boys would go for lunch and it would be a bowl of soup and toasties – I never used to bother. Then it was up to your room to get your boots and everything packed, then down to the team room to wait for the bus. The telly would be on and we'd watch Bill McLaren doing the build-up from Murrayfield.

There was no dress code really, but they wanted you to wear a shirt and tie on the way to the game. You were meant to wear your blazer too, but you had to buy it at Jenners and I didn't get one until my 21st birthday when my mother bought it for us, so I just wore a sports coat.

The bus to Murrayfield was good. We'd pass all the folk in their kilts on their way to the game and they'd give us a wave. We used to sing a lot on the bus – we used to sing 'Flower of Scotland' before it became the national anthem. Billy Steele was a bit of a singer and he liked the Corries so we sang a lot of their songs – and there were other songs that had been picked up. In rugby most teams have their own songs and 'Flower of Scotland' and some of the other Corries' songs were what we sang.

The older players would spread out on the bus and sit with the young ones to try and ease them over if they were feeling nervous – I think Nairn McEwan sat beside me the first time. Obviously you're pretty anxious – you don't know what you're going into, you've never played in front of a crowd like that before and you know its going to be fast but you're not sure how fast. Everybody wants to do it, but you're apprehensive anyway.

We usually got to Murrayfield about an hour and a quarter before kick-off. We'd go and look at the pitch, and try to take in the atmosphere. Then it was back into the dressing rooms and the coach would be shouting key objectives while you're getting changed and trying to get warmed up. In those days you couldn't get out for a run before the match, you had to do as much warming up in the dressing room as you could. I remember one year later on in my career when I had a bad leg and I went to get warmed-up in the car park between the cars.

Quite often I used to be sick before the game – not all the time, but fairly often. I don't think that was a bad thing, it was just nervous tension and it's good to be on edge before a big match – it sharpens your senses.

Half an hour to go and you would get your photo taken, then the President of the SRU would come in – you could tell he had arrived because you could smell the gin and tonic in the dressing room. Usually it would be the same old stuff: 'You're playing for your country today, and remember we don't want any dirty play.' But some presidents were pretty straight and would tell you to go out there and kick their arses. When Lex Govan was the president he used to say things like: 'I've got only three words to say to you boys: Fire and F-ing Fury'. It was always four or five words instead of three and I remember McGeechan used to aye laugh at that.

Once the President had said his bit he would leave and the captain would take over, and it was him from then on in. Every captain has got his own way of doing it – of trying to get you pumped up – but the bottom line is that you don't need pumped up because you're pretty much there already.

PC was captain for my first cap and he was pretty good. He was quiet but you could tell he had this confidence in his own ability. He maybe wasn't as inspirational as others in the changing room, but with him it was more about what he did on the pitch.

There was be a lot going on during those last few moments in the changing room, and a lot would go over your head, especially for that first cap. You would find that maybe the half-backs might get together, the three-quarters might get together and the forwards would get together, and they'd all be doing what they needed to do to get ready. Then, before you know where you are, the ref comes in and you're down the tunnel and onto the pitch.

There was no 'Flower of Scotland' in those days, they played 'God Save the Queen' and 'La Marseillaise'. We didn't line up for the national anthems like they do now. Sometimes we would be in a huddle, but other times we just stood where we were when the music started, so you might be down in the in-goal area by yourself and you just had to stand there and wait for the music to finish. To be honest it was something that the players could have done without because they had done all their preparation and they just wanted to get on with it. Having said that, it was a good chance to calm down and get your thoughts together. It maybe wasn't so good for the forwards because they want to get stuck in and make contact; but as a back you have to have a different sort of psyche because your first touch might be catching a high ball or rifling a kick into the corner – it might be a contact situation, but nine times out of ten it's not, it's you getting the ball and having to see what's on.

There was one time later on in my career when they were playing 'God Save the Queen' and I must have been caught spitting on camera. I got pulled in for an interview with Dod Burrell – who was the chairman of the selectors at the time. It didn't come to anything, but we were all told that in future we had to stand to attention during the national anthems and we weren't to spit. Maybe it looked like I was giving a bit of dissent – but it wasn't that, I was just trying to clear my throat. You know what it's like when you come out into the fresh air and you're looking to get the rubbish out your lungs.

There weren't that many there for my first cap, I think only about 40,000 because French games weren't that well supported in the early seventies. I can't remember much about the game to be honest, I was young and it was all happening around me. I think in your first cap you're just playing on your wits.

Maybe the French didn't play as well as they could. They had some big players in the side – Benoit Dauga, Jean-Pierre Bestiat, Armand

Vaquerin and guys like that, but I suppose they've never been good travellers. What I do remember is that we had a good scrum, with the Mouse [Ian McLauchlan], Sandy Carmichael, Bobby Clark, Gordon Brown and Alastair McHarg in the front five. Broon and McHarg got us the ball in the line-out. So, basically, it's what I've always said about rugby. If your front five are producers in the scrum and line-out, it makes life easy for the rest of the team. And the front five definitely was the strength when I came into the Scottish side – no doubt about that.

In fact Scotland did not dominate the scrum, as they lost five strikes against the head and managed to steal the French ball only once; however they were superior to the visitors in every other facet of the game with Nairn McEwan and Roger Arneill dominating proceedings and ensuring a wealth of second phase possession for the home side.

France started the match in lively fashion and it took a fine cover tackle from Colin Telfer on Jack Cantoni to prevent the visitors taking an early lead after Pierre Villepreux had created an overlap on the left wing. But it wasn't long before the Scots took charge and after twelve minutes they took the lead with a fine Telfer try. As was the case with much of Scotland's good work that afternoon it came from some impressive scavenging play by the back row. MacEwan charged down Jean-Michel Aguirre's clearance kick after a wheeled scrum close to the French line, recovered the ball, fed PC Brown, and the Scotland captain sent Telfer over in the left-hand corner.

A few moments later Telfer extended Scotland's lead with a sweetly struck drop-goal from outside the 25, after a line-out take by PC Brown. Just before half-time PC Brown made it 10–0 with a 35-yard penalty after a French line-out infringement.

Scotland started the second half with the same gusto as they had exhibited throughout the first 40 minutes, with Clark hacking a loose line-out ball up the left touchline, for MacEwan to pick up and feed Renwick. Having cut back infield towards the posts, Renwick was eventually closed down and couldn't quite get his pass away to Ian McLauchlan for what would almost certainly have been Scotland's second score of the match.

Instead it was France who struck next. Having taken a painful blow to the ribs, Ian McCrae retired from the match and Arthur Brown had to deputise at scrum-half whilst Alan Lawson made the long journey from the main stand at Murrayfield, through a labyrinth of corridors to the changing rooms, from where he could get the match doctor's permission to join the action as a replacement. During that time Brown was penalised for a squint put-in, giving Villepreux the opportunity to kick the points from inside his own half and only 15 yards in from the touchline.

Scotland responded with what was perhaps the best of the three fine tries they scored that afternoon. It was Renwick who eventually touched down after some admirable composure and impressive foresight by Telfer and Arthur Brown transformed a promising French counter attack into a fine Scottish score. It came about after MacEwan spilled the ball when he was flattened on the French 25-yard line and Jean-Pierre Lux hacked ahead. Telfer was first back and scooped the ball up off the deck, but with a blanket of French players bearing down on him his options appeared to be limited. However he showed the presence of mind and the adventurousness of spirit to carry on running backwards towards his own goal line, thus giving Arthur Brown the time and space he needed to sweep left so as to receive an intelligent pass from Telfer which immediately transformed defence into attack. The full back was eventually half held by a French opponent but still managed to feed Alastair Biggar, and when he was eventually closed down Renwick was on the inside ready to receive the ball. From 25 yards out the debutant scampered home.

These were the days before neutral touch-judges were used in internationals, with a representative from each of the competing countries running the line instead. On this occasion Eric Grierson, a former international referee and Hawick stalwart, was doing the job for Scotland. In the press the following week there appeared a photograph of Grierson forfeiting any pretence of impartiality by jumping in the air and raising his arms in triumph as Renwick touched down over the line.

With 20 minutes to go Scotland were 14–3 ahead. They were in a commanding position but they were not yet out of sight, and when Benoit Dauga crashed over after a mix-up at the base of a scrum close to the Scottish line, and Villepreux kicked the conversion, it looked like a tense finale was on the cards. France were now within a converted try of winning the match.

However the Scots kept their composure and Renwick twice pinned the French back with cleverly angled kicks towards the right touchline. Then, in injury time, Arthur Brown followed Renwick's lead and rifled a kick into the corner. PC Brown stole possession at the subsequent line-out and Lawson's long pass found Telfer, who fed John Frame with the neatest of reverse flicks. The Gala centre hit the line at a devastating angle, but he still needed to use all of his considerable pace and power to make the most of the situation – first of all he shrugged off the despairing tackles from Dauga and Villepreux, before carrying Jean-Pierre Bastiat, the heaviest Frenchman on the field, over the line.

"Schoolboys went wild, invading the pitch. Though everyone knows, including themselves no doubt, that they should not have done it, they had an excuse, having seen a try that typified just what Scotland had done in the match – broken the French," wrote Bill McMurtie in the *Glasgow Herald* the following Monday.

Arthur Brown's conversion brought the score to 20–9, giving the Scots their biggest margin of victory over France in the 31 games since their 23–6 success at Murrayfield in 1927.

"Jim Renwick did almost everything with the minimum fuss and the maximum of efficiency: not tall but well made and packed full of those rugby virtues that have stood the test of time," opined Norman Mair in *The Scotsman* . He had done more than enough to justify his selection.

And so it was on to the post-match celebrations.

JMR:
After the game there was a bus to the NB [North British Hotel]. You got changed into your DJ and then went up to the President's room for a few drinks. If you won you were allowed to drink champagne, if you got beat it was cans of Export. So that night we had a couple of glasses of champagne and then went down stairs to dinner.

In the early days I had to rent my DJ. They used to refund you the money – £4.50 it was if I remember – but then guys started claiming the DJ on expenses even if they had one of their own, so they had to do away with that. A few years later my mother bought me a bottle-green velvet dinner jacket – they were all the rage and it was in Hawick colours, so it was perfect as far as I was concerned. Later on boys started wearing kilts but I've never had a kilt on. What do I want wearing a skirt? I don't like them. Even at my son Scott's wedding they were all in kilts, but I just wore a suit.

At the dinner the players sat in the centre of the room and the delegates from the clubs were all round the side. There was a guy playing the piano, and you always got a cigar. I remember Berot, the French stand-off, was a nightclub singer so he got up and sang a few numbers. Then the presidents would speak and the captains would speak and it would be the same old patter, thanking the referee and the touch judges and all that stuff. The French dinners were a nightmare because you had to listen to the interpreter as well so it went on for ages.

After dinner there was a players' bar and nobody else was allowed in, so we used to smuggle drinks out to Robin Charters who would be at the dinner as Hawick's representative but was stuck in the lobby. In the mid-seventies Gordon Brown and boys like that started getting things organised and they started having a player's dance which you were able to bring your wife or girlfriend to, which was a better way of doing it.

After my first cap there was a disco on at Boroughmuir and some of us went up there for a drink in our dinner suits – it was me, Hovis [Arthur Brown] and Colin [Telfer]. We stayed there until eleven o'clock, when the place closed, then it was back to the NB and I think the President's room was still open so we went in and had a few more beers.

Then it was back to Hawick on the Sunday. Sometimes I'd get a lift if there was someone else going down the road, but Colin lived in Edinburgh and he was the only Hawick boy in the side, so I had to get the bus that time.

To be honest it didn't matter how I got back to Hawick because I was that goosed and I just wanted to sit by myself and relax. It had been a big week and a big build up, starting the Sunday before with the second national trial, but Derrick still wanted you to train at Hawick on Tuesday, and then you were with the squad from Thursday morning. So with the game on the Saturday, and then the drink afterwards, well you were knackered by the time Sunday came around. You'd had a week of thinking and worrying about the game, so now that it was out the way you felt pretty flat.

In the changing room before the match there had been a bundle of telegrams which I hadn't had time to read. I'd had a quick glance at them but the first time I really got to read them was on the Sunday. I've still got them all, from folk wishing me well – the PSA, the Quins, teachers I'd had, the swimming club, folk like that. I got one from Arthur Brown's

mother and father; now she'd be the first to shout at you at a Hawick–
Gala game – she'd hit Robbie Welsh with a brolly at a Hawick–Gala
game a few years before – but there you go.

It took you a couple of days to get over it physically, but the thing
about Hawick was that you didn't get to walk around with your head in
the clouds – they kept your feet on the ground. So it was back to work
and that was it.

As expected Renwick retained his place for Scotland's match against
Wales three weeks later, though this was not quite as joyous an occasion.
Things started off well enough, with Renwick (kicking in place of the
concussed PC Brown) opening the visitors' account with an early penalty.
Despite playing well below the high standards set in their previous
match, Scotland found themselves 12–10 ahead after an hour of play.
But in the final twenty minutes the hosts were able to cut loose, with
Gareth Edwards (twice), Roy Bergiers and John Taylor adding to Gerald
Davies' first half touchdown, to make it 35–12 to Wales at the end – thus
condemning Scotland to their heaviest ever defeat in Cardiff up until
that point.

Renwick's friends at the Quins were in Wales for the match and at the
end of the game they ran onto the pitch to greet him. Then, having failed
to sneak down the tunnel, they quickly made their way round to the back
of the stand, where they caused an almighty fuss as they tried to get into
the changing rooms to visit the boy who had been part of their own squad
only two years earlier.

Despite Scotland's late collapse Carwyn James, the Llanelli coach who
had masterminded the successful British and Irish Lions tour of Australia
and New Zealand in 1971, was impressed by Scotland's baby-faced centre.
"I like Jim Renwick. He's going to be very good," he said. Renwick's most
vivid recollection of that afternoon is of being mightily impressed by the
length of Gareth Edwards' pass – which meant Barry John at stand-off
was able to line up opposite the Scottish inside centre.

Scotland did not play Ireland that year, with the SRU deciding after
much procrastination that it was a risk not worth taking given the
prevailing political climate – especially with two servicemen in the
team. In Scotland's final game of the season they defeated England
23–9 at Murrayfield. It was Scotland's fourth successive defeat over the
Auld Enemy and meant that England picked up the wooden spoon that
year.

Hawick finished the season top of the unofficial championship, having lost only one match away to Edinburgh Wanderers and drawing another against Melrose at the Greenyards two weeks later.

The All Blacks

The 1972–73 season promised to be a busy one for Renwick, with both Hawick RFC and the SRU commemorating their centenary years. On top of that New Zealand were to tour Europe, which meant he would get his first chance to play against the mighty All Blacks.

However, his season got off to an inauspicious start when he took a blow to the face during Hawick's impressive 24–21 victory over a Scottish Presidents XV which was essentially a Scotland B side with players such as Dougie Morgan and Andy Irvine playing. Renwick was in considerable pain but made himself available the following week when the SRU kicked off their centenary celebrations by hosting a match between a composite Scotland–Ireland side and a composite England–Wales side at Murrayfield.

Renwick had not been in the initial team but was called into the side during the week leading up to the match after first choice stand-off Colin Telfer, and then his initial replacement Barry McGann, both called off. Mike Gibson took on the number ten jersey and Renwick took the great Irishman's place in the centre. Norman Suddon also played, as a late replacement for Ireland's Ray McLoughlin.

In front of 40,000 spectators the team in green and blue won by 30 points to 21. Gibson was the star of the show with three tries. The rest of his team's points came from Tom Grace, the Irish winger, who scored a brace, and Arthur Brown, who slotted two penalties and two conversions.

Just over a month later Renwick played in his first ever match against the All Blacks, on 25 November 1972. He was selected at centre to play for the rather clumsily named Rest of Scottish Districts XV against Ian Kirkpatrick's touring side.

The Scottish Districts team was:
A.R. Brown (Gala); W.C.C. Steele (Bedford), J.N.M. Frame (Gala), J.M. Renwick (Hawick), L.G. Dick (Loughborough Colleges); I.R. McGeechan (Headingley), I.G. McCrae (Gordonians); N. Suddon (Hawick), F.A.L.

Laidlaw (Melrose), R.D.H. Bryce (Bristol), A.P. McHarg (London Scottish), P.K. Stagg (Sale), N.A. McEwan (Gala), P.C. Brown (Gala), W. Lauder (Neath).

On paper it was a pretty strong side. There were thirteen capped players in the starting fifteen, and the two uncapped players would go on to win international honours in the not too distant future: Ian McGeechan winning the first of his 32 caps when Scotland played the All Blacks three weeks later, while Hamish Bryce appeared as a replacement against Ireland during the 1973 Five Nations tournament.

JMR:

The game was played at Mansfield and it was a real eye opener. They were a good side and I'd never played against anything like that before. We had a strong team out, we had some big time players like PC, Alastair McHarg and Splash (Nairn MacEwan) in the side, but we were never beating them. In fact we got blown away that day. We got screwed in the scrum, we hardly won any line-out ball, and they were a lot more dynamic than us around the park. I was just tackling forwards all day. We ended up getting beat 26–6.

To be fair it would have been the first time that most of our boys had played against New Zealand and it was a bit of a learning curve. It was a different feeling when you played against the Blacks. They had an aura about them which was overpowering.

I remember going down to Mansfield to see the South of Scotland playing Wilson Whineray's All Blacks in 1963. There was 16,000 folk there and they put their best side out – with guys like Colin Meads, Kelvin Tremain and Ken Gray playing. But the South got stuck in and they only lost 8–0 in the end. I remember Christie Elliot from Langholm and Elliot Broatch from Hawick were the two centres that day, and they tackled everything that moved.

But even though the score in that match was close you knew that you had seen something special. They were huge, they were scary, and with memories like that you always had it at the back of your mind that you were playing against rugby gods. So you wanted to get out there and have a go at them, but deep down you were intimidated as well.

And the All Blacks were focused tourists. New Zealand is so far away from everyone else that even Australia was a pretty major expedition for them in those days, so if they wanted to play international rugby they knew they had to come away from home on long trips and they were used to it – they had it sussed.

That was the first time I faced the Haka and I never really thought much about it to be honest. I just thought it was a ritual that you should show respect to, but it didn't scare you or anything like that. Mind you, back in those days they didn't do it with the vigour that they do now, when they're in your face and it's like a war cry. Half of them didn't know it, you could see them looking round and copying the boy next door. I'm not saying it was like that for the Maori boys, but certainly a lot of the rest of them weren't very convincing.

The other thing that sticks in my mind was that it was a dark day and we wanted to play with white balls, but the All Blacks wouldn't let us. They had to have leather balls with the lacing because in those days their kickers were toe bashers and their wingers threw in at the line-out and they had to get a grip of the old lace. So in a lot of ways they were ahead of their time, but because they were that isolated from the rest of the rugby world I suppose they were in some ways a bit out of touch with the way the game was changing. Not that they were ever in any danger of getting left behind – rugby was that important to them that they would pick up on these things pretty quickly and adapt them to suit the way they wanted to play.

The Combined Districts team's chances were not helped by the SRU's insistence that a Saturday morning meet (and not a Thursday evening or Friday morning assembly) would give the team sufficient time to prepare for the challenge of taking on the mighty All Blacks.

The first National Trial of that season was played on 2 December and Renwick scored a try and kicked a conversion as the senior Blues team defeated the Whites by 31 points to 12. He was named in the Scottish Districts XV to play the Combined Services the following Wednesday, and it was the stated intention of the national selectors to give a run-out in this match to the provisional Scotland team for the imminent Test match against the All Blacks – save Billy Steele (RAF) and Bobby Clark (Royal Navy) who the forces team had first refusal on.

The Districts side played poorly in this match and only managed a 13–12 victory after a last-gasp Renwick try. Despite this poor showing the selectors stuck to their guns, bringing Steele and Clark back into the squad but apart from that sticking with the team they had pencilled in after the Trial – although injuries altered the composition of the side slightly.

With Colin Telfer (knee ligament damage), John Frame (severe concussion sustained during the trial) and Arthur Brown (fractured tibia) all unavailable due to injury, the Scotland team for the All Blacks match featured four new faces in an inexperienced back division.

Ian McGeechan had performed solidly at stand-off in difficult circumstances in the game against the All Blacks at Mansfield Park three weeks earlier, and that was enough to convince the national selectors that he should wear the number ten jersey ahead of Fraser Dall of Heriots and David Bell of Watsonians.

Andy Irvine was selected at full back after a performance of breathtaking impudence during the National Trial, during which he was moved from the junior White's team to the senior Blues team at half-time after several sparkling intrusions into the line. Another break in the second half set up a try for Renwick. Irvine had missed the game against the Combined Services with an injured knee, but when Davie Aitchison, his main rival for the number fifteen jersey, broke his collar bone in that game, and Irvine declared himself fit the following day, the decision became a simple one for the selectors.

Ian Forsyth, a powerful centre who was at that point playing for Stewart's FP in their last season before they amalgamated with Melville Colleges FP, was also given his first cap. He had only made it into the Whites side for the National Trial because Bob Keddie, who had been capped in 1967, had to withdraw from the match with an injured shoulder. But he ended up doing a superb job as a replacement for John Frame in the Blues team when the Gala player retired from the match concussed, and on the Wednesday before the match he was called into the national side when it became clear that Frame would not recover in time.

David Shedden, the West of Scotland winger, was another debutant on the wing. Of the capped players in the Scottish backline, Renwick was still two months shy of his 21st birthday and was only winning his fourth cap, scrum-half Ian McCrae had been capped five times before, and Billy Steele had nine international appearances under his belt in an international career stretching back to 1969. That meant the Scottish backline had a grand total of 17 caps between them, which was half as many as the 34 which had been accumulated by their opposite numbers.

The teams were:

Scotland: A.R. Irvine (Heriots FP); W.C.C. Steele (Bedford), I.W. Forsyth (Stewart's FP), J.M. Renwick (Hawick), D. Shedden (West of Scotland); I.R. McGeechan (Headingly), I.G. McCrae (Gordonians); J. McLauchlan

(Jordanhill College), R.L. Clark (Edinburgh Wanderers), A.B. Carmichael (West of Scotland), A.F. McHarg (London Scottish), G.L. Brown (West of Scotland), N.A. MacEwan (Gala), P.C. Brown (Gala), R.J. Arneill (Northampton).

New Zealand: J.F. Karam (Wellington); B.G. Williams (Auckland), B. Robertson (Counties), R.M. Parkinson (Poverty Bay), G.B. Batty (Wellington); I.N. Stevens (Wellington), S. M. Going (North Auckland); J.D. Matheson (Otago), R.W. Norton (Canterbury), G.J. Whiting (King Country), P.J. Whiting (Auckland), H.H. McDonald (Canterbury), I.A. Kirkpatrick (Poverty Bay), A. I. Scown (Taranaki), A.J. Wylie (Canterbury).

JMR:
When we went to Murrayfield we had a good chance. They had most of the play but we might have stolen it in the last minute. It was 10–9 going into injury time and we were putting them under a bit of pressure, but Sid Going intercepted a pass inside from Alistair McHarg and ran the length. We ended up getting beat 14–9, but there was no shame in that because that was a good side they had brought over.

Kirkpatrick was the captain and he was one of their all-time greats. He was big, strong, fast, a ball handler – he had it all – and he was a nice bloke too.

Then there was Alex Wylie who was also in the back row, and he was a really hard man – as tough as they come. And their front-row of Jeff Matheson, Tane Norton and Graham Whiting were three big powerful guys, so we maybe didn't have the same advantage there that we were used to against European sides at that time.

I was against Bruce Robertson and that was an education. He was a tough boy to go up against because he had pace and he had the deft little touches. He was a good runner with the ball but he also knew when to kick and when to pass. He was a tricky player and I always thought he wanted to play rugby. Sid Going was at scrum-half and he was a livewire. Bryan Williams on the left wing was another one of the stars of the show – he was big, fast and had a great side-step. And of course Grant Batty was a wee guy but a real handful on the other wing.

As a team they were probably fitter than Scottish rugby players at that time and they had high skill levels too, but the key to their success was their aggression. They were more aggressive than anything we were used to. Whatever they did they did with conviction and it was relentless. I suppose they were ahead of the game in that sense.

They didn't make many mistakes either. They just didn't give much away and they would never do anything daft. They ground you into the mud first and if they were going to play then it would be in the second half after they had done the hard graft. There weren't many weaknesses and they were a well-organised outfit that knew what they had to do to get the win.

It was another step up for me, and I remember thinking after that game that I had a long way to go if I was going to be able to live with these boys. I realised that I was going to have to work on my pace, because although I wasn't slow I wanted to be faster. I could get away with it in Scotland but against teams like New Zealand you're in danger of getting burned. You can never be too fast.

Tackling was a problem too. I wasn't big and I was never going be a knocker downer like Cranny [Alistair Cranston], but if I was going to hold my own against men like Bryan Williams and Bruce Robertson then I was going to have to improve my physique which was something I had never thought about before. The communication in defence wasn't there either.

Off the pitch Renwick was not quite so impressed with the tourists.

They were pretty dour. I remember going to a reception after the Scottish Districts game in the Vic Hotel in Hawick and you didn't get to know them much. I think it was just that they were tough guys – the likes of Alex Wylie and Jeff Matheson were hard men – and they were there to do the business, not to have fun.

Kirkpatrick was a good guy, but they said he wasn't tough enough with the discipline and that was maybe why they had a few problems – Keith Murdoch was sent home. There were obviously problems there and maybe that was why they came across the way they did.

They were alright, but they wouldn't sign autographs and things like that. Other All Blacks teams I've been involved with since then were a lot more friendly – guys like Stu Wilson, Bernie Fraser and Duncan Robertson were better boys – but that tour was pretty dour.

The story of Murdoch and his fall from grace is one of the more intriguing in the history of rugby. A mountainous prop by the standards of the time, weighing more than seventeen stone at his peak, he had punched a security guard who was trying to stop him raiding the kitchen at the Angel Hotel in Cardiff, just hours after he had scored New Zealand's only try during their 19–16 victory over Wales on 2 December. Murdoch had a history of getting into trouble as a result of his wild behaviour off the pitch and, under pressure from the Home Unions, the All Blacks management decided to send him home. But Murdoch didn't make it back to New Zealand, stepping off his homeward bound plane during a break in Sydney and disappearing into the Australian outback, where he has lived ever since – although apparently he has made frequent low-profile visits back to Otago over the years to visit family and friends. Even while trying to live in obscurity Murdoch has frequently found himself an unwilling participant in major news stories – the latest episode being in 2001 when he was summoned to attend a coroner's hearing as a witness in a case involving the homicide of a young Aborigine, who had been caught breaking into Murdoch's farm. No charges were ever brought against Murdoch. Ian Kirkpatrick has since said that he regrets not standing up for his erstwhile team-mate at the time of his expulsion from the tour.

The All Blacks lost five of the 32 matches they played on that 1972–73 tour – against Llanelli, North-Western Counties, Midland Counties (West), the Barbarians and France. The Barbarians game in particular will be long remembered as one of the great matches in the history of the game. It started with a bang when, after two minutes Phil Bennet fielded a Bryan Williams kick ahead, bobbed and weaved past several tacklers, and then launched a thrilling counter attack down the left touchline. The ball passed through the hands of JPR Williams, John Pullin, John Dawes, Tom David and Derrick Quinnell, before Gareth Edwards appeared from nowhere to take on the running, surging past several All Blacks before diving over in the corner for one of the greatest tries of all time. The Barbarians went on to win the match 23–11. The All Blacks also drew two matches on that tour – against Munster on Tuesday 16 January 1973 and against Ireland four days later.

Andy Irvine

One Scottish player in particular made a big impression during that defeat to New Zealand at the tail end of 1972.

Andy Irvine made his Scotland debut in that match despite the fact he had not yet fully recovered after flaking the bone and damaging the ligaments in his right knee during the National Trial two weeks earlier. Then, before half-time, stitches were inserted into a mouth wound. Despite all this he managed to set the match alight on a number of occasions with some electrifying breaks. He also kicked six of Scotland's nine points and his second penalty in particular was a truly magnificent effort from just inside the New Zealand half. The headline above the match report in *The Scotsman* the following Monday read: "Irvine's unforgettable debut – and he was only half fit."

Irvine's efforts prompted Carwyn James to ask: "Can I take that full back of yours home with me?"

It was the start of a glittering international career for Irvine, who was at that time only three months past his 21st birthday. He would go on to win 51 caps for Scotland, captain the national side fifteen times, score 273 points (a record which lasted until Gavin Hastings overtook it against Argentina in 1990) and play in nine Tests for the British and Irish Lions during three separate tours to South Africa in 1974, New Zealand in 1977, and South Africa again in 1980.

At this point Irvine had played against Renwick on a number of occasions for Heriots against Hawick, and for Edinburgh against the South – however the New Zealand match was the first time the pair had lined up on the same team (although Irvine had been scheduled to play alongside Renwick for Scotland B in Oyannax in November 1971, but injured his leg ten days before the match playing for Edinburgh against Scottish Universities).

They would go on to play in 43 international Test matches together over a ten-year period, during which time they would establish themselves as Scotland's two outstanding backs of that era.

Over the years the two players would forge a mutually beneficial understanding of each other which Jim Telfer would describe in 2003 as "magical" when naming both players in his best ever Scottish back division for *The Scotsman* newspaper.

Renwick rates Irvine as the best attacking player he has ever teamed up with.

> He was a hard man to play against because he was so difficult to pin down, he had the pace to get out of trouble and he had a boot on him that could take you from being under the kosh to putting the pressure on the opposition. He was also a hard man to play alongside because you never knew what he was going to do next, but I enjoyed that side of things – it kept you on your toes and it was good fun. He was maybe not as good a defender as some other guys I played with – but his attitude was always: 'If you score three I'll score four.'
>
> Andy was in the fortunate position that he was playing full back, he was coming into the line and he had a licence to try things. He would make a few mistakes but he was one of those types of players who would make up for it with a try or a penalty or a great break. Every team he played in would give him a free rein if they had any sense.
>
> He sometimes got a bit of stick for being too flash, but the folk that said that didn't know what they were talking about – there was a lot of steel there too. I remember that game against New Zealand in 1972 and he wasn't right, he had a bad leg, but he was gutsy that day. It was the same when we were in South Africa with the Lions in 1980 and he was struggling with a dodgy hamstring. So there was more to him than met the eye.

Irvine is equally complimentary of Renwick.

> Jim is about as close as Scottish rugby has ever got to producing a genius. He had a tremendous side-step, he had a lot of pace, he was very quick off the mark, and he had great balance. He did actually have everything. He could dummy, he could swerve, he was a tremendous tackler, he was a tough boy with a very strong and powerful upper body from the swimming he did in his youth. He could kick goals, he could drop goals, he could control the game, and to be honest he could have played anywhere on the park if he put his mind to it. He played most of his career at centre but he could easily have played stand-off at the

highest level, and if he'd wanted to he could also have played on the wing or at full back quite easily.

He was only 5'9", but even today, although the boys are a lot bigger and more physical, he would have been a great stand-off. He could have easily coped with the big hits and the power because he was tough and he was awfully strong.

And of course he has a great sense of humour. I remember in New Zealand in 1975 we were all trying to do a crossword at the back of the bus, Jim was reading out the clues and everyone is really struggling to get the answer except Duncan Madsen – who was a bit of a know it all. So all the boys are getting really hacked off with this until Jim eventually says: 'Hell, this is a really tough clue.'

'What is it?' says Madsen.

'Seven down – Postman's delivery,' Jim says.

'How many letters?'

And Jim says: 'Thoosands.' Hook, line and sinker.

In 1982 we were playing England at Murrayfield and we were in the teamroom at the Braid Hills Hotel, when in came Jim Telfer, who sticks a video in the machine and says: 'Right boys, we're going to watch England's last game against Wales. I want you to have a good look at this and then we'll have a discussion afterwards.'

So the lights went out and after five minutes we're all nodding off. At the end of the match the light came back on and Telfer says: 'Right boys, we've seen the opposition, we're going out to play them tomorrow, has anyone got any comments?'

Absolute silence.

'I can't believe this,' says Telfer. 'We've been watching them for an hour and a half, has nobody got anything to say?'

Slowly up goes Jim's hand.

And Telfer says: 'I might have guessed, only a Border boy would show any interest. Yes Jim – what's your point?'

'You couldn't open the window could you? It's roasting in here.'

Nobody would have the balls to do that except Renwick. The place just erupted. Even Telfer saw the funny side of it.

That was typical of Jim. He was a pretty laid-back character no matter what the circumstances were. You get guys in the changing room who are banging their head off the wall and thumping their chest. Jim would look at them and you could tell he was thinking: 'What the heck are they doing?' But in his own quiet way he would build himself up, and when that whistle went he was a very determined individual. He was always as competitive as you could ever hope anyone to be, but maybe he was a wee bit unemotional about it all and some people might have got the impression that he was a bit cool, a bit laid back, and that his heart wasn't really in it.

Maybe that is part of the reason why Jim, in my opinion, was a very under-rated player. Although he got a whole barrel of caps and he went on a Lions tour, he should have had more caps and been on more Lions tours. He was dropped once or twice by Scotland but he's the best player from this country that I ever played with or against. Certainly I loved playing with him because we were on the same wavelength – he was always looking to have a go and so was I.

As a full back it's pretty important that your stand-off and centres can time a pass and read a situation so Jim was great to play behind. That was especially the case towards the end of the seventies when John Rutherford came into the side – Jim and John together were a tremendous combination.

Jim has got a brilliant rugby brain. He doesn't say all that much, but when he does talk people listen because they have a lot of respect for what he says. I've sat down with Jim and had beers on numerous occasions after games, and he's just a breath of fresh air to listen to – he's got a great analytical mind when it comes to rugby.

Irvine is in no doubt that Renwick's excellence as a rugby player and his single-minded yet under-stated approach to the game can be directly traced to his Hawick background.

Jim was a bit younger than me but they started young down in Hawick so we both hit the scene at the same time. Our first game against each other would have been at Mansfield Park on New Year's Day 1971, it was my first ever game against Hawick and it was a massive match because they always had a fantastic record against us, especially down there where we very rarely came away with a result. I remember scoring a try and kicking three penalties in that match, and getting snowballs thrown at me from the terracing.

In those days we would play them at Goldenacre at the end of September, at Mansfield on New Year's Day, and when the leagues came along we had that match as well which would take place whenever the SRU scheduled it to be played. So we usually had three games against Hawick in a season and they were always tremendous games.

Heriots, as a club, had a tremendous respect for Hawick and we always took the New Year's Day game very seriously. It was a tough one because it was an early start, and although we would never drink too much the night before a few of the guys would have sat up until one, maybe even two o'clock. And there was always an aura about Hawick at Mansfield Park which wasn't helped by the crowd still being a bit merry from the night before and very vocal as a result. I got off to a great start when we beat them 17–6 down there but I don't think we won again in Hawick for ten years at least.

The game against Hawick at Goldenacre on the last Saturday of September would invariably attract our biggest crowd of the season. It was always the biggest game on in Edinburgh that weekend, and it was a holiday weekend in Hawick so their supporters used to come up in their droves. The stand would be packed with Heriots supporters and the area in front of the stand would be packed by Hawick supporters who liked to be closer to the action so they could bait us.

There would be about 5000 supporters there and the game would always be a cracker. We were one of the few teams in Scotland at that time to get any sort of change out of Hawick. We didn't often win at Mansfield, but we very rarely lost at Goldenacre, and we always had great games – there was very few 6–3 sort of score-lines, more regularly it would be 28–22 or something like that.

I remember towards the end of the 1975–76 season when we went down there and they beat us 69–6, but when we played them in the league at the start of the next season we won 13–10. That particular victory took place during my first year as captain and I remember I had a suspicion we would do well that day because just before kick-off, Norman Pender called off, and without him the Hawick scrum tended to struggle. It was a wet day and so it turned into a bit of a forward battle, and while Hawick won most of the loose ball, we out-scrummaged them and did enough in the end to win. Hawick had this tremendous tradition that you were playing for the green jersey, and that you were playing for the town. Jim used to say to me: 'If we get beat then on Monday morning we have to go into hiding because we get so much abuse from the locals. If you walk down the High Street it's like a wake, the whole town is in mourning.' Most of the Borders sides had that, but I think it was epitomised more at Hawick than in any other place.

I would say that Hawick were the most organised, the most committed and the most forward-thinking club in Scotland during my playing days, and it was Hughie McLeod and then Derrick Grant who were behind that. They had been inspired by their experiences in New Zealand with the Lions, and playing Hawick was like going up against Otago – who didn't have big forwards compared to Canterbury and Auckland but were always really fast and fit and would ruck you off the park.

Similarly Hawick were never the biggest guys in the world, particularly in the back row, but they had great technique. People used to say they were dirty but I don't think that is right – they were very physical and you knew that if you were on the deck against Hawick they would ruck you out, but they would ruck their own boys out as well. So it wasn't underhand or anything like that, it was just the way they played.

They were always fantastically fit, and it was their ability to manufacture quick ball which I think was the hallmark of Hawick. Unlike teams such as Gala, West of Scotland and Edinburgh Wanderers – who all had big strong packs – Hawick rarely ever mauled it, they would ruck it because that produced quick ball for the backs to play with.

You watch the professional game now and you regularly see the ball recycled fifteen to twenty times in one passage of play. In the seventies that didn't happen – you were lucky if you got two or three rucks on the trot – but I remember playing Hawick and they would sometimes have an overlap after the seventh ruck, which was very unusual at that time.

Every time Cranny got the ball he used to come in on a rangy or a scissors, and the first tackler would often miss him because he was so big and powerful, so it would be the second or third guy that eventually stopped him, but he always hit the deck and they always rucked over, and that was when they started playing rugby. It was great to see.

And with such a good set of backs they were always going to be lethal. They had Colin Telfer at stand-off, they had Jim and Cranny in the centre and in the early days guys like Robbie Welsh were playing too. They always had good scrum-halves like Raymond Corbett, and they had Ian Chalmers and Kenny McCartney on the wing.

So when we played Hawick we used to basically give them the ball at the breakdown because we knew they were going to get quick possession even if we did compete, and in order to stop the overlaps we used to do in the seventies what teams do now – which is stand off the ruck and fan out. Hawick used to get really hacked off with that and complain about us fringing, but of course it worked. The alternative for Hawick was to go right through the middle because then we would have had to put our forwards back in, but it took them a while before they started doing that.

Our matches against Hawick tended to be real tactical battles and I used to love having chats with Derrick Grant after a game. He would ask about how or why we did things – he wasn't shy. I think Derrick used to always worry about what our backs would get up to because with Fraser Dall, Harry Burnett, Jimmy Craig and guys like that in the side we had a pretty useful backline.

Another impressive thing about Hawick was that they had this tremendous ability to replace one player with another one who was just as good, if not better. They would lose someone like Norman Suddon at prop or Wat Davies in the back-row, and Renwick used to say: 'Not to worry, Derrick will just go up into the hills around Hawick, and he'll chop one down and carve out another great player.' And that's basically what happened: when anyone retired there was always another player ready to take over. Derek Deans retires as hooker and Colin Deans comes along. Norman Suddon retires and Norman Webb comes along. Donnie McLeod retires and Sean McGaughey comes along. The number of top players Hawick produced during that period was astonishing.

I suppose in the professional era they are going to have to use that knack of producing good players more than ever before because they are always going to lose their best players to the Borders or one of the other pro teams. In a way that is sad because I don't think the boys have the same fun and camaraderie as we used to have when guys would play for the same club for ten or twelve years and you really got to know your team-mates – and you also got to build up friendships with the opposition from playing games against a team and then afterwards socialising with the same guys twice a year over several years.

If you look at rugby now, I would think that most players will average three to four seasons with a club because the pro teams are sucking up the best players and guys are a wee bit more mobile and likely to move away. If you look at a club like Heriots, there will be five or six, maybe even seven or eight, major changes every year. So you don't get much continuity at clubs and you tend not to build up the same loyalty and the same friendships. We quite often have reunion matches against Watsonians or Stew-Mel, and I just wonder if they'll be able to do that in ten or fifteen year's time.

That's not a criticism of anyone or anything, it's just an observation on the way the game has changed, and I fully appreciate that the game had to change to survive. Professionalism has brought a lot to rugby, it's just a shame that it meant we also lost a little bit of what used to make the game so great when Jim and I played.

The great rapport between Hawick and Heriots is exactly the sort of thing I am talking about – they were fierce rivals but there were also a lot of very good friendships built up. For instance a few years ago Jimmy Simpson, a former Heriots club president, died; and there was quite a few Hawick guys up at the funeral – which was nice to see. Right up until recent seasons a lot of the older guys from the sixties like Jack Hegarty and Robbie Welsh would come up to Goldenacre to watch the game, and likewise lots of Heriots guys like Hamish More would go down to Mansfield.

When I was playing the bus used to always stay down for a late night, particularly after the New Year's Day game when the bar would be chock-a-block after the match. There was usually a dance on at Mansfield or we would go up to the Tower or along the High Street. We wouldn't leave until about half-past-one and there was the odd no-show when guys would miss the bus – I wouldn't like to think what had happened to them but they always turned up for training on the Tuesday with a big grin on their faces.

A lot of people didn't like playing the Borders' clubs because they thought they were dirty and they were scared of them. But tradition is a great thing and if you look at that small population you can't help but think that what they have achieved in Scottish rugby is tremendous. It's just a shame that with the way things have gone it's much harder for them to be the force that they were – and for the good of the game in this country I hope things don't get too tough for them because we are not a big enough nation to go without a club like Hawick, which has contributed so much to Scottish rugby over the years.

Dropped

By the time the 1973 Five Nations came around, Jim Renwick, at the tender age of twenty, was Scotland's second most experienced back. He had played in each of Scotland's last four matches and had not let anyone down, though some observers still harboured doubts about whether he was quite ready to play international rugby. "For the first couple of years he was in the side a lot of folk in Hawick said he was a lucky man to be where he was. I don't think they thought he was a bad player, they just thought it had come a bit easy for him," recalls Addie Renwick.

The Scotland selectors did not seem to share those concerns, naming him in the Scotland team for the first match of the campaign against France on 13 January. Renwick had missed the final trial at Murrayfield on the penultimate day of 1972 in order to attend his grandfather's funeral, but this had perhaps worked in his favour because it was a less than convincing performance by the Blues team in which he had been scheduled to play as they only just managed to scrape an 11–10 victory.

For the game against France there were three changes from the side which played against New Zealand. Alan Lawson was at scrum-half ahead of Ian MacCrae, Ron Wright was called into the second row after Gordon Brown pulled out of the side with an ankle injury, and Wilson Lauder was at flanker instead of Roger Arneill, who had been forced to retire from international rugby to concentrate on his business commitments in Germany.

In the first ever match at the newly opened Parc de Princes, Scotland were unable to cope with France's power up front and they eventually lost 16–13. Perhaps the most memorable thing about this encounter was that Ken Pattinson, an Englishman making his debut as an international referee, pulled a muscle in his leg in the thirteenth minute and had to retire, to be replaced by Francis Palmade, the French touch judge. The significance of this was not that it gave the home team an advantage, for it was agreed by all concerned that he had been very fair, but that he was extremely strict which meant that the game rarely flowed.

With barely a trickle of possession, most of which was kicked away, the Scottish three-quarters had few opportunities to impress with the ball in hand. However, Renwick, along with his centre partner Ian Forsyth, earned praise for their efforts in defence. And he played a crucial role in Scotland's try, flattening Jack Cantoni, the French full back, in a tackle that dislodged the ball and allowed Bobby Clark to send Alan Lawson in for the score.

Despite this it was Renwick who gave way when the selectors decided to bring back Colin Telfer, who had proven his fitness after a two-month lay off with damaged knee ligaments. As ever Renwick was philosophical about that setback to his fledgling international career.

Any of the backs could have been dropped after the French game but it just so happened that it was me. We never got the ball much in our hands, all we could do was come in and tackle, so I didn't have much chance to prove myself. But I can see why they wanted Colin in at stand-off and I suppose they wanted to see how Geech and Forsyth got on in the centre.

We met France on one of their good days and we were done up front, so we were chasing shadows a lot of the time. I remember sitting next to Geech in the changing rooms after that game and we were feeling right sorry for ourselves. He was really down and I was trying to console him, but it was tough because I thought he was going to be dropped as well. But in the end it was me that missed out.

You had to watch because I was brought up to be fair and honest but maybe I was too honest. In the changing room after the match I found myself talking about the mistakes I'd made and the things I should have done differently. Then, when I stopped and looked around . . . well . . . there weren't many others saying much. So maybe I did talk my way out of it a wee bit, and that's something you learn. There's times when it's better to keep your mouth shut.

There were a few folk who had bad games in Paris, but they must have thought it was easier to drop me. They didn't tell you why you were dropped in these days. If you were selected for Scotland you got a letter from John Law, who was the secretary of the SRU, but if you were dropped you were dropped and you didn't get a phone call or a letter or anything like that.

But there's no point taking the huff – I wasn't brought up to do that. You just have to train harder, roll the sleeves up and do better. And you have to listen to folk if they're telling you that you're weak somewhere, or need to work on something. You need to stick at it and get better.

Renwick was one of four players dropped for Scotland's next game against Wales. Dougie Morgan came in for his international debut in place of Lawson at scrum-half, Brown returned ahead of Wright in the second-row, but perhaps the most notable change was at flanker where Wattie Davies, Hawick's 22-year-old all-action hero, was selected ahead of Wilson Lauder. Davies had been on the verge of making his international debut two years earlier but a knee injury sustained during the New Year's Day game against Heriots had put him out of contention. Injury and illness had robbed him of a lot of rugby since then, but it now seemed that, at long last, his time had come. Sadly another knee injury, once again sustained against Heriots on New Year's Day, would not clear up and he had to withdraw from the side a few days before the match. Jock Millican, the Edinburgh University student, took his place. Davies would play another four years at Hawick, win a Scotland B cap against France in 1976, but he never made it back into the Scotland team.

Renwick might have shrugged off his removal from the Scotland set-up with the nonchalance which has come to be recognised as a trade-mark characteristic over the years; however the fact that he scored four tries and 36 points for Hawick in their next match, a 56–9 demolition of Edinburgh Academicals, must surely be regarded as proof that deep-down the player felt he had a point to prove.

A week later, with Renwick watching the action from the Clock End at Murrayfield having played that morning for Hawick against Musselburgh, Scotland defeated Wales 10–9. Colin Telfer scored Scotland's first try and Billy Steele the second, which Dougie Morgan converted to give the home team a 10–6 lead at half-time. Three weeks later it was Ireland's turn to lose to Scotland at Murrayfield. This time the score was 19–14, with McGeechan dropping a goal while Forsyth handed-off Mike Gibson for Scotland's only try. Scotland's other points came from Dougie Morgan's boot.

JMR:

I knew after that game that there was no way I was going to get back into the side any time soon. But I was quite happy – I'd got my caps. I was content to play for Hawick and take my chances when they came along. International rugby was extra, but Hawick was the main thing, trying to keep your place in the Hawick team was your biggest priority in life. I mean nobody likes getting dropped, but I always thought I'd get back in at some point and I knew why I'd been left out as well. There was competition for places, there were other more experienced players coming through, and the selectors obviously felt that these were the boys that could do the best job for Scotland at that point.

I'd played quite well for Hawick and the South during 1971, and I'd done alright in the B game in France and in the National Trials, so I suppose they had to pick me really. But that doesn't mean it couldn't come back on you. There's loads of guys get in quickly and their game goes back a wee bit, some guys get in and they are ready straight away, but I was young and maybe it wasn't the case with me.

I think that happens with a lot of players when they come in on natural ability. They eventually have a season when they start thinking about it and trying to improve their game. You see it in football with guys like Michael Owen and Wayne Rooney. Obviously those two made a bigger impact than I ever did when they arrived on the scene, and they're still good players – but there is no way they could carry on forever playing the way they did when they were eighteen. It's the same kind of thing as happened to Iain Balshaw, the English full back, after the 2001 Lions tour. People will always get wise to the way you play eventually, so you have to start boxing clever and you have to learn when to have a go and when to play it safe. There has to be more to your game than just a few tricks. If you're going to last then you have to be able to do the less glamorous stuff as well.

A lot of people thought I was too young when I first got into the Scotland team and they were maybe right. I didn't really know what I was doing and I was having to learn on the hoof. I hadn't played a lot of rugby so I was living on my wits, which was alright because I had a bit of ability and I was quick enough to get myself out of trouble. But then I went through a period when I was beginning to understand what I was trying to do, and when that happens your game slips back a wee bit because you start worrying about things that didn't even enter your head before. It takes you a while to learn how to process all the information you need to take on board during a game if you want to be a good all-round player. It's a bit like golfers when they start thinking about their swing.

McGeechan was 26 when he got his cap, Forsyth was older still, so they maybe had a head-start on me. Andy [Irvine] was young as well but he was in the fortunate position that he was playing full back, so he was coming into the line and he had a licence to try things.

Renwick's plight was not helped by that nasty blow to the face he had sustained playing for Hawick against the Scottish Presidents XV at the start of he season. The injury had not stopped him playing but it was uncomfortable and was affecting his vision.

I had to go and see an eye specialist because I was seeing double all the time when I looked upwards. It was bad news as far as my rugby was concerned but it also made life difficult at my work. At first I thought it was just a black eye, but I got another bang on it during the Scotland–Ireland versus England–Wales game in the middle of October so I had to go for an x-ray. That's when I found out that I had cracked my cheekbone and that there was a trapped nerve. So I went to see the specialist and he told me that if the nerve is still trapped after the bone heals then I will be seeing double all my days. But, he said, with any luck it will release the nerve and I'll be alright – and that's what happened in the end, although it still feels numb sometimes.

"Jim Renwick seems at present in something of a recession – probably due as much to a natural reaction to last season's meteoric rise as to his recent eye injury. Not that he played all that badly. Just that he has it in him to play so much better," wrote Norman Mair in November 1972. It seems a pretty fair assessment.

With the Triple Crown up for grabs Scotland went to Twickenham for the last game of the 1973 Five Nations competition with high hopes. For the third match running they fielded the same starting XV but on this occasion were out-muscled by England's pack. Despite this, two late tries by Billy Steele brought Scotland to within a point of their hosts, before Geoff Evans sealed an English win with a late try which was converted by Tony Jorden. Ian McLauchlan played in that game despite breaking his leg three weeks earlier against Ireland.

At the end of March caps were awarded for another game organised as part of the SRU's centenary celebrations which had a Scotland team matched against an all-star SRU President's XV. Renwick once again missed out. Scotland eventually proved too strong for the guest side which had only congregated for the first time a few days earlier, winning 27–16 on a rain-swept and blustery day. Ian McGeechan had to retire from the match with an injured neck after only thirteen minutes, to be replaced by John Frame, who was fit again following his head injury.

The President's XV for that match was:

A. Carlson (South Africa); J.J. McLean (Australia), D.R. Burnett (Australia), D.A. Hales (New Zealand), G.B. Batty (New Zealand); I.N. Stevens (New Zealand), G.L. Colling (New Zealand); J. Iracabal (France), R. Benesis (France), D.A. Dunworth (Australia), B. Dauga (France), A.R. Sutherland (New Zealand), J.H. Ellis (South Africa), A.J. Wyllie (New Zealand), P.J.F. Greiling (South Africa).

It was a season of mixed fortunes for Renwick at club level. Hawick ended up finishing third behind Boroughmuir and Gala in the last ever Scottish championship to be played before the introduction of an official national league structure the following year.

They did, however, retain the Border League with a 31–6 victory over Gala in the last game of the season. This was a magnificent result given that Jim Scott was injured early on, meaning that Hawick had to play 75 minutes with only fourteen men. Bruce White grabbed a hat trick of tries but the score of the match belonged to Kenny McCartney, who handed off the burly John Frame and ran home from inside his own half. As he made his way back into position to receive Gala's kick-off McCartney passed Renwick, who was preparing to kick the conversion. If McCartney was expecting a compliment from his old friend then he should have known better. "Aye Crab, fear is a great propellant," was Renwick's wily observation.

A few weeks later McCartney was once again on the receiving end of his teammates' caustic humour. At the Gala Sevens he retreated back behind his goal-line to collect a long kick ahead. He looked left and then right before kicking his heels and setting off on an audacious counter-attack. Unfortunately he ran straight into one of the posts, knocked himself out, and Hawick conceded a try. "If you could've beaten the post you would have scored," noted Brian Hegarty.

*   *   *

As Renwick's exploits as a seventeen-year-old in 1970 has shown, his pace, fitness and eye for the gap meant that he was ideally suited to seven-a-side rugby. It is therefore slightly surprising that in early April 1973 he was overlooked for the Scotland VII which played in the one-off international sevens tournament which was held at Murrayfield at the conclusion of the Scottish Rugby Union's centenary year celebrations.

His club-mate Colin Telfer was preferred at stand-off whilst John Frame was selected at centre. The other notable omission from the Scotland team was Andy Irvine.

The pair did, however, get to play in the tournament, making it into the SRU President's VII – along with fellow Scots Dave Shedden, Jim Henderson (who picked up an injury and was replaced by Dougie Morgan the day before the tournament) and Bobby Clark. The final two places in the side were taken up by the South African forwards Piet Greyling and Jan Ellis.

Given the predominance of Gala in sevens at that time it is not all that surprising that the Scotland side was made up of five Gala players – Drew Gill, Frame, PC Brown, Kenny Oliver and Johnie Brown – in the middle of whom were sandwiched the Hawick half-backs of Telfer and Stan Davidson.

In the event neither of these sides did as well as expected. In Group A Scotland defeated Australia but lost to New Zealand and Ireland, while in Group B the President's team was beaten by England and Wales before managing a 20–16 victory over France after extra-time. Both teams finished third in their respective groups whilst Ireland and England topped the two league tables and competed in an arduous final which England eventually won by 22–18 – thanks largely to a lung bursting final break by Keith Fielding for the decisive try. Even then Ireland might have stolen the victory at the death, but with an overlap outside him Fergus Slattery decided to go it alone and lost the ball.

Despite the excitement which surrounded this pioneering rugby venture, which many hoped would become an annual event, it was a pretty undistinguished afternoon for the Scottish players who took part. For Renwick the longest lasting memory of the experience was the gruelling training session inflicted upon the President's squad on the day before the tournament.

They put Jim Telfer in charge of the team and he ran our guts out the day before the tournament. When we got out of bed on the Saturday we were all stiff. The South African boys were out of season and they were really toiling. They felt we had done too much and I think they were right. But that was typical Jim – it's just the way he does it.

Glory Days

From the end of the war until the late eighties Hawick Rugby Club just kept getting better and better. The whole structure in the town was right, with four thriving junior clubs playing in a strong league, and the school, the PSA and the Wanderers producing player after player. You have to remember the times, you hadn't any money, you hadn't any TV, so you trained during the week, you went to the pictures on a Friday night, and you played rugby then went out on the town on the Saturday. Then you hadn't any money left and it was back to the start of the week again. And the whole town was the same.

Robin Charters

When Hawick played Jed-Forest at Riverside Park on a Tuesday night in a rearranged Border League fixture at the tail end of the 1975–76 season, an oversight meant that the famous green jerseys of the visitors had been left back in Hawick. But the show had to go on, so the players took to the field wearing an assortment of vests and t-shirts – apart from Kenny McCartney, who would not compromise when it came to sartorial elegance and took to the field wearing a cashmere jersey.

As would be expected in a Border derby, the home crowd were delighted by Hawick's self-inflicted misfortune and had great fun at the players' expense.

JMR:
It was embarrassing. They booed us when we ran onto the pitch and all the way through the first half they were giving us all sorts of stick. 'Get off ya scruffs,' they were shouting. I was taking the kicks and I was getting stick off the crowd because I just had my vest on. Of course all the kicks seemed to be right out on the touchline and I was having a nightmare. I was desperate to score because I was getting hassle off the crowd, but I was missing everything and I only got one over. In fact, one

time the ball blew over and I said to George Murray, who was the ref that day: 'Can I set it up again? I've no started my run up yet.' And straight away they were shouting: 'Yi might as well gie him the points, yiv been giving them everything else all day onyway.' It was a typical Jethart crowd, a typical Border crowd.

Hawick were only 3–0 ahead at half-time. However, by that time Hawick's strips had arrived, and it was a different story in the second half.

"We got the green jerseys on at half-time and took thirty points off them to win the match 33–0," recalls Renwick. "It was like Superman getting changed into his costume. Of course the chat after the game was that they were scared of the green jersey."

Derrick Grant:
When you achieve a level of fitness, and set a high standard of what is expected of the players, then you hit a level of consistency that has other sides worrying about you. We played a lot of very good sides but when they came up against Hawick they started thinking about what they have to do to stop us – when they should be thinking about what they should be doing to beat us. You build up an aura of invincibility, but to do that you've got to get the wins under your belt in the first place, and once you have done that you have to keep winning and winning and winning, because as soon as you slip up that aura is gone and life gets a lot harder.

Hawick dominated the first five years of the official league championship after it was introduced by the SRU in season 1973–74, although there were a few slip-ups along the way – usually against West of Scotland.

In the first season of the official championship their only defeat in the competition was against the Glasgow side in front of a huge crowd at Mansfield in a rearranged fixture on a Wednesday night in April. Renwick was not playing that day having injured his ankle against Boroughmuir two weeks earlier. It was, however, a hollow victory for West, as they needed to win by thirteen clear points to lift the championship but only managed a 13–9 scoreline. After the match Hawick were presented with the league trophy, which perhaps made up for the loss slightly. Hawick had one draw that season, against Heriots.

In 1974–75 Hawick finished two points clear of Gala at the top of the table, but once again they lost to West. This time it was a 4–6 reverse at Burnbrae when the team was shorn of several leading players – including Alistair Cranston and Colin Telfer in the back division and, perhaps most significantly, props Norman Suddon and Norman Pender, which meant Hawick struggled to attain parity in the scrum against a pack containing Sandy Carmichael, Quentin Dunlop, Gordon Brown, David Gray and Robert Haldane. "West had a big, strong pack and we always struggled up-front against them, especially when Pender wasn't available," says Renwick. "That meant we couldn't get on the front foot to play the fast rucking style of game that we were used to, so they were a bit of a bogey team for us at the time."

Because of the difficulties Hawick had encountered against West in the first two years of the official championship, it was particularly gratifying for all involved the following season when they smashed their great rivals by 23 points to nil at Mansfield Park on 14 February 1976, with Kenny McCartney scoring a hat-trick of tries, while Colin Telfer scored a drop-goal and Renwick kicked two penalties and a conversion.

The Hawick team that day was:
Bruce Elliot; Kenny McCartney, Jim Renwick, Alistair Cranston, Bruce White; Colin Telfer, Raymond Corbett; Norman Pender, Colin Deans, Norman Webb, Alan Tomes, Ian Barnes, Wat Davies, Donnie McLeod, Brian Hegarty.

Hawick finished that league campaign with eleven wins from eleven games.

If 1975–76 represented the high water mark for that Hawick side in terms of their superiority over the rest of Scottish rugby, then 1976–77 has to take the plaudits in terms of suspense and excitement.

Having lost the first match of their league campaign away to Heriots (13–10), Hawick rallied well and swept all before them before meeting West at Burnbrae on 26 February, when once again they came unstuck and lost 12–6. However West had already lost to Gala and Boroughmuir at the start of the season, while Gala had also lost twice, to Hawick and Langholm. All of which meant that by the last Saturday of the regular season Hawick, Gala and West were tied at the top of the table, and unless two of these three teams lost in their final match the championship would be decided on points differential. Sure enough all three sides won. West defeated Edinburgh Wanderers 16–6, Gala blew away Highland 31–3, while Hawick fought back from being 7–19 down to Selkirk at the interval to win 52–19.

When the points differential column was tallied up it emerged that West had managed to score 110 more points than they had conceded, while both Gala and Hawick had positive point differentials of 186. To decide the title, a play-off was organised, which took place at the Greenyards on the evening of Tuesday 12 April, with a crowd in excess of 10,000 turning out. A Donnie McLeod try, a Colin Telfer drop-goal, and a drop-goal, a penalty and a conversion by Renwick, eclipsed Arthur Brown's solitary late penalty to leave a final scoreline of 15–3 in favour of Hawick.

The following season Hawick won ten of their eleven league matches and drew the other against Boroughmuir as they marched to their fifth title in as many years.

There could be no argument that Hawick were the dominant force in Scottish club rugby at this time, and they were also a force to be reckoned with on the fairly regular occasions when they took on the best clubs from England, Ireland and Wales. Among their scalps were Sale, Bath, Coventry, Headingley, Abertillery, Newport and Ballymena – but the highlight came on Hogmanay 1977 when they went down to Newcastle and defeated Gosforth, the John Player Cup winners in both the previous two years, by 18 points to 16. It was a ferocious battle upfront with Hawick clinching it with a Renwick drop-goal near the end, much to the delight of their large and enthusiastic travelling support.

JMR:

They were great times. We had a good team full of guys that were on the same wavelength. We had a lot of talented players who thought a lot about their rugby. We trained hard, played hard and then enjoyed ourselves. We were maybe not guaranteed to win, but it was unusual to lose, and if we did we got hammered at training, and that's what we expected because we had been brought up believing that Hawick were the best and if we didn't win then we hadn't worked hard enough.

Derrick and Robin made sure there was a good spirit in the club. When we were playing in Edinburgh we'd leave early and have a bowl of a soup at the Donmarie on Minto Street and have a chat about the game and the conditions before heading off to the ground. Afterwards we'd always have a few beers and quite often we'd stop for a steak in Lauder on the way back down the road to keep the boys together. Then it would be back on the bus and we'd have a sing-song. Usually it was everyone singing together but a few of the boys had their own party pieces. I had a few different songs over the years – in the early days it would probably be a Common Riding song, later on I liked 'Amarillo'; Ian Chalmers would sing 'Three Wheels on My Wagon'; Toomba [Alan Tomes] sang 'There's a Tiny House'; Derrick Grant sang 'Nothing Like a Dame'; and

Heg [Brian Hegarty] was one of the boys who couldn't sing so his party piece was 'The Old Woman Who Swallowed a Fly', but I've never heard him finish it.

About three or four times a season we'd organise a late night in Edinburgh or Glasgow and we'd try and make a point of having those nights together as a team – quite often it was at Boroughmuir because they'd be having a disco. We drank vodka and fresh orange after games. That was the drink – vodka fresh. The pubs shut at ten o'clock in those days, but we'd drink on the bus on the way back down the road and make our own entertainment. We stopped in Carnwarth on the way back from Glasgow once and there was a dancing competition so all the boys entered – Eck McCallum and Glynn Hobkirk, two of the Quins boys who used to get odd games for Hawick, were dancing with each other for a laugh.

That's Scottish culture for you – we bonded by drinking together. In Scotland, if you have a rugby club then you have to have a bar along with it. If you have a football club there's drink involved. If you have a cricket club there's always a bar. It's the same with bowling clubs and almost every other club I can think of. I know there's financial reasons for that, but its no the same in many other countries. It's the way we do things in Scotland, its part of our culture. I don't know why it's like that, but I'm glad it is because I've always enjoyed the banter in the bar after the game.

Obviously that's not the case anymore for the top rugby players and even a lot of the guys in the club game. It's turning into more of a science, whereas in my day even the internationalists were playing for fun and enjoyment and to have a few beers. There was a good feeling in club rugby back then. There were good supporters who would follow you all over and you always got good chat from everybody involved in the game. There was one guy called Archie Hume who used to always come up after the game to congratulate you, he'd stick out his hand and when you went to shake it he would say: 'So you do have hands.'

That was typical of Hawick supporters. They were good at keeping your feet on the ground. They never let you get carried away with yoursel'. If you had a bad game you were told about it, and if you had a good game they didn't say anything. That's the way it has always been in Hawick. They keep telling you your faults and where you have gone wrong, it's aimed at keeping your feet on the ground, but sooner or later you start thinking: 'Am I not good enough for this?' It stops you getting carried away, but does it also inhibit you as a player. I remember playing in Baa Baas games and in other invitational sides, and I never felt I was comfy there. All the superstars were there and I wasn't pushy like some of them, and I don't know if part of that was from years of being kept in place.

But I suppose it didn't do me any harm. I'd rather be the way I am than be bumptious. And when I think about it, the reason Hawick managed to stay on top for so long was probably because we were never able to relax, we were never allowed to get carried away with ourselves, and we were terrified of losing because it would mean big trouble.

Gala

I'd rather be a lamp-post in Hawick than the Provost of Gala.

Jim Renwick

"I'll always remember my first training session at Hawick," says Jonny Else, who played at the club for two seasons in the late- 1990s. "I was one of the guys holding the rucking pads while Alistair Imray, Roddy Deans, the Landels brothers and the rest of the pack charged through some pretty ferocious rucking drills. Every time they stopped for a breather there would be chat about 'Gallic Aunts'. I was pretty new to the Hawick accent but I could make out the gist what they were saying – yet I couldn't understand why they were so keen to get stuck into these Gallic Aunts or what these Gallic Aunts had done to get them so angry. It took me half the session before I realised that Hawick were playing Gala on Saturday."

Hawick had some major rivalries during the seventies. Their perennial bogey team West of Scotland was always a key fixture, while Heriots' dazzling backline meant that those games were always eagerly anticipated. But no match in Scottish rugby incited as much passion and as much vitriol as those between Gala and Hawick.

JMR:
Norman Mair once suggested to me that because Hawick and Gala knew each other so well, tactics must have a huge influence on the game. I told him that it was the total opposite. When you go into a Hawick–Gala game all the tactics you worked on during the week go out the window. It's you against him, and the first to lie down loses. Certainly from a Hawick point of view it was a battle of wills. We would just keep on going, keep on going, and keep on going. We would never back off.

We used to talk about tactics at training during the week, but the main thing in your mind wasn't the tactics, it was the focus of beating

Gala. And I sometimes think we forget it's not all about moves and strategies. Tactics are going to help you win but you need the mental side to do it when the going gets tough. You can't coach that. You can speak about it but only one man can give you a tough mental attitude and that's yourself.

Gala had a lot of good players, but I think they were under-achievers – certainly in the early days. They just never quite lived up to their potential and we always seemed to have an edge on them. I think we worked harder than them and we wanted it more – they might not agree with that but that's the way it seemed to me.

I remember playing Gala at Mansfield at the end of my first season and there was a strong wind coming down the pitch, which we had behind us in the first half. But at half-time we were only winning 6–3 and in the second half they piled on the pressure. With about twenty minutes to go they kicked a penalty and I thought: 'We're in trouble now.'

Jock Turner was clean through but slipped on the turf, Duncy Paterson was over but knocked the ball on, and it seemed like they just couldn't score. Then, right at the end, we were in our own 25 and I got the ball and kicked for touch, but it skewed off my boot and it went away to the left wing. Drew Gill came across to kill it, but Chalmers had come flying up and got his boot to it first. He kicked it on again, and two metres from the line it just bounced up into his hands and he scored in the corner. We beat them 9–6 and I thought to myself: 'How can we have won that today? We should never have won that game.'

Colin Telfer and Norman Suddon weren't available that day, Derek Deans had been capped once in 1968, but the rest of us were just boys – and they were meant to be the big shots. They had five guys in their side that played for Scotland against Wales the week before – John Frame, Turner, Paterson, Nairn McEwan and PC Brown – but we went out there and beat them. I think that was an important day because that was when a lot of the young guys who would be the backbone of the team in the seventies came of age. We didn't deserve to win, but the fact that we did gave us a bit of confidence and from then on we always seemed to have the Indian sign over them.

The teams that day were:

Hawick: D.S. Cranston; D. Gray, J.M. Renwick, A.G. Cranston, I. Chalmers; C.G. Hogg, B. Elliot; N. Pender, D.T. Deans, I. Cranston, I.A. Barnes, C. Wright, C.B. Hegarty, R. Broatch.

Gala: A. Brown; A.D. Gill, P.B. Townsend, J.N.M. Frame, J. Barthinussen; J.W.C. Turner, D.S. Paterson; A. Mitchell, B. Rutherford, K. Dodds, J. Gray, R. Dickson, J.G. Brown, P.C. Brown, N.A. McEwan.

JMR:
In later years Gala came into their own, and they beat us a few times, but it always went to the wire and they were always huge matches. Hawick and Gala are the two biggest towns in the Borders and I suppose the rivalry came from that. In Hawick we were brought up calling them 'Dirty Gala' and 'Pale Merks' because they were the last town in the Borders to get indoor toilets.

Given the ferocity of the rivalry between the two towns, Galashiels would be the last place you would expect a Hawick man such as Renwick to set up home, but fate had a role to play.

I had known Shelagh Kinghorn for a couple of years when we found out we were going to have to get married. I was eighteen years old and it was just before I got capped, so it was a lot to take in at the time. I remember telling the Hawick boys about it. We were playing Watsonians up there, and before the game we were all sitting round the table and I said: 'I'm getting married on 29 April, so I won't be able to play at Langholm sports.' Well, it was obvious what the situation was. There was just silence, nobody knew what to say, then Eddie Murray, who used to drive the bus for us, started laughing and one by one they all started laughing.

The week before we got married I had my 'Foy' [stag party] at the Quins on a Friday night. Andy Irvine came down and it was a good night. And the next day we won Jed sports — we beat Edinburgh Wanderers in the final after extra time. And a week after that I got married, while Hawick got knocked out in the semi-finals at Langholm by the Barbarians.

For the first month we stayed with my mother and father, but I was just coming out my time as an apprentice and I was working in Gala because the SSEB [South of Scotland Electricity Board] office in Hawick had closed down. I didn't drive in those days so it was a hassle, and we were struggling to get the money together to set up a house, so when the SSEB said that they would sort us out if I moved to Gala . . . well . . . it was what we had to do.

I always knew I'd move back to Hawick eventually, that was always the plan, but it took us a couple of years to get organised — we ended up being in Gala for eight or nine years. Scott was born on 14 August 1972, and on 12 September 1973 we had Andrew. They went to primary school in Gala – but I think they managed to get over that. They seem to be alright now, at least.

Addie Renwick:

A Hawick man living in Gala – Jim got some stick for that. But he loves that sort of thing. He loves the banter, even if it's at his expense – in fact I sometimes think he enjoys it more when it's at his expense.

Later on, when he was thinking about moving back to Hawick, he was wanting to buy a car. I served my time in a garage, so I told him to come and ask my advice once he had found something he fancied. A few days later he's found this car and we go and have a look at it. I gave it the once over then said to him: 'Aye, that's quite a good car – a wee bit expensive, but quite a good car.'

So he goes off and has a think about it, and eventually he says: 'Right, I'm going to buy that car, I'm away to get it now.'

But he comes back with a Skoda, a brand new Skoda. Now in those days Skodas got a lot of stick. Nobody wanted to be seen dead in a Skoda. So I says: 'Jeepers creepers, you hannae got a Skoda have you?'

'Oh aye,' he says. 'I got a Skoda. The fella gave us twae grand off it. I got it for the same price as the other one, and I don't need an MOT for three years because it's brand new.'

Well, when he used to drive it to the golf club everybody would be out cheering and clapping and giving him stick. But he loved it – absolutely loved it.

Around that time Renwick was invited by his Scotland team-mate David Leslie to speak at a sportsman's dinner in Dundee, and was asked if he could pick up Richard Noble, one of the other speakers, at Edinburgh Airport.

JMR:

A few weeks before the dinner I was reading the paper and I noticed an article about a guy called Richard Noble who has just broken the world land speed record. So I gave David Leslie a call and said: 'This Richard Noble – is it the same one that has just broken the world land speed record?'

'It's the same man, is that a problem?'

'Not for me,' I says. 'But I thought I should let you know that I'm driving a Skoda at the moment. I don't know what your boy Noble will think of that.'

Leslie thinks about this for a while, then says: 'You're right Jim. Just leave it. I'll organise a taxi for him.'

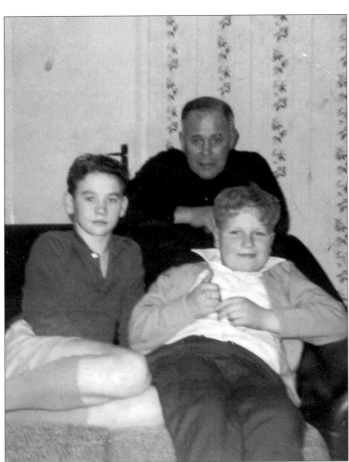

Left: A young Jim Renwick with his father and Terence Froud – his oldest and closest friend. Circa 1963.

Below: Jim Senior and Teenie Renwick in 1991 with their grandson Neil – younger brother to Scott, Andrew, David and Lindsey, and elder brother to Stuart and Alex.

Top: The Hawick team which won the East of Scotland junior men's 100 yard freestyle, *c.*1964.
From left to right: James Renwick, Brian McConnell, Ian Wilson and Fraser Scott.

Above: Bill McLaren, the Voice of Rugby, was an inspirational coach responsible for introducing several generations of Hawick youngsters to the game. He remembers spotting the potential in a ten-year-old Jim Renwick.

Top: During the lead-up to his international debut in 1972, Renwick struggled to keep his mind on his job as an apprentice electrician.

Above: In action at Mansfield Park, Hawick, with Bruce White, Norman Suddon and Kenny Douglas looking on.

Top: After making a spectacular debut in senior rugby playing for the victorious Hawick Seven which won their own sports in 1970, Renwick played for the Greens for most of the following season and throughout the spring sevens tournaments. This is the seven which retained the Paterson Cup at Hawick in 1971. *Back row (l to r):* Ian Chalmers, Kenny Douglas, Brian Hegarty, Alistair Cranston; *front row:* Jim Renwick, Rob Broatch, Robbie Welsh.

Above: At the other end of his career Renwick continued to play for Hawick Harlequins well into his forties. This seven won at Lismore in the early 1990s. *Back row (l to r):* Gregor Sharp, Graham Livingstone (a replacement from Heriots in the final), John Ainslie, Jim Renwick; *front row:* Keith Douglas, Rocky Johnston, Derek Hope.

The Scotland team for Renwick's first cap against France on 15 January, 1972. *Back row (l to r)*: Eric Grierson (touch judge), Billy Steele, John Frame, Roger Arneill, Alistair McHarg, Bobby Clark, Colin Telfer, Meirion Joseph (referee). *Middle row*: Ian McLauchlan, Alistair Biggar, Gordon Brown, Peter Brown, Sandy Carmichael, Nairn MacEwan, Arthur Brown. *Front row*: Jim Renwick and Ian MacCrae. *Photograph © Yerbury*

Renwick made a dream start to his international career, scoring the second of Scotland's three tries in a 20–9 victory over France. These were the days before neutral touch judges and on this occasion Eric Grierson was Scotland's representative on the touchline. Seen in the background here with a broad grin across his face, the Hawick club stalwart was so delighted at seeing this youngster from his home town scoring that a few seconds after this shot was taken he jumped in the air with his arms raised in triumph – all pretence of neutrality laid to one side. *Photograph © Scotsman Publications Ltd*

Top: Hawick coach Derrick Grant was probably the most influential individual in Renwick's rugby career. He's seen here during his playing days, tackling MacHerewini on the day 16,000 people, including an eleven-year-old Jim Renwick, turned up to watch the South of Scotland take on the mighty All Blacks at Mansfield Park in 1963.

Above: Brian Hegarty receiving the trophy after defeating Selkirk in the final of the Gala Sevens in 1978, with some famous Hawick faces in the background.

The Hawick team which won National League Division One and the Border League during season 1976–77, as well as the Hawick, Gala and Langholm Sports. *Back row (l to r):* Colin Telfer, Dick Polson, Kenny McCartney, Harry Graham, Ian Cranston, Billy McCracken, Ian Douglas. *Middle row:* Mel Graham, Alistair Campbell, Alan Tomes, Norman Webb, Norman Pender, Donnie McLeod, Billy Murray. *Front row:* Colin Easton, Colin Deans, Raymond Corbett, Alistair Cranston (Captain), George Penman (President), Brian Hegarty, Bruce Elliot, Jim Renwick, Alistair Taylor.

Terence Froud showing his athleticism as the final whistle blows after Renwick had kicked the injury time penalty which sealed a famous 12–10 victory over Gala at Netherdale in 1982. That result effectively brought Hawick the National League title. *Photograph © Scotsman Publications Ltd*

Against Wales and England during the 1978 season the Scotland team contained six Hawick players:
Alistair Cranston, Norman Pender, Brian Hegarty, Jim Renwick, Alan Tomes and Colin Deans.

Renwick and Andy Irvine forged a great friendship with each other based on a similar approach to life and rugby. Here the dynamic duo elude Clive Woodward of England. *Photograph © Colorsport*

Renwick loved touring, but he was always anxious to hear the news from home, especially during his two months in South Africa with the Lions in 1980.

Top: Bill Beaumont and Roger Uttley charge at a very small looking Renwick. This photo prompted Andy Irvine to comment: 'Jim Renwick against two Englishmen: it seems like a fair contest to me.' *Photograph © Colorsport*

Above: Renwick makes a break during Scotland's famous victory over Wales at Cardiff Arms Park in 1982. He was one of the stars in that match, scoring a try and a drop-goal. *Photograph © Colorsport*

The Scotland team for Renwick's last cap international at Murrayfield, against Wales in 1983 *Back row (l to r):* Touch Judge, Rob Cunningham, Gordon Hunter, Ron Wilson, David Leslie, Bill Cuthbertson, Alan Tomes, John Beattie, Iain Milne, Jim Calder, Gerry McGuinness, Jim Pollock, Iain Paxton, Touch Judge. *Front row:* Keith Robertson, Roger Baird, David Johnston, Jim Aitken, Roy Laidlaw, Jim Renwick, Peter Dodds, Colin Deans, Bryan Grossman. *Photograph © Yerbury*

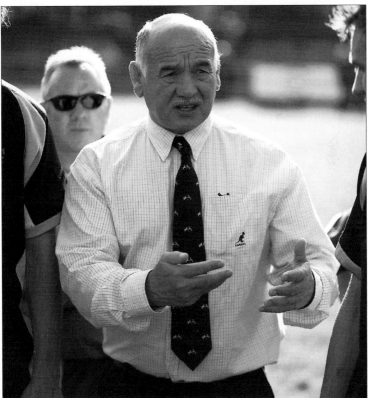

Top: Renwick with South Africa's Mr Rugby, Danie Craven, during the Lions tour of 1980.

Above: Still coaching. Passing on some words of advice at half-time during a recent Edinburgh Accies match. *Photograph © Ryan McGoverne, www.ryanmcgoverne.co.uk*

Top: A reluctant public speaker, Renwick also finds it hard to say no. Here he addresses the Hut at St Leonards during the 2006 Common Riding. On the left is Cornet Reid, and Renwick's old friend Provost McCartney. *Photograph © Alistair Learmonth, www.borderfestivals.co.uk*

Above: And it all ends like this. The life of a retired international rugby player throws up all sorts of strange scenarios. Here Renwick and Finlay Calder pose for photos towards the end of another rugby club dinner.

Whilst living in Gala, Renwick continued to travel to Hawick at least three times a week to train and play. Before buying his Skoda he would usually be picked up by team-mates travelling down from Edinburgh, but often he would have to get the bus. He eventually moved back to Hawick just before heading off to New Zealand for Scotland's tour there in the summer of 1981.

A month after his return from that trip David , his third son, was born on 21 July 1981, and on 20 February 1983 daughter Lindsey arrived.

Derrick Grant

Ian McLauchlan was one of the hardest men ever to pull on a Scotland rugby jersey. He was fairly small for a prop but he was technically superb and very, very strong. He played 43 times for Scotland between 1969 and 1979 and took part in two successful Lions tours to New Zealand in 1971 and South Africa in 1974. On the first of those trips he earned the soubriquet Mighty Mouse when he was thrust into the Test side after the Lions' first choice props, Sandy Carmichael and Ray McLoughlin, were sent home from the tour injured after a particularly brutal encounter against Canterbury on the Saturday before the first Test. McLauchlan scored the only try in that match in Dunedin, which set the tone for a famous Test series victory.

But even the indomitable Mighty Mouse used to regard the Hawick players he came across with a combination of admiration and bemusement. "Those buggers haven't got blue blood, they've got green blood," he would mutter.

It is a sentiment with which Derrick Grant wholeheartedly and happily agrees. "Hawick was my first love and my last love, I must admit," says the man who coached the club to six official league championships during a ten-year period as headcoach between 1973 and 1983.

> I played for Scotland and the Lions, I coached Scotland and I was involved with them right up to the 2003 World Cup – and although it was a great honour and privilege to get these opportunities, none of it was more important to me than Hawick. I was involved with coaching Hawick for fourteen seasons and I never lost the desire to beat everybody.

In his playing days Grant had been a hard-hitting, no-nonsense flanker who was always prepared to put his body on the line for the cause but perhaps lacked the extra yard of pace which would have transformed him from being an exceptionally good open-side into a great one.

He had first played for Hawick in 1959, won the first of his fourteen caps in 1965, and was a member of Mike Campbell-Lamerton's British and Irish Lions touring squad which visited Australia, New Zealand and Canada in 1966 – although a groin injury limited the number of games he played and he didn't manage to pick up any Test match appearances.

Two years later Grant had been lined up to tour with the Lions again, this time in South Africa with Tom Kiernan's successful 1968 squad. Ronnie Dawson, who was to coach the Lions on that trip, had spoken to Grant during the season and assured him that the he was definitely picked; but not long before the tour was due to get under way Grant was forced into early retirement, at the age of 29, after suffering one concussion too many.

By the time Jim Renwick was entering senior rugby, at the start of the 1970s, Grant was assistant coach to Robin Charters at Hawick, and he was determined to use the experience and expertise gleaned from touring with the Lions in 1966 to make Hawick the best side it could possibly be. At the start of the 1973–74 season he took over as head coach for the first ever season in which the official league championship was played in Scotland. He brought in his friend Elliot Broatch, who had tackled so bravely in the centre for the South against the All Blacks in 1963, to coach the backs.

Derrick Grant:
I'd learned a hell of a lot from Robin and I knew the kind of fitness we needed to be top dogs and I just worked it from there. Elliot was a friend of mine and I knew he had a good rugby brain so we did it together. I think Hawick at that time were unique because Scotland only appointed their first coach in 1971, but we already had two coaches. That was an idea that I first noticed in New Zealand – they always had a forwards and a backs coach – and I think we would be one of the first sides over here to do it.

In this professional era when 30 backroom staff are taken on Lions trips (as was the case on Sir Clive Woodward's tour to New Zealand in 2005), it is easy to forget just how much our approach to coaching has changed in a relatively short period of time.

Traditionally the responsibility for organising rugby teams on both the training paddock and the pitch had been part of the captain's remit, and such was the resistance to the idea of coaching in the northern hemisphere that it wasn't until the 1966 Lions tour that a coach was named as part of the tour party – with John Robins, a Welshman who had toured with the Lions in 1950 and gone on to become a PE lecturer in Sheffield, being given the job. However old habits die hard and it was not an easy trip for Robins, whose position was not helped when he tore ligaments in his knee whilst refereeing a charity match in Wellington.

"John Robins was a very honest guy and he certainly got our fitness levels up," recalls Grant. "But he didn't coach any of the international sides because they didn't have coaches in those days and Campbell-Lamerton, who was an army captain, tended to overrule him. He wasn't the brightest as far as that was concerned."

But the precedent had been set and more and more coaches began to be accepted as part of modern rugby culture, although the SRU were typically reluctant to embrace this change. For example, Jim Telfer was captain when Scotland toured Argentina in 1969, and as such he was put in charge of all training and coaching of the players during that trip.

It wasn't until 1971 that Bill Dickinson was given the rather mealy-mouthed title of 'adviser to the captain' for the Scottish international rugby team. This meant he was responsible for preparing the national team before matches but only had an advisory role in the process of naming the side – that was still the preserve of the selection committee known as 'The Big Five', consisting of a representative from each of the five districts – Glasgow, Edinburgh, the South, the North and Midlands and the Anglo-Scots.

The idea of having two coaches for one team was still a long way off – at least on this side of the world – and it wasn't until 1981 when Colin Telfer was made assistant to his namesake Jim Telfer (no relation) that Scotland accepted that development. It was 1989 before the Lions had two coaches, with Roger Uttley working alongside Ian McGeechan in Australia. With this in mind, it is clear that in the early seventies Hawick were some way ahead of the game when it came to coaching.

At Hawick a committed group of former players – including Grant, Charters, Hugh McLeod and Jack Hegarty – were determined to do everything in their power to ensure that the success they had achieved on the pitch during the fifties and sixties was built upon in the years that followed.

And if that meant breaking with normal practice and having both a forwards coach and a backs coach then so be it.

While Renwick had very little direct contact with Hugh McLeod during his playing career, the former Scotland prop was a major influence in the background at Mansfield Park throughout the seventies and early eighties. Not least because of his close relationship with Grant.

Derrick Grant:
I remember Hugh McLeod used to tell us all about what he had seen in New Zealand when he was there with the Lions in 1959, so when I went there in 1966 I wanted to do the same for Hawick. A lot of the players at that time weren't really thinking about coaching but I had it in my head that I would like to coach and Hugh had me primed to learn as much as I possibly could to bring back to Hawick. And when I saw the set up in New Zealand I knew that we had a lot to learn or we were going to be left behind.

Jim Telfer was on that trip too, and the pair of us used to go along and watch their training sessions and see how they did it. The other guy who used to come along with us was Don Rutherford, the English full back, who had a remit from the English Rugby Union. They had said to him that they were thinking of introducing coaching in England at club and school level and they wanted him to keep his eyes open. He went on to become the RFU's technical director.

We came up against a superb All Blacks side on that trip with guys like the two Meads brothers, Ken Gray, and Brian Lochore at their disposal. They beat us 4–0 in the Test series so you can imagine there was plenty to pick up on. Their pack was just something else in terms of the quality of rugby they played. They could do all the spade work – they could scrummage and they could win ball in the line-out as well as anybody – but when they got loose in the open field it was unbelievable.

I remember Stan Meads making a break from the tale of the line-out when we played Wanganui–King Country and our backs couldn't catch him. They were just so fast and powerful running with the ball in hand and that was the kind of rugby I wanted Hawick to play – to win possession, go forward, and cause the opposition all sorts of problems with our physical presence and our skill. Then at just the right moment, while the big boys were still moving forward, I wanted them to deliver quality ball to the scrum-half so that the backs could roll into gear.

It doesn't sound like rocket science, and it wasn't – but in those days what we were trying to do was ahead of our time in Scotland. I've sat in the stand and listened to spectators criticise the way Hawick played – people saying there was too much forward work or complaining about Alastair [Cranston] hitting up in the centre – but there was more to Hawick than that. To me that was sour grapes.

I wanted us to be the best pack of forwards that Scottish club rugby had ever produced and I worked towards that objective using the experience I'd had in New Zealand to guide me. I always wanted to play fifteen-man rugby but to do that you have to have a powerful pack.

And Hawick were that much fitter than everyone else at that time. Because the one thing I learned going on the Lions tour was what fitness was all about. If you want to play at the highest level and handle the demands that are put on your body, then you have to have the fitness. As a selector and a coach you look at the quality of the players you had and say: 'Right, this is the way I want to play the game.' And the type of rugby we wanted to play meant our fitness levels had to be at an exceptionally high level.

You build a team, it doesn't just happen for you – you have to build it by getting the right guys doing the right job. At the start of the seventies it was a young side but by the time the official championship started in 1973 we were ready to build a great team.

Just as he had been happy to learn from New Zealand, Grant was also happy to learn from other sports.

There used to be quite a lot of athletics meetings in the Borders and I used to speak to those guys about how to achieve certain types of fitness. I used to speak to sprinters and longer distance runners and you picked up little tips. I used to get information from a guy who worked in the Pringles mill who was in touch with coaches in America.

The other valuable thing that I learned from the professional runners was through speaking to one guy who was a half-mile and miler. He said that if you are building up for a big run – or in our case a big game – then three to four weeks beforehand you should run yourself into the ground. What he said was that he'd 'bottom' himself. It was something you couldn't use too often, maybe only twice or thrice in a season for the top challengers.

So what we used to do was work them really hard a fortnight, maybe three weeks, before the big game, and after that we used to work on nothing else but short sharp sprints. And it was almost like having a racehorse, when the horse wants to go and the jockey has got to hold him back, and they were bursting to go, and when it came to the game you just let them go and on those days, when we had got it right, they were superb – we were unbeatable.

Funnily enough I picked up a few tips about fitness from a fellow from Heriots called Peter Hill – he was an athlete but he was helping out with the fitness at Heriots. Elliot Broatch and I spoke to him on every opportunity we could, and he gave us a lot of stuff about how he prepared Heriots. It was basically the same format as I had adopted at Hawick, but with a more professional approach. I had written down what I wanted them to do, but he broke it down even further. He broke it down to a certain amount of yardage and he built up their fitness by increasing the yardage. At the start of the season he would have them doing maybe 400 yards of quality anaerobic running, and he would build it up and build it up until he had the players running the number of yards that they would run in an average rugby game. He had it down to specifics and I picked up on that because it was a better way of training – it was a gradual build-up and less haphazard. It was common sense when you think about it, but it was what he had learned at Loughborough College.

Our season fell into a basic format. The early part of the season was based on building up your stamina levels, and once you've got that aerobic fitness in the bank then you start working on anaerobic fitness, so we would then do a lot of sprinting over short distances which could be anything from 25 yards up to 110 yards, and we were looking for the ability to run that distance again and again with a short recovery time so that they were running without the chance to take oxygen on board. I know it is a lot more scientific now, but that system worked and it gave us wonderful fitness levels where you had the stamina to keep going for the whole game – even against tough opposition.

They used to say that Hawick could win in the last fifteen minutes, but that wasn't an accident. It was because our fitness levels meant we could maintain the standard we were playing at for the full 80. In fact we could raise our game at the end while the opposition were beginning to tail off.

There were weights at Mansfield but a lot of guys worked in manual jobs and they were naturally strong, so we did quite a few drills that worked on strength but it wasn't like it is now. We did a lot of running and passing because that is what rugby is all about – passing is everything in rugby.

It was all planned. The boys maybe thought I just liked running the backside off of them when I felt like it, but I can assure you that it was all planned – there was a method in the madness. They were good trainers at Hawick and the great thing in those days was that all the international players were the best trainers. That was partly because there was the incentive of playing for Scotland and even the Lions – but it was also because we developed a culture of that being the way it is, so that anybody coming into the side knew right away what the standard was and what they would have to do if they wanted to play for Hawick.

That has been one of the secrets to Hawick's success over the years – we've had a constant stream of players going away with Scotland and the Lions and bringing back new ideas to the club. Success breeds success and we were fortunate because we always had guys playing representative rugby, who would come back and pull the level up, and I suppose that a lot of clubs didn't have that same sort of outside influence.

I remember when Jim came back from the Lions tour in 1980 and he got the boys doing a little extra training after the session was over. They would jog round the four corners of the field and do so many press-ups, sit-ups and burpies. It was a way of warming down but getting a wee bit extra work in as well. He often brought back tactical ideas form international trips as well.

I always listened to Jim and the other guys who had been away with the international team or the Lions. You couldn't afford to ignore them. Some guys might let their ego get in the road, but it wasn't about ego for me, it was about Hawick. You took every opportunity going to make the team better and keep Hawick one step ahead of the rest.

All things considered it was a tough regime, but the intensity of training at Mansfield was a crucial factor in the level of success enjoyed by Hawick during the seventies and eighties.

JMR:
We only had fifteen down to train, because anyone who wasn't in the side trained with their junior team, so you got specialised stuff. And with two coaches there and only fifteen players, there was no hiding place – it was tough, very tough.

If you dropped balls you were telt, if you missed tackles you were telt. You might score three tries on Saturday, but if you missed a kick or slipped off a tackle you were telt about that. You had played well if Derrick never spoke to you.

And if there was a team that did more running than us, well, they'd worked their tail off because Derrick really punished us. You always had to do your set runs, every Tuesday and Thursday, and there's no doubt that was one of the reasons for being able to make the grade when you moved up – because you'd done all the groundwork.

If you think of a game of rugby and your team are getting 60 percent of the ball and the other team are only getting 40 percent, then you can waste 20 percent, which is a third of the possession your getting, but the other team can't afford to waste any. So, rather than being boring we were being exciting, because our domination up front meant the backs had the freedom to try things. That was one of the principles of Derrick's game, that the forwards were there to win the ball and really set the platform for winning the game.

In 1971 the Lions had beaten the All Blacks with hardly any possession by throwing the ball about – but the game was changing and it was getting harder and harder to do it without having at least parity upfront. Derrick was a hard driving forward himself and obviously he wanted to coach that, and I think he was right.

Maybe in the early days I wasn't aware of how lucky I was to have so much good ball to play with. Colin was a good enough player to weigh up the possession and decide if it was good stuff that the backs could have a go with, or whether to kick it, or keep it tight with the forwards.

But I learned fairly early that while you can get good ball there's no such thing as bad ball – its all possession and you've got to use it all. The key is using it wisely. Teams playing against Hawick would struggle that way because they knew that they weren't going to get that much ball so they had to move everything and take risks that we didn't have to take.

The fundamental principle of rugby is to go forward with the ball. Derrick's thing was that it's a momentum game and that's what we worked on – basic number eight pick-ups, going round and going forward. And in the days before they changed it to 'use-it-or-lose-it' the team that was going forward got the put-in – it didn't matter whether it was a ruck or a maul, if you were going forward then you got the put-in.

Mind you it wasn't all about winning the battle up front – folk often forget that the backs played some nice rugby too. We never got a row for having a go, never got a row for trying things, if it was silly things you tried then you would get a row, but not for having a go and trying to beat a man or off-loading out the tackle and things like that.

I mind some boys would get a hard time from Derrick, he used to flip sometimes and call them out and give it to them. It wasn't about the player, it was about Hawick and the team, and if there was a weak link there you had to sort it out.

Crab [Kenny McCartney] used to get a lot of stick and a lot of it was pretty unfair because there was only a couple of lights covering the whole pitch at Mansfield in those days which meant you could hardly see where you were going on a dark training night, and by the time the ball got to Crab on the wing during unopposed he had to be flying – and it wasn't easy catching in that light, especially when you're going full belt.

I remember at the time of the miners' strikes when there was no lights because they were having power cuts to save their coal. We all went down to Mansfield and it was pitch black – you couldn't see a thing. I said to Heg: 'We can't do much in this. We'll be inside the night, we'll have an easy night.'

I should've known better. Derrick turns up and says: 'We can't see what we're doing but we can still run.' He had the car headlights on and had us running hard for two hours. We were on our knees, but it did us no harm at all.

There can be little doubt that all this hard work did Hawick an awful lot of good. In winning each of the first five official league championships after the competition's inception in 1973, they lost only four league matches and drew two matches out of 55 played. They scored 230 tries and conceded only 29.

They won the title again in 1982 and didn't finish outside the top four in any of the ten years in which Grant was at the helm. During that time Hawick produced three British Lions, seven Scotland internationalists and six Scotland B caps.

Derrick Grant:
I'd been brought up believing that Hawick was the greatest club side in Scotland and when the official leagues started in 1973 I was very determined that Hawick would be the first name on the cup

We achieved that, but we didn't win it with a 100 percent record, we got beat by West of Scotland at Mansfield. The next year we got beat by West again, this time through there. But in the third year we absolutely took them apart at Mansfield Park and I think that was the best I've ever seen Hawick play. It was really heart warming for me to watch Hawick that day. We really played superbly – we started to play like a New Zealand pack and I think that was the ultimate. The backs played well too, but for me it was most satisfying to see the forwards play like New Zealanders. I think I got a bigger kick out of that performance than winning the league trophy.

The league was important and we had to win that but we didn't want to be beaten by anybody because we wanted to be the best ever. That side had a great mentality and they hated losing – and when they did lose it was a mistake. The only time it wasn't a mistake was when Heriots came into their own at the end of the seventies.

Maybe it wouldn't have been the same if everything hadn't been going so well, but it was a great time. Hawick were a special side in those days and it was a tremendous achievement to get five championships on the trot. Amazing consistency. I remember we lost six games in a row at the start of the 1969–70 season. We were inexperienced and we got into a rut that we couldn't get out of. That experience taught me a valuable lesson – it highlighted to me that you have to win at all costs. It's very hard to get your message through to players when you're losing but if you can win one game then you've got a platform to go onto the next game. The end justifies the means, so you might have to be negative sometimes to win a game and then win another game, but once you start winning then your message gets through to the players a lot more easily than it would if you were losing and you can start thinking about playing more exciting rugby. The kind of rugby you want to play is always in the back of your mind, but to achieve that you have to do some navvy work and dig the foundations first – you have to do the basics and give nothing away to the opposition just to win the game.

Grant was unrelenting in his determination to drive Hawick onwards and upwards. He was fiercely proud of the club and the town which it represented, and as an antidote to the threat of complacency in the future he fed on the pain of previous disappointments.

I always had a long memory and I never forgot the bad things that happened, and that's what motivated me, kept driving me forward, and stopped me ever getting complacent. I always erred on the right side because too much is better than too little when it comes to training. You have to stack the odds in your favour.

When I came into the Hawick side in 1959–60 it was a great team playing superb rugby. Jack Hegarty, Adam Robson, George Stevenson, Hugh McLeod and my brother Oliver were all internationalists and we wiped the board with everybody. Hugh had come back from New Zealand in 1959 and he introduced a lot of the methods he had picked up when over there, and we did a lot of running even then.

But then four or five boys went to rugby league, a few others moved on and it all disappeared so quickly. I never ever forgot how quickly a side can come up and how quickly it can go down, and that was possibly the main driving factor for me as a coach. It's like having a butterfly in your hand, and you open up to see what its like, and before you know it the butterfly is away. If we stopped for too long to enjoy it then it would be gone – we had to keep our noses to the grindstone. I might have been demanding, but those boys have got it in the bag now and nobody will ever take what they achieved away from them. You can't lose those memories.

Make hay while the sun shines because the years go by so quickly – that's a pretty good motto. Looking back now, I can see that I was lucky that during my playing and my coaching career at Hawick I was surrounded by men who believed in that motto too.

Back in Blue

Renwick was one of ten Hawick players in the South of Scotland side which drew 16–16 with Argentina in November 1973, and he was then recalled to the Scotland set-up for their non-cap international against the tourists a fortnight later. It was a strong Scotland side, with only three uncapped players in the starting fifteen. They were Mike Hunter of Glasgow HSFP alongside Renwick in the centre, Duncan Madsen of Gosforth at hooker, and Bill Watson of Boroughmuir on the flank. All three would be capped during the course of the next Five Nations campaign.

Despite the experience in their ranks, Scotland were fortunate to win this match against an Argentinean side which impressed with some great running rugby. The final score was 12–11 to the hosts, but both tries in the match were scored by the tourists. Hugo Porta, the great Argentinean stand-off who played 57 times for the Pumas between 1971 and 1990, got the first Argentinean try, and Renwick's opposite number, the equally impressive Alejandro Travaglini, scored the second. It took a late Colin Telfer drop-goal to separate the sides. The day ended on a sour note when Gordon Brown was punched by an opposition forward in the tunnel after the match, and the Argentinean manager accused the Welsh referee of bias.

Two months later Renwick retained his place in the Scotland team for the game against Wales in Cardiff, which finished 6–0 to the home team thanks to a disputed score by Terry Cobner, who was playing in his first international.

The try came about after Wales had stolen their second strike against the head in quick succession and Gareth Edwards sent play down the blindside with a clever reverse pass to Phil Bennett. Gerald Davies took up the running but when he was caught by Nairn McEwan just short of the line, Cobner was on hand to receive the ball and dart over the line. The rules of the time dictated that if the ball touched the ground after a player had been tackled then he had to release it, but the referee ruled that on this occasion the ball had been prevented from touching the deck when Davies was tackled so the score was allowed to stand.

At the time Renwick thought that the Scots had been hard done by, but after the game he accepted Davies' assurances that the try was legitimate. Besides, Wales had probably done enough to deserve the win.

During the final moments of the match Renwick broke out from his own 25 to create a two-on-one with Lewis Dick against Davies. The Welshman gambled on taking the ball carrier. He bet right and Scotland's last chance to salvage something from the match was lost.

Two weeks later Scotland faced England at Murrayfield. Since 1880 the Calcutta Cup match had been played in March as the last game of the season, but because of a new system of rotating international matches it took place on the second weekend of the championship on this occasion.

Scotland raced into a 9–0 lead in less than eleven minutes thanks to an Andy Irvine penalty, a Wilson Lauder try and an Irvine conversion. And it might have been more had the full back been on target with two other long range penalty efforts, but instead England pulled it back to 9–7 at half-time with an Alan Old penalty and a Fran Cotton touch-down after some strong running by Peter Squires, Andy Ripley and Tony Neary. After the break England dominated, but Scotland's stubborn defence meant it wasn't until the game reached its final quarter that the visitors were able to take the lead through a Neary try from a short penalty move.

Some heroic Scottish tackling – particularly from Ian McGeechan (who at one point felled three Englishmen in quick succession with a series bone-crunching hits), Nairn McEwan and Wilson Lauder – had kept the Scots in the game, and it was only when they went behind for the first time in the match that they managed to move into attacking mode. With ten minutes to go Telfer collected a long line-out throw from Drew Gill, dummied to go left but instead switched the ball to the right, via MacEwan, to Irvine. The Scottish full back cut inside Old and though half tackled was able to propel himself over the line.

The conversion was missed which meant Scotland's lead was only two rather than four points, and it looked like this would be crucial when Telfer hacked a loose ball down field and Peter Rossborough, the English full back, gathered the ball, steadied himself and dropped a goal from 35 yards. That put England's noses back in front, and as the game entered injury time it looked like the opportunity for a famous Scottish victory had slipped away.

But then Old missed touch as he tried to clear the ball from his own 25, and Irvine fed Gill who hacked forward. A hapless Englishman tried to collect the ball but knocked forward in the process, and the error was compounded when David Duckham instinctively picked up from an offside position. In the third minute of injury time Scotland were awarded a penalty and one last lifeline. The penalty was from 40 yards out and close to the touchline, but Irvine showed supreme self-confidence and composure under pressure. His kick sailed long, straight and true though the posts to make the score 16–14 for Scotland. The final whistle sounded a few seconds later.

It was a dramatic conclusion to a thrilling match full of theatre and tension, in which the lead had changed hands four times in the last twenty minutes. In their delirium at having stolen a famous win with the last kick of the match the players carried Irvine off the pitch on their shoulders.

JMR:
That was a bit of much I thought, but sometimes when you've worked so hard in a game, you've lost it and you've won it again . . . well . . . emotions run high. But it's not the Hawick way to go over the top about things. When I scored I used to make sure that I didn't show that I was smiling. I just tried to touch the ball down and run back without showing emotion. There's a few times I've been in the vicinity when Andy Irvine has scored a try and I've just turned and run back. I've not jumped up and down and waved my arms about. It's not that I'm not pleased, it's just not the way we did it at Hawick.

Scotland were brought back down to earth in their next match with a 9–6 defeat to Ireland in Dublin. Playing with the breeze at their backs during the first half Ireland had raced into a 9–0 lead, and despite dominating possession in the second half the Scots were not able convert pressure into enough points to win this match.

Scotland did however finish the season on a high with a 19–6 victory over France when for the first time that season their handling play began to click and they scored two very good tries. First of all McHarg crashed over after a passage of play in which Renwick, Dick, McGeechan, Hunter, Irvine and Gill were all involved. Then Irvine, McHarg, Carmichael, Lauder, McGeechan and Renwick all played a role in creating an equally impressive try for Lewis Dick. This victory denied the visitors the championship, which went instead to Ireland.

That summer Willie John McBride captained the Lions tour of South Africa. Andy Irvine, Ian McGeechan, Billy Steele, Gordon Brown, Sandy Carmichael and Ian McLauchlan were the six Scots selected for the trip. It is often said by his friends and admirers that Renwick should also have gone, but he believes that the selectors were right to overlook him on that occasion.

> I wasn't ready for it. McGeechan hadn't played many more games for Scotland than me, but he was a bit older and a bit more experienced. However, I think we did well out of that trip. All these boys came back from that tour with a bit more strength and some new ideas. If you have the right players on these tours you benefit and I think that happened for us that year. It was the same in 1990, after Finlay Calder had captained the Lions in Australia with eight other Scottish guys in the squad – including the Hastings boys, Craig Chalmers, Gary Armstrong, David Sole, John Jeffrey and Derek White. They came back and won the Grand Slam that year.
>
> You could say the same about the 1983 tour, even if it wasn't a success in terms of results. Guys like Rudd [John Rutherford], Roy [Laidlaw] and Deano [Colin Deans] would have learned a lot over in New Zealand, and they would have been fit and raring to go when they got back – remember these were the amateur days and the Scottish boys were always good trainers which meant that they would really benefit from two months living like a professional.

Renwick played for Scotland throughout the 1974–75 season, which started with a 44–8 victory over a free-running Tongan touring side in a non-cap international at Murrayfield. In the new year Scotland won both their home games in the Five Nations – against Ireland (20–13) and Wales (12–10).

Against Ireland Renwick scored one of Scotland's two tries from a dummy scissors move with David Bell of Watsonians, who was making his international debut alongside Renwick in the centre. Billy Steele got the other score, while Dougie Morgan dropped a goal and Andy Irvine kicked two penalties.

The Wales result was particularly pleasing. Wales had already defeated France away and England at home in their first two matches of the tournament, and brought a huge crowd north for this game. In the end a world record 104,000 supporters packed into Murrayfield on the day, with several thousand more unable to squeeze their way in. Wales would go on to win the championship that year, but because of their defeat to Scotland they would have to wait another year to win their first Grand Slam since 1971.

The teams that day were:

Scotland: A.R. Irvine (Heriots FP); W.C.C. Steele (London Scottish), J.M Renwick (Hawick), D.L. Bell (Watsonians), L.G. Dick (Jordanhill College); I.R. McGeechan (Headingley), D.W. Morgan (Stewart's FP); J. McLauchlan (Jordanhill College), D.F Madsen (Gosforth), A.B. Carmichael (West of Scotland), A.F. McHarg (London Scottish), G.L. Brown (West of Scotland), M.A. Biggar (London Scottish), D.G. Leslie (Dundee HSFP), N.A. McEwan (Highland).

Wales: J.P.R. Williams (London Welsh); T.G.R. Davies (Cardiff), S.P. Fenwick (Bridgend), R.W.G. Gravell (Llanelli), J.J. Williams (Llanelli); J.D. Bevan (Aberavon), G.O. Edwards (Cardiff), A.G. Faulkner (Pontypool), R.W. Windsor (Pontypool), G. Price (Pontypool), A.J. Martin (Aberavon), M.G. Roberts (London Welsh), T.J. Cobner (Pontypool), T.M. Davies (Swansea), T.P. Evans (Swansea).

As a spectacle of rugby the match proved to be a bit of a disappointment. Three Dougie Morgan penalties against two from Steve Fenwick gave Scotland a 9–6 lead at half-time, and in the second half both sides continued to struggle when it came to opening up the opposition's defence. Ian McGeechan's drop-goal was the only score during the second period until the fourth minute of injury time, when at long last JPR Williams was able to spark a sweeping attack which eventually led to Trefor Evans scoring in the corner. Alan Martin kicking for Wales in the absence of Fenwick, who had been forced to retire injured from the match before half-time, missed with the long-range conversion attempt which would have given the visitors a draw.

Throughout the seventies Scotland struggled to get results away from home and 1975 was no exception. They lost narrowly away to both France (10–9) and then England (7–6). The French game in particular was an opportunity missed. In a bad-tempered match the ball was twice dropped by Scotland as the try line beckoned, and Irvine managed to convert only three out of his nine penalty attempts.

In the England game Scotland were once again playing for their first Triple Crown since 1938, and also for a share of the championship. But their failure to capitalise on the pressure they exerted throughout the match meant they came away empty handed. Despite being a long way from the action, Irish referee Patrick D'Arcy awarded a controversial try to Alan Morley when he was judged to have beaten Irvine to an awkward kick ahead. That was midway through the second half and for the remainder of the contest Scotland pressed England, but the home side were able to absorb the pressure fairly comfortably. That was until two minutes into injury time when Scotland were awarded a penalty 35 metres out and slap in front of the posts. Another last ditch Scottish victory over England appeared to be on the cards, but Dougie Morgan pulled the kick wide. In the dressing rooms afterwards the Scottish heads were understandably down. Morgan's was about his ankles. There was a deadly silence, until Renwick piped up: "Hell, Dougie, I could have back-heeled a chest of drawers over from there."

This match reinforced the impression that if Scotland could score tries then they would go from being a pretty good side to being a very good one. Renwick and Steele had scored against Ireland at the start of the championship, but since then they had failed to cross the line.

Colin Telfer:
It probably had something to do with the way we were playing at the time. Bill Dickinson was still coach and he played a forward dominated game. We had a good front five with Carmichael, Madsen, McLaughlan, Brown and McHarg, but to my mind we didn't have a back-row which suited a wider game.

Nairn McEwan and these guys were good players but I always felt that there was no link between that power in the front five and a more expansive game. With Jim and Andy Irvine there we had the capability in the backs to play a wider game. You've got to play to your strengths and the front five was ours, but I don't think we gave the backs enough opportunities to cut loose. We did at times, but not enough for my liking.

JMR:
We had the ability. There were some good attacking players there, but I suppose we were out the habit of scoring tries and when that happens

it quite often becomes a monkey on your back. You've got to believe you can score and expect to score.

But you've got to remember that in those days you didn't score as many tries. If you got three tries in an international you were lucky, so it maybe isn't as bad a statistic as it seems. And the other side of it is that at least we were getting a few results, whereas later on in the seventies we were scoring tries but couldn't buy a win. I'd rather win 3–o with a disputed penalty than score five tries but lose by a point.

Toomba

Jimmy Graham used to be fond of telling his workmates at Jaeger's mill on Commercial Road in Hawick about his grandson, who was a strapping lad playing rugby in Gateshead. It didn't take Robin Charters long to get wind of this and when he did he was straight on the phone, inviting the youngster to a trial match.

Alan Tomes:
It was the start of the 1973–74 season and it was the first time I had been inside Mansfield Park. Robin said: 'Go and get changed and introduce yourself.' So I went down the tunnel and took a left into the changing rooms. When I walked in Jim Renwick was in the middle of telling a story and he just stopped dead and looked round at me. There was total silence, it was a horrible moment. I think I said: 'I'm Alan Tomes – the replacement for Jim Scott,' or something stupid like that. Still silence. Eventually Norman Pender saved me. He pulled me down onto the bench next to him and handed me a strip. Slowly the rest of the guys started carrying on with what they were doing before. I always had a soft spot for Norman after that.

I'd come from a pretty poor side that never won any games and this was a team full of internationalists. I'd never seen an internationalist in the flesh before. So I was pretty intimidated, and when I got that reception I just wanted the ground to swallow me up. But I soon realised it wasn't personal – Hawick people are just a bit reserved. It took me about a year before I was really a part of it. They are friendly enough, but they won't push themselves to get to know you. It got to the stage that I thought I better make more of an effort and start pushing myself, so I started staying in Hawick for nights out after the game. And once I had proved myself as a player they started to accept me.

Anyway, I played that trial match, but I didn't have a car and had just started a new job so I was back playing for Gateshead Fell at the start of the season. Then I guested for Hawick when they played a

Northumberland select side in 1973, and after that I knew I had to make the effort. So I saved up and bought an old Morris Minor and started travelling up and down the A68 to train and play for Hawick.

In those days the roads were quieter so I never used the brakes and it used to take me an hour and ten minutes travel each way – an hour and a half maximum. I left Hawick one night and didn't see another car until I was passing Newcastle Airport. It was a lot of travel, but I never regretted it. Never once did I consider playing for Gosforth or a team like that.

I found it tough at first. Before coming to Hawick I'd received no coaching whatsoever and I played for a rubbish team. They were nice guys but they weren't successful and they got picked on, so you have to decide what you are going to do about that and I started being a fighter. That was okay in Gateshead, but at Hawick they weren't looking for brawlers. They wanted hard boys but not guys that gave away lots of silly penalties, so I had to get the discipline under control.

After a less than promising start to the relationship, Renwick and Tomes soon became firm friends. Together they were stalwarts of both the Hawick and Scotland teams through most of the seventies and into the eighties. And they shared the same sort of laid-back approach to life and rugby.

Alan Tomes:
We'd get team-talks in the changing rooms before internationals and guys would be talking about this being the most important thing you'll ever do and all that sort of stuff. Then you'd catch Jim's eye and you could see he was thinking: 'What a load of crap.' I'd have to stare at the floor so that nobody could see me smiling. Jim and I were very similar in that sense. We took the game seriously but we didn't take ourselves seriously.

I remember playing Wales in the late seventies and I was marking Jeff Wheel, who was a pretty tough character. Nairn McEwan was giving the team talk and he turned to me and said: 'Wheel is going to punch you, he's going to kick you and if you go down he's going to stand all over you. So what are you going to do about it?'

I said: 'Let him have all the ball he wants.'

It was the most inappropriate thing I could think of. I didn't like all this mouthing off about what I was going to do. I preferred to do my talking on the pitch.

Jim and I had some great times playing for Scotland, even if we went through a long losing spell at the end of the seventies when we hardly won a game. After the games we used to go back to the North British, have a quick change and nip across the road to the Abbotsford for a pint. I remember one time we were getting a lot of stick because we were in the middle of that losing run and we had been beaten by France, again. One guy must have been in the band which the French used to always have, and he had his trumpet with him. He was taking the mickey, and asked if any of us could play his trumpet because we certainly couldn't play rugby. Of course Jim could, so he got up and did *The Last Post* – which was quite appropriate given our losing record.

JMR:

We were playing sevens at Selkirk once and Toomba was in the side. He was quite big, he was fairly mobile, and he was quite a good ball handler, so he used to play a few games for us in the sevens. Anyway, on this occasion we were playing Melrose and he ends up with the ball right where you don't want to get it – between the posts on your own line. In that situation I would always aim for the tramlines and use the touchline as a defender, but Toomba hoofed it right down the middle, Melrose ran it back and Keith Robertson scored between the kindling.

We're all back behind the posts waiting for the conversion and I'm not happy. So I go over and tap him on the shoulder. 'Listen Toomba, this is how it works. You get the ball for us, you don't kick it, you just get it and give it to us. If you're ever caught like that again don't kick it, just pass it to one of the backs. We'll do all the kicking and decision making, you just get the pill.'

Two minutes later one of their boys pulls me back as I run past him, so I turn round and smack him and he smacks me back – penalty to Melrose for me punching. Melrose get the ball, tap it and score. I'm standing behind the posts feeling sorry for myself and Toomba taps us on the shoulder. I turn round and he says: 'Listen Renwick, I'll do the fighting; you do the running and scoring the tries. If you're ever caught like that again, then don't hit the boy. Leave that to me. You just wait for me to get the ball and give it to you.' That was typical of his style.

I think it was difficult for Toomba when he first came to Hawick because he was a bit of an outsider. But he fitted in well with guys like Pender and Donnie McLeod because he was hard. And over the years he's been one of the most dedicated players Hawick has ever had. He played 386 games for the club which is more than anyone else except Alistair Cranston. It's some going when you think he was travelling up and down the road from Gateshead the whole time.

Even after he retired when he was 37 he still came back and answered a few SOS calls for Hawick when they were struggling. I think he was into his forties by this point. We used to joke that Toomba would be sitting in his living room in Gateshead watching the TV then the Hawick selectors would send out the 'Batman Beam' over Carterbar, and Toomba would jump in his car and come to the rescue.

New Zealand 1975

Scotland's seven-match tour of New Zealand during the summer of 1975 was Renwick's first major rugby expedition. The trip can be considered a qualified success, with Scotland making a fairly good impression on both the rugby field and with the New Zealand public.

Renwick was impressed by the friendly welcome extended to the touring party by the locals he encountered on the trip, and he enjoyed the fanatical approach to rugby prevalent in New Zealand. In many ways he felt at home, because the culture of the place was very similar to that of the Scottish Borders.

That couldn't be said of Hong Kong, where the Scotland squad spent a night on their way to New Zealand.

JMR:
I remember in the hotel Barney [Ian Barnes] and I were getting the lift up to our room and two smart looking Chinese women get in. One of them says to Barney: 'Are you here on business?'

He gives her the usual: 'I'm here to play rugby for Scotland, I'm an international sportsman.' Then he says: 'How about yirsel? Are you here on business?'

'Monkey business,' she said. All the way from Hawick and the first person we meet is a hooker. It was a culture shock. I'd never come across anything like that before.

By the time the squad eventually arrived in New Zealand several members of the party were suffering from stomach bugs picked up in Hong Kong, and there was only limited time available to prepare for the first match of the tour against Nelson Bay on 24 May. All of which was of no major concern to Bill Dickinson who believed that jet-lag was all in the mind and nothing that a good hard training session wouldn't sort out, so the squad were put through their paces in typically robust fashion before the Borders contingent in the party were invited along to an interview for Borders TV, which was to be conducted by John Dawson from the *Tweeddale Press*, who was the only journalist to make the trip and had turned up at Heathrow with one battered old case held together with string.

JMR:

We were all lined up and he moved along the line asking each of us a question. It was the usual stuff, John Dawson would say: 'John Frame, a well known face in the Borders, how's the tour going so far?' And Frame would give him his spiel, then the camera would move onto the next guy.

It came to me. 'Jim Renwick, another centre, a Hawick man on tour, have you met any locals?'

'Aye, the locals have been great,' I replied, and then gave him the usual patter.

Eventually he got to the end of the row and he must have miscounted because he'd run out of questions and he still hadn't spoken to Barney. You could see him trying to think on his feet – but it wasn't happening for him. Eventually he says: 'Ian Barnes, another Hawick man, how are the women out here then Ian?'

Barney says: 'Well you better ask Jim – he is doing a lot better than me.'

Well I was right in: 'Cut that – cut that.' I was a married man!

Of course Dod Burrell, who was the tour manager, heard all about it and he called a team meeting. He got us all in the team room and he says: 'Right boys, we've got a problem. There's yin man in this room who has let himself down – he has let his team down – and he has let his country down.'

Barney's sitting right in the front row and he's looking over his shoulder – shaking his head and tutting – trying to work out who it was and what they've done. He doesn't even realise that it's him that's being talked about.

So he got his knuckles rapped, and the tape never went back.

Renwick played in the Nelson Bay match, in which Scotland fielded what was thought to be their strongest team against probably the weakest opposition they would encounter. The management were keen to get the trip off to a good start and they achieved that with a 51–6 victory, with Renwick scoring one of Scotland's eight tries. The result was built upon a domineering performance by the touring pack, Duncan Madsen taking thirteen heels against the head – which was a massive total even in those days when the strike was much more keenly contested than it is now.

It was a different story three days later, when a Scotland side shorn of several key players including Renwick, Andy Irvine, Sandy Carmichael, Alastair McHarg and David Leslie, lost 19–15 to Otago in front of a hostile crowd at Carisbrook – 'The House of Pain' – in Dunedin, the place where Vic Cavanagh had invented modern rucking in the 1940s. Otago had a proud record of giving British touring teams a bloody nose, having beaten the Lions in 1950, 1959 and 1966. It was a tradition they would carry on in 1993, when Gavin Hastings' side came a cropper in Dunedin on the Saturday before the first Test in Christchurch

The Otago match was Alan Tomes' first in a Scotland jersey and he almost made the perfect start to his Scotland career when, in the fifth minute of that match, a Colin Telfer pass put him into space. The try was there for the taking, but he chose to force a pass to Mike Biggar instead of backing himself to go it alone.

Renwick returned to the team for Scotland's next match against Canterbury in Christchurch which was played under the spectre of the barbaric attack on Sandy Carmichael during the 1971 Lions tour. Despite starting well, the Scots eventually went down 20–9, with all of Scotland's points coming courtesy of Andy Irvine's boot. The visitors were once again comprehensively out-rucked – in fact they didn't win a single ruck all day, while Canterbury won ten. The line-out stats were not much better, with the home team winning 24 to Scotland's six. Alex Wylie, the Canterbury and All Black number eight, said after the match: "It was an easy game for us."

Things got back on track in Scotland's next match, a 30–0 victory over Hawke's Bay, who were one of the stronger provincial teams in New Zealand at that time. Once again Renwick sat the match out. Clearly the Scots had learned the lessons which had been unceremoniously handed out by both Otago and Canterbury. Their victory was built upon domination of the set piece – where they won ten scrums against the head, and won the line-outs 22–11.

Scotland's best performance on the tour was in their next match against Wellington in front of 35,000 spectators at Athletic Park. It was an exhilarating encounter which Scotland eventually won 25–36, with Renwick scoring one of Scotland's three tries. John Frame and Ian McGeechan also touched down. Bizarrely, a power-cut just as the two teams were preparing to leave their changing rooms had plunged both sets of players into darkness, and they were left bumping into each other and feeling their way along the walls as they tried to make their way up a narrow staircase to the tunnel which led to the pitch.

That match was played on 7 June, which happened to be the Saturday of Hawick's Common Riding festival. There were five Hawick players on that trip and as the Common Riding song points out: 'Absent Teries' thoughts fly homewards, on each Common Riding morn'. To mark the occasion the Scotland squad had their own re-enactment of the Hut at St Leonards, with the Hawick players in the party taking the principal roles.

> JMR:
> They made Colin the Cornet, Barney was the right-hand man, Toomba was the left-hand man, Pender was acting-fither, and I was nothing. I was a bit peeved by that. I'd rather've been left out the Test team. They put me in charge of the drink – I had to pour the rum and milk for the boys.
>
> I was the only West Ender there, but I was nothing. They had Barney who was from Burnfit, they had Colin from Edinburgh, Tomesy from Gateshead and Pender was born in Bridlington – and here was me pouring the drinks. Barney was the only one that knew the Common Riding songs, but he never sings. I think Telfer sang: 'Dinah, Dinah, show us your legs.' Mind you Dod Burrell picked the office-bearers and he was a Gala man, so it shouldn't have been a surprise.

Renwick got his own back on the morning of the Test match when Burrell, who had been a highly decorated Regimental Sergeant Major in the King's Own Scottish Borderers during the war, marched into the team meeting, stood to attention, and said: "Thirty-two years ago today I sent a squad of young Border boys over the top at Flanders. None came back."

There was a stunned, prolonged silence before Renwick slowly raised his hand. "What is it Jim?" snapped Burrell.

"Dod," said Renwick tentatively.

"What?"

"I would like to come back."

Renwick hadn't played in Scotland's 16–10 victory over Bay Of Plenty on the Tuesday before the Test, but enjoyed fishing and experiencing the Maori culture in Rotorua. Meanwhile those playing in the match were having a far less enjoyable time.

Alan Tomes:
We'd been getting a bit of a doing up front so before the Bay of Plenty match Bill Dickinson gave the forwards a real roasting, and Duncan Madsen was on the receiving end of some really harsh words. In the changing room he was bouncing around trying to look as angry as he could when he kicked the door leading into the showers. Well his foot went right through it and it was like a fish hook – the studs got caught and he couldn't get his boot back out. Just then the referee came in to give us the usual chat about behaving ourselves and not getting too rough – and Madsen was hopping around with his foot stuck in the door.

The Test match, was played at Eden Park in Auckland after a downpour on the morning of the match.

JMR:
I've got a picture of myself on the pitch the day before the game and its fine – nice conditions to play the match – but the next again day it was six inches deep. I didn't go out onto the pitch beforehand, but there was boys coming back in saying that it was wet and that the water was lying on the surface. I thought to myself: 'These boys haven't seen Langholm on a bad day, it can't be any worse than that.' Then we got out there and . . . flipping hell . . . I've never seen anything like it.

It was a joke. Grant Batty tried to drop a goal, and the ball just died in the water. The game should never have been played, but we were flying home the next day and 50,000 folk had turned up to watch – so I suppose they didn't have a choice.

We were playing into a gale in the first half and we were only 6–0 down at half-time, which wasn't bad considering. But the wind changed at half-time and we got beat 24–0. If the wind had stayed we might have done better, but that's rugby for you.

They were a good side. You're talking about Bryan Williams, Duncan Robertson, Sid Going, Ian Kirkpatrick, Andy Leslie and guys like that. They were good lads and they were good players. If I'm being honest I don't think we were ever beating them.

With Andy Irvine moving to the wing, Bruce Hay was winning his first cap at full back that day, but he broke his arm after fifteen minutes and was replaced by Billy Steele. However Renwick is loath to use either the weather or the loss of their hard-hitting no-nonsense full back as an excuse for Scotland's defeat.

After the game Andy Leslie, the New Zealand captain, said: "This was one of the greatest moments in New Zealand swimming." Ian McLauchlan, his opposite number, congratulated the All Blacks on their win, but commented that it was "just sheer luck that nobody drowned."

JMR:
Overall I think it was a good tour – hard but good. We would train in the morning and they were tough sessions. Dickinson was good at getting you working hard, and guys like McLauchlan, Carmichael and McHarg had been around a while and they set the standard. They were good players and they pushed us on a bit.

But we also got the chance to see New Zealand too. To be fair it was the amateur days and guys were taking time off their work. You got an allowance every day and that was enough to live off, but a lot of guys were losing pay by being there, so there had to be a balance between doing the hard work and having a bit of fun. That was the beauty about playing in those days, we would train hard in the mornings but we played golf, went jet boating, went canoeing, and did things like that in the afternoon. And there were a lot of free nights, so you got to know boys.

That trip was also Renwick's first opportunity to carry on the Hawick tradition, initiated by Hugh McLeod when he toured with the Lions in 1955 and 1959, of bringing the lessons learned on tour back to Mansfield Park.

I remember before we went away on these sorts of trips Derrick used to say: 'If you find anything out bring it back to training.' So I kept my eyes peeled and because New Zealand were the best in the business, there is no doubt that there was plenty we could learn from the way they did it.

One thing I picked up on was that they worked hard on organising their defence. They were all very vocal and everyone knew what they were doing and had something to add, it wasn't just the stand-off calling the shots.

Their size, power, aggression, skill levels and body position were all things we could learn from too. But their all-round attitude was the big thing for me. Because it was so important to them they all had a lot of knowledge about the game, and it was impressive how quickly they picked up on what you were trying to do. It was after that trip that I really started studying the game properly and really watching folk closely, because that was when it struck home how important it was to use every little thing to your advantage.

From then on, at dinners after international matches, I used to always ask the opposition questions like: 'How do you defend that?' or 'Why don't you do it this way?' Some of them wouldn't say anything, but some would tell you. That's the way you learn, because everybody does it differently, you might do the same thing but you go about it in different ways.

That probably was the secret to our success at Hawick during the seventies – the experienced players bringing the messages back. And that was especially the case that year because there was five of us there, and when you come back from New Zealand you come back with a different outlook on the game.

I thought that I took rugby seriously until I went to New Zealand, then I saw that they take it twice as seriously as anyone in Scotland – the players, the fans, everybody. They thought about it more than us because it was more important to them than it was to us. Wherever you are in the country they talk about rugby. If you met a lassie and you said: 'I'm a prop.' She would say: 'Loose-head or tight-head?'

Far East 1977

In the summer of 1977 the British and Irish Lions toured New Zealand and Fiji. Renwick, who had just been named player of the year by *Scottish Rugby* magazine, was named as a reserve but was not selected in the travelling 30. His exclusion from the squad was a controversial decision.

Andy Irvine:
Jim should definitely have gone in '77 and I would have taken him in '74 as well. The thing is, in '77 there was a huge Welsh bias in the Lions selection. Phil Bennet was the captain and John Dawes was the coach, and they took a guy called David Burcher who, to be honest, just wasn't in the same league as Jim. They also took a guy called Gareth Evans as a utility player, and he wasn't fit to lace Jim's boots. But that's selection. Everyone is entitled to their opinion but unless you are picking the team then yours isn't worth a thing.

Renwick was typically self-effacing and philosophical about being overlooked. "I'm really a bit fed up hearing about whether or not I should have gone on the Lions' tour. Of course I would have been chuffed to have been picked, but I wasn't and that's just life. It was an honour to be standing by as a reserve," he said at the time.

With the benefit of hindsight he points out that bad weather and some hostile media coverage in New Zealand meant that this was not the happiest of tours. The Lions lost the Test series 3–1, and to add insult to injury they were defeated by Fiji on the way home.

JMR:
I suppose I had a chance of getting on that tour, but I didn't make it, and when I think about it now – why should I have been picked to play for the Lions. I had been in and out of a Scottish side that had been struggling a wee bit over the last couple of seasons. I mean, if you look at the 1977 season . . . well . . . it's nothing to get excited about. We had

got humped by England (26–6) and I wasn't even picked for that game, I came back for the Ireland game when we beat them (21–18), but then we got hammered by France (23–3) and Wales (9–18). The year before wasn't much better – we had beaten Australia just before Christmas, but had lost to France and Wales in the New Year, and then I had been dropped for our victories over Ireland and England. So I can understand why the selectors maybe felt they didn't need too many Scottish boys, and why I wasn't one of the five selected.

Besides, I was just as pleased not to go because it wasn't a great trip and I wouldn't have got to go to the Far East with Scotland if I had been with the Lions – and that was one of the better tours we went on during my time as a Scotland player.

Obviously everybody says the rugby on that trip was easy and it was, but it was perfect for our purposes because it was a pre-season tour in September, just before the leagues started in October; and it was what you would call a developmental tour nowadays. We took a lot of young guys like Colin Deans, Bill Gammell, John Rudd [Rutherford] and Roy Laidlaw, who were all just beginning to make their names as big time players.

There were a few older heads like Mike Biggar, who was the captain, Ian McLauchlan, Lewis Dick and myself. Nairn McEwan was the coach and he didn't have anyone to do the backs for him so, because I was one of the more experienced players, he asked me to help out with that.

We had a good squad of boys, we had a good committee, and the tour went well. Everybody had little jobs to do – for example, Gordon Dixon, from Gala, was the team photographer, and he kept that job right through the tour even though he didn't have a camera.

We played five games and won them all fairly easily, but it was tough because of the temperature and the humidity.

I remember flying into Bangkok and one of the boys grabbed the tannoy and started saying: 'We are about to land at Bangkok Airport. This is a fully automatic flight so nothing can go wrong, go wrong, go wrong . . .' If you pulled that stunt nowadays you'd end up in a Thai jail!

The tour manager was a guy called Tom Pearson, who was a schoolteacher from Fife. He was a good guy but very straight, and I remember when we arrived at the airport in Bangkok we all had to be dressed immaculately in our number ones – which was a pair of tartan trousers, shirt, tie and blazer. Now, normally when you arrive there's somebody at the airport from the St Andrews Society playing the bagpipes – but not this time. We got off the plane and it was bloody hot, we were sweating away in our number ones and we were looking aroond for the Thai rugby official, but we couldn't see anybody at all. Then this wee guy comes over – he's wearing a pair of flip-flops, shorts and a t-shirt, and written on the t-shirt it says: 'F*** work, go fishing.' It turns out he's our liaison officer, and I don't think Tom Pearson liked that at all. From then on we all wanted to be in t-shirts and shorts, but Tom liked us to be in our number ones.

There wasn't much rugby in Bangkok, I think it was just to break the journey up. But we did get a game against the Thai national team; there were a few ex-pats out there who were keen to get the rugby going, but it just didn't work. We won 82–3 on the hottest day of their year. It was too hot to play rugby in Bangkok really.

The tour party moved on to Hong Kong where they played one game, again against the national team. The tourists won 42–6 although they were made to work for their victory against a spirited home side that defended heroically during the first half, before Scotland's superior class began to show in the second half. Renwick scored his second try of the trip from a penalty rebound.

That was a tougher game because there was a lot of British boys out there and at least they had the physique – Drew Lamont who had been a hard prop with Boroughmuir was playing for them. Everybody that didn't play in Thailand got a game in Hong Kong, and a few guys, like myself and Barney [Ian Barnes], played in both games. We won but it was a tough mission, especially for the big boys, because the humidity was unbelievable. They had big fans in the changing rooms to try to cool us down even before we got out on the pitch, and we had tubs of water right along the touchline so that we could get some fluids on board – but even still some of the boys lost ten pounds during the game.

Maybe because it was at the start of the season we weren't as fit as we might have been at the end of the season – but we'd done a lot of training before leaving Scotland, so I think it was just that we weren't used to the humidity. We were on sixteen salt tablets a day while we were out there, and we were drinking gallons upon gallons of water. Some of the boys were getting the shakes after training.

They looked after us well in Hong Kong. We were guests of the Hong Kong Jockey Club at the Happy Valley racetrack, and we played golf at the Hong Kong Golf Club. We were also guests of honour at a banquet at the Hilton Hotel. Everyone was in dinner jackets and bow-ties while we were in our number ones – again. No expense had been spared, they had the Young Generation group dancing on the stage and everything was going well until they brought the starter out, which was sliced pineapple with a lotus leaf as decoration.

I was sitting next to Gerry McGuinness and before I'd even started he was coughing and spluttering with an empty plate in front of him.

'My throat's on fire – I need some water,' he says.

'What's wrong wi' you?' I asked. I thought he was taking the mickey.

'It's that leaf, there's something wrong with it.'

I said: 'Gerry, you greedy bastard, your no supposed to eat the leaf, its part o' the decoration – it's like eating the skewer as well as the kebab.'

His throat had swollen up and he was frothing at the mouth. We were shovelling ice-cream down his neck and the head waiter was running around in a panic because nobody had ever eaten the leaf before, so he didn't know what was going to happen. Gerry was alright the next day but he was in quite a lot of distress at the time. He got a right gliff.

So at the next court session we had Gerry up on a charge of gluttony. Toomba was judge so he was handing out the sentences, and Gerry's fine was that he had to eat this massive big cake we'd bought. We we're just going to let him start and then shove his face in it, but Gerry ate the whole thing – no bother to Gerry.

In Bangkok and Hong Kong it was fairly relaxed. If you wanted a drink you went and had one. There was quite a bit of free time – we trained in the morning then had a few beers later on.

When we got to Japan the first place we stayed in was like a monastery and we were all sleeping on the floor with the Buddhist robes on. We went on the bullet train and one night some of the boys went to a disco where they met John Lennon and Yoko Ono.

The rugby was a bit tougher, but not as hard as we thought it was going to be. Japan had been over to Scotland the year before and given us quite a tough game (Scotland won 34–9), but we wiped the floor with them this time. We had trained hard and we played well. We won 74–9 in Tokyo with Bill Gammell scoring four tries. The game was played in the Olympic Stadium, and I remember standing next to the pit and looking up and wondering what Lynn Davies had felt on that night when he had won Olympic Gold in 1964.

They are always going to struggle in Japan because of their size. There was plenty of effort from the boys we played against, but they were just a lot smaller than us. Their manager was called Shiggy Konno and he was almost at the end of his tether. They'd had Wales there in 1975 and he felt that they had shown signs of progress, so the match against us was big set back for him.

At the dinner they gave us all Seiko watches, which were the first digital watches and were worth quite a bit of money at the time. In fact there was talk that we might have to give them back because you weren't allowed gifts of more than £50 in those days. In the end we got to keep them but we should have given them back out of courtesy because all we gave them in return was a tie with a thistle stamped on it. Typical SRU – they gave us the state of the art watches and we give them a tie.

During their time in Japan Scotland also defeated a combined Meiji and Waseda Universities side 59–13 in front of 30,000 fans in the National Stadium, and a Japan B side which they defeated 50–16.

Heg

Scotland's tour of the Far East during the summer of 1977 was a success in terms of blooding several young players who would go on to become key performers in the future. However, the benefits of this trip were not instantaneous. Scotland's record during the next two seasons did not make pretty reading: in nine matches played, they lost seven and drew two.

JMR:
We went a lot of games without a win. But we weren't playing that badly and we weren't getting beat by a lot. Nairn McEwan had taken over as coach from Bill Dickinson, and I felt sorry for him because he put a lot of work in and he didn't always get the breaks. We were maybe just a few players short of being able to win these games that we were losing by one or two points.

The 1978 championship was particularly disappointing, with Scotland losing all four games. However it was a memorable campaign as far as Renwick is concerned because Brian Hegarty made his international debut and earned all four of his caps that season. Hegarty had initially only been drafted into the Whites team for the national trial after his Hawick team-mate Donnie Maclead was forced to withdraw from that match with a knee injury, and then when David Leslie withdrew from the Scotland team on the Wednesday before their opening match of the championship with an ankle injury, he was called into the starting team for that match against Ireland.

JMR:
Heg was probably the most impressive Hawick player I've ever seen because of his attitude. He played the same position as Derrick had played so he was always going to get it hard, but in terms of playing week-in and week-out, his training, and just his general attitude . . . well . . . you couldn't fault him. And I don't think he got the credit he deserved.

He got four caps in 1978 but I don't think Scotland got the best out of him because he was a key player for us for a long time. For Hawick he played at the tail of the line-out and the right hand side of the scrum, but when he got picked for Scotland he was picked at six and played on the left hand side of the scrum. That's a big difference.

I remember training with Scotland in the early days and the back-row wanted to know where the ball was going off every line-out and every scrum. They wanted to know if the backs were coming down the middle, going wide, or whatever. So when I went back to Hawick I said to Heg and Kenny Douglas: 'From now on you'll need to know where the ball's going because that's the way they're doing it up the road.'

Heg says to me: 'But we know where it's going.'

Now he was a step in front of these boys at Murrayfield because he was thinking: 'It's a line-out here, Cranny will be coming doon the middle.' And he didn't need to wait for a call. He was a hard but honest player, and he had a good rugby brain.

He was good fun as well. We used to call him Babble, because of some of the stuff he used to come out with. When he was captain at Hawick he would say things like: 'Right boys, get roond the kicker' or: 'Come on, let's pull our socks doon.'

And when Toomba first joined Heg was wanting to encourage him but had forgotten his name, so he was saying: 'Well done number four' and: 'Good play number four.' I remember one week he strapped up his knee and stood up to go out, then realised it was the wrong leg.

His first cap was over in Dublin and he was sharing a room in the hotel with Donald McDonald, a South African boy who played in the back row for West. After we'd all checked in we came down for our tea and I asked him who he was sharing with.

'I'm sharing with Bill,' he says.

'Bill who?'

'Bill McDonald.'

'His name's no Bill,' I said. 'It's Dave.'

Of course it wasn't, it was Donald, but Heg kept calling him Dave after that. He's some man. You can wind him up like anybody's business.

It would be unfair to use this breakdown in communication in the back-row as the reason for Scotland's 12–9 defeat in Ireland. Their problems were far more fundamental than that. It was a period of transition for the Scots, with Nairn McEwan taking over from Bill Dickinson as coach, Dougie Morgan newly appointed as captain, and several senior players reaching the twilight of their long and distinguished playing careers. The junior Whites fifteen had defeated the senior Blues team 20–18 at the national trial two weeks before the championship kicked off, but despite this the selectors had stuck with their old guard for the Ireland match, with seven of the starting fifteen over the age of 30.

Not surprisingly the Irish dominated the loose play in that match, though for most of the first half they were unable to capitalise on this supremacy and just before the break the scores were tied at 6–6 through two penalties apiece. Then Stewart McKinney came on as a replacement for John O'Driscoll and made an immediate impact, scoring a try off a Fergus Slattery break from the base of a scrum, which was converted by Ward to give the home team a 12–6 half-time lead. In the second half Irvine, who was playing on the wing, missed with a long-range penalty, before Morgan kicked a penalty to make it 12–9, but also missed one. Then, in the closing stages Hegarty almost scored in the corner, but was bundled into touch. From the line-out Scotland were awarded a penalty and Morgan elected to run it and go for the win, rather than kick for the draw – but the ball was knocked on.

> JMR:
> I remember thinking at the time that a draw away from home isn't bad, but Dougie decided to have run at them and Mike Biggar dropped the ball. It was Dougie's call, he was captain, and if we'd scored he'd have been a hero, so maybe he was right.

Despite being out-played, the Scots had come within a whisker of getting a result against a strong Irish team away from home. However the need for fresh blood was becoming increasingly apparent and could no longer be ignored. For Scotland's next match, against France two weeks later, several significant changes in personnel were made – most notably at tight-head prop, where record cap holder Sandy Carmichael gave way to Hawick's Norman Pender, who had been on fine form for his club in recent weeks and had caused the Blues all sorts of problems in the scrums during the national trial. There was also a change at hooker, where another Hawick man, Colin Deans, replaced Duncan Madsen.

Against France the score was once again close, but ultimately unsatisfactory. Scotland led 13–4 at half-time thanks to tries from Irvine and Dave Shedden, and a penalty and a conversion from Morgan. It might have been 13–0, had Irvine not landed awkwardly and injured his shoulder in scoring his try. He went off for treatment and because it was just before half-time Scotland chose to wait until the break before deciding whether to replace him. In the meantime Hegarty was moved from the back-row to the wing, while Bruce Hay moved to full back. "I was trying to hide behind the bigger forwards so that they wouldn't spot me and send me out to the backs, but it didn't work," recalls Hegarty.

JMR:
France kicked off into the corner, got a line-out, and Jerome Gallion stuck up a box kick. Heg dropped it behind his own line and Gallion scored. I looked at him and said: 'Yi daft bugger.'

Heg just shrugged his shoulders. What else could he do? I felt sorry for him. He normally had good hands but everyone makes mistakes. Every Christmas from then on we asked him if Gallion had sent him a card that year.

In the second half Francis Haget scored a try for France, while Jean-Michel Aguirre (who had starred for France B against Scotland B in 1971) kicked three penalties and a conversion, to give the visitors a 19–16 victory.

Early in the second half Alistair Cranston had replaced Irvine, making it six Hawick players on the park at once – Cranston, Renwick, Deans, Pender, Tomes and Hegarty. All six started two weeks later against Wales in Cardiff. Then, within three minutes of kick-off, Graham Hogg replaced Dave Shedden.

JMR:
Greco's my cousin. He was born and raised in Hawick but had moved to Edinburgh and joined Boroughmuir in 1972. So when he came on I turned to Bruce Hay and said: 'That's seven Hawick boys on the pitch now.' Then a few moments later Greco went for a loose ball but it bounced through his legs and they almost scored.

Bruce says: 'Aye, look at the seven bastards frae Hawick.'

'Six frae Hawick and one frae Boroughmuir,' I replied.

It was a tough mission for Greco that day because he wouldn't have been expecting to get on – especially not that early in the match – and he was marking Gerald Davies. At one point he went up to tackle him and Davies just went whoosh, and left Greco flat on his arse. At the dinner that night I says: 'Have you still got Gerald Davies in your back pocket there?'

Of course that was the patter all night. 'Gerald, you can come oot now.'

Mind you, Davies didn't score that day, so Greco must have done alright.

Playing with the wind in the first half the Scots took an early lead through a 40-yard Dougie Morgan penalty; but the Welsh soon responded with a typical Gareth Edwards try – the scrum-half erupting from the base of a scrum and darting over the line in a shimmer of dummies.

With McGeechan having moved into stand-off from centre the Scots backs looked sharper than they had been all championship, and this was demonstrated when the visitors regained their lead through a marvellous Renwick try. Alistair Cranston made the initial dent on a crash ball, then Mike Biggar and Morgan combined to send McGeechan through a half opening. JPR Williams brought the stand-off down but Bruce Hay was ready to take up the running. In turn Hay fed the ball back inside to Renwick, who side-stepped back inside JJ Williams and darted over the line. It was the first of three tries which Renwick would score on consecutive visits to the Principality.

Scotland's lead was short-lived. Before half-time Ray Gravell crashed over for his first try in Welsh colours, then in the second half Steve Fenwick's try was sandwiched between a dropped goal and a penalty for Phil Bennet. With twenty minutes to go Derek Quinnell powered over to make it 22–7.

During the final quarter the Scots tried to claw their way back into the match, and they did manage to narrow the gap when Dougie Morgan kicked another penalty and then Tomes bundled himself over after a neat short penalty move, but it was too little too late. It finished Wales 22 Scotland 14.

The match had been played in arctic conditions with both in-goal areas frozen solid. Afterwards the weather deteriorated and almost claimed Renwick as a victim.

Brian Hegarty:
The dinner had been at the Angel Hotel and we were walking back to our hotel. It was the middle of a blizzard so it was a case of keeping your head down and just ploughing on. We got to a shopping precinct and Jim started trying to trip me up by kicking my heels. I just kept my head down and ploughed on and he eventually stopped. I must have walked 50 yards before I looked back and saw him lying in the snow almost covered. I thought he was joking but when I eventually went back

he was out-cold. I picked him up and dragged him back to the hotel, but he's a lucky boy I turned round when I did. Because if I'd got back to the hotel before noticing he was missing I wouldn't have bothered going back out.

The snow meant that Cardiff airport was closed the following morning, so the squad had to get a bus to Birmingham and fly out from there.

JMR:
We were just about to get on this plane at Birmingham and Norman Pender's wife says: 'There's something wrong with this plane. I dinnae think we should get on.' That was all we needed. We just said it'll be fine and not to worry. Then, halfway down the runway the engine went on fire, so she was right.

Once we got off the plane she was in a bit of distress, so Kenny Lawrie gave her a cigarette to help calm her down. But the night before they'd been mucking about with these dummy fags that blow up in your face. Someone must have sneaked one into his packet and he gave it to her by accident. I thought Pender was going to kill him.

Scotland's final game of the championship was against England at Murrayfield.

JMR:
Neither of us had won a game that season so it was a big match because nobody wants to end up whitewashed. But we didn't play very well that day and we lost 15–0. I nearly scored in the corner but got pulled down just short. But I've no complaints about the result – we got what we deserved.

It was a pretty disappointing season really. We used three different stand-offs – Ron Wilson, Geech and Richard Breakey – which is an indication that things weren't quite right. It also meant we lacked continuity.

But as I said before, we weren't that far away from getting results, and although we didn't win anything the next season [1979], we got two draws [against England at Twickenham and Ireland at Murrayfield], so I think we were moving in the right direction. And with John Rutherford coming in at stand-off we were beginning to get a bit more consistency. Another guy that made a difference was Keith Robertson, who gave us a bit more spark in the backs.

Before that, in December 1978, Scotland put up a credible performance against New Zealand at Murrayfield, and might even have claimed an unlikely win. With the All Blacks leading 12–9 Scotland were piling on the pressure, when McGeechan attempted a drop-goal which was charged down and hacked ahead by Bruce Robertson for a breakaway try.

> The trouble was that Andy [Irvine] was in the line. I remember them asking the question at the team meeting afterwards: 'Why was Andy in the line if we were going to drop the goal?' Geech must have just decided to try it off the cuff.

Defence

Defence is an area in which Renwick has never been given much credit – despite the fact it was his heroics in facing down onrushing Frenchmen, for Scotland B in Oyannax in November 1971, which catapulted him into the reckoning for an international call-up at that early stage in his career. In fact it is amazing how often newspaper reports of Renwick's big matches comment on the efficiency with which he dealt with opposition attacks.

The reason this part of Renwick's game is often forgotten about appears to be that he was not spectacular enough in the tackle for some observers.

JMR:
My defence was more round the waist. Some folk want to hit guys and hurt them: Cranny [Alistair Cranston] was like that, so was Bruce Hay, Derrick Grant and Elliot Broatch. They were tough, tough tacklers who wanted to hurt you and I'm not going to criticise that because you always want a few guys in your side who the opposition are a wee bit feared of. But that wasn't what I wanted to do – I didn't want to kill the boy, I just wanted to tackle him, get him down, but be able to get back on my feet as quick as possible so I could play the ball. Which, funnily enough, is what the modern coaches are now teaching.

Maybe it was because I came through as a stand-off and stand-offs were never tacklers in those days – there wasn't many who could. Colin Telfer was a good player but he wasn't known for his tackling. You wouldn't pick your stand-off because he could tackle. So maybe if I'd been brought up in the centre all my days, I might have been more aggressive. But I was thinking more about the team thing, and not the hits.

Renwick's approach was maybe not quite as spectacular as the crash tackling style of play favoured by the likes of Cranston and Hay, but his methods could be just as effective, if not more so.

Andy Irvine:

I used to always have a hard time playing against Jim. I fancied my chances against most guys at club level because I was a wee bit quicker than most, but he was the one guy that I always had a problem with. He used to lay off in the centre, looking for me to come in the line, and he was very, very difficult to beat. He had the pace. If Alistair Cranston got you he would put you through the back of the stand, but quite a lot of time he would be going for the big hit and miss you completely. Jim, on the other hand, would lay off you, and because he had the luxury of pace he could show people the outside and you would have to be immensely quick to get round him.

People go on about the crash tacklers like Alistair Cranston and Bruce Hay, and there's no doubt that in a one-on-one situation with a big guy running at them they were super tacklers because they were big powerful blokes with lots of guts. But it's not only the big guys you have to stop, and Bruce and Alistair used to struggle against the wee jinky guys because they didn't have the pace.

Jim might not knock you back five yards, but he would get you. He was like Ian McGeechan in that sense. Because of their size they weren't noted as great tacklers, but very few players got past them – and I think if you had the kind of match statistics that are available now it would have made interesting reading.

As John Rutherford points out, rather than being a weakness defence was in fact an area where Renwick was often ahead of his rivals. "Before the late seventies drift defence hadn't been heard of, but Renwick picked up on it very quickly," he says. "The French invented it but Jim was probably the guy that first got us playing it over here, and Scotland really did play it well during the early eighties. Maybe it was because Renwick, David Johnston and I were all fairly slight, but we really played the drift well together."

JMR:

In the seventies there was a lot of folk that didn't understand drift defence. Derrick Grant used to say it was an abdication of responsibility, but I used to say: 'No its not. It's the opposite. It's taking on responsibility.'

The thing is, when Derrick played it used to be that backs went up and hit their opposite number, and as a tail-gunner at the line-out he would come up to hit the stand-off and if the stand-off got it away then he would loop back out behind the centres, because all the other backs would be in their opposite number's face already. But then the laws changed in the late sixties so that the three-quarters had to get back ten yards at the line-out instead of being level with the back man, and in the scrum they had to be behind the back foot whereas before they were onside as long as they were behind the ball. That meant that the wing-forwards were almost always first there to take the stand-off, and all the other defenders could move out one. So if you were playing inside centre and you went up you would be able to go for the outside man. It meant I could take Cranny's man, Cranny could drift out to the full back, who was coming into the line, the wing stayed on his man, and you stopped them getting an extra man – and that's all drift defence is.

But what you had to remember was that sometimes boys come back into the pocket, and if you drift then sometimes you leave a hole. So you've got to think about how you cover the hole because the last thing you wanted was a flyer having a run at your forwards. How we dealt with that was by making sure that Colin never drifted – he was responsible for taking anyone that was coming back into the hole. The centres were stopping them outflanking us, and the number seven and the stand-off were stopping them coming back into the heavy traffic.

Sometimes, when the opposition got wise to you drifting, they'd play a couple of moves with runners coming back inside. So we would vary our defence too, we'd say: 'Right, we're no drifting, we're going up to hit.' Your defence has got to be as good as your attack, because if they work out how you defend they can work out how to beat it, so you have to be able to change it or you get made to look stupid.

And the drift didn't always work. Sometimes you would shout drift and Cranny would already be hitting the boy. Then you would just have to cover round. But that wasn't my style, I would go up and if the boy passed it I would move out, and if the boy passed it again I would move out again.

Nowadays you don't even bother drifting at the line-out. You have the stand-off marking the inside centre, the inside centre marking the outside centre, the outside centre taking whoever is coming into the gap, and the winger still takes his man. Basically you don't often see overlaps from the line-out.

But off scrums it's a lot harder to drift because you get confronted with players earlier. That's why I think scrum ball is the best ball for backs, because you can pull the opposition in and they can't drift.

So as a defender you might decide to defend from the wing in, with the winger and the centres coming up fast, meaning that the stand-off can't move it – you trap him in a position which he doesn't want to be in.

If we were playing a team like Heriots who had Andy Irvine you would use Australian defence – or what I call Australian defence because that's where I first saw it. In Australian defence you don't want your full back to come into the line at all so you bring your blind-side winger in, and he stands right behind the stand-off at a line-out. His job is to get across and hit the man coming down the channel between the outside centre and the winger, which is usually the full back but depending on whether they've worked a move could be any of their players.

But if you do that then you're leaving the box wide open, so we used to have our hooker dropping back into the blind-side winger's position to cover the box kick. But really, if you could get Heriots kicking into the box, well you're laughing, because that's the last thing they wanted to do.

We used to use the Australian defence system against Heriots quite a lot because they had a lot of good players in their backs – Jimmy Craig, Harry Burnett, Fraser Dall, guys like that. And you knew that any of them could go, so you couldn't concentrate just on Andy. We were struggling to mark both them and Andy, so Australian defence was ideal.

You can't use that Australian defence off a scrum, because you can't bring your winger round that far or they'll attack the blind side if they have any sense. So I remember asking Roger Gould, the Australian full back, how they do it off a scrum and he said: 'You bring your number eight out.' You can't do that now, but then you could bring your eight out and he took the stand-off and you all moved out one.

So, it's just a bit of organisation. It's about doing it, and once you do it a couple of times it becomes easier. I think the professional boys these days spend a lot more time thinking about defence than we did, and I suppose that's one of the key areas where the game has changed a lot.

Attack

*Who attacks who in rugby? Is the guy with the ball attacking the defence?
Or is the defender attacking the guy with the ball? I think it comes down
to the ability of the guy with the ball. The more strings you have to your
bow – in terms of kicking with both feet, side-stepping, timing a pass and
so on – the easier it is for you to be the attacker, because the other guy
doesn't know what's coming. If you're limited with what you can do then
you're going to struggle because you're just waiting to see what happens
and hoping you get away with it. You're not making the decisions. The
more options you've got the better the player you are. I'd like to think
that when I had the ball I was always attacking.*

Jim Renwick

As far as Jim Renwick is concerned, when it comes to rugby, defence is
a science, but attack is an art form.

Renwick is remembered as one of the outstanding attackers in Scottish
rugby history. He scored eight tries in 52 Scottish caps, 129 for Hawick
in 341 appearances and countless others during his career for various
representative, invitational and sevens teams. He scored a try on his debut
for Scotland, and a number of his international touch-downs rank among
the most exciting and instinctive scored in a Scotland jersey. In statistical
terms others have notched up a higher hit-rate of tries, but as most of
those who played alongside him would acknowledge, Renwick's breaks
more often created scores for others rather than himself.

While the science of defence merits deep thought and careful consid-
eration because of its value to the team when fully understood and properly
applied, the art of attack relies heavily on natural ability and instinct,
which means that it is important that players are given the freedom to
express themselves.

However, all great artists need to hone their talent, and it concerns

Renwick that, because coaching attacking rugby requires a different approach to coaching structured rugby, it is a discipline which is becoming increasingly neglected in the modern game. It doesn't help that professionalism has ushered in an attitude in rugby whereby errors will not be tolerated and gamblers are seen as a liability.

JMR:

The easiest bit of coaching is defence because you are working to patterns so all you need is somebody calling the shots and everyone else carrying out the orders, and its easy to stand around at a training session and talk through why it makes sense to defend one way and not another.

Working on attack is harder because it's about reading what is on in front of you and everyone sees it differently. Most of the time nobody is right and nobody is wrong. So rather than just letting guys play what is in front of them coaches tend to create move after move so that everyone knows where the ball is going. That makes sense in a way, but it takes away the individuality which is what rugby, for me, is really all about.

I worry that the attitude is getting more and more to be that players shouldn't try to beat their opposite number because it is a higher risk than playing it safe, taking contact and making sure they can present the ball. Folk say that a good ruck is better than a bad pass, but we're in danger of forgetting that nothing is better than a good pass which puts a player in space. If you don't take a chance once in a while then you're not going to have many opportunities to throw a good pass.

You've got to have a culture in the team where guys aren't scared to take a chance, and everyone is expecting the good runners to have a go. It's a self-fulfilling prophecy. If the team believe that they can run at the opposition and cause some problems then they are geared towards doing that, and even if it goes wrong then they are ready to tidy up, and when it works it is worth it. But if the team as a collective unit isn't thinking that way then you have no chance.

It's not a risk moving it on your own try-line if everybody in the team knows that you're going to do that; but if you're the only guy thinking that way then it's a big risk.

I know it's difficult. I remember from my own playing days that there would be times when I hadn't had a go for a couple of weeks, so I had to force myself because it's easy to get out the habit.

But it was always at the back of my mind that I was going to have to take a wee risk sometimes, and I was usually happy to back myself. And I was lucky because guys like Donnie McLeod, Heg and Billy Murray could read the game and they knew what I was going to do so, they would be on my tail, and it's not so much of a risk then.

Some guys will never be front-line attackers. Some guys are made to be supporters, but if you do that well then you can at least be a front-line finisher. If you can get three backs in the same team who are on the same wavelength then I would say that's enough. At Hawick I think it was me, Colin and Cranny who gave the platform for how we were going to play; and then we had guys like Crab [Kenny McCartney] and Chalmers, who were good rugby players and great finishers, there to get on the end of moves.

You look at old videos of games, some of the stunts that guys like Andy Irvine and David Duckham tried to pull were crazy, but when it worked it was great. I'm glad that in my day if I wanted to have a go from my own line I could do that. If it didn't work I would have had to justify myself to the coach but all I would have to say was that I thought I could make it and that would be enough. Nowadays folk are a lot more critical, especially with professional players who we expect to be flawless because they get paid to play. We took it seriously but we were still playing for fun, these guys are playing for their livelihoods and they can't afford to take risks.

There's no doubt that the game is better for having had folk like Andy Irvine, Gerald Davies and David Campese doing what they did. I'm glad I've seen these risk takers in action and in a hundred years from now it's these guys who will be remembered, not the boys that rarely did anything wrong but rarely did anything exciting either.

They always show that great Gareth Edwards try in the 1973 Baa Baas versus New Zealand game, and there was a few risks taken there and a few wild passes thrown, but it was a fantastic try and that's what I want to see – not guys hitting up fifteen times until eventually they barge over the line.

Rugby is big business today, but how much is that down to boys like Campese that had kids copying his goose-step? We should maybe remember that as we get more worried about stifling individuality.

Part of the problem is that the current laws mean that the ruck situation, while being the safest method of recycling ball, fails to draw in defenders – with the consequence that there is very little scope for any sort of attacking enterprise, regardless of how good the player is at creating something out of nothing. In response to this Renwick advocates a high risk strategy whereby the ball is kept alive, even when contact cannot be avoided.

I'd prefer that the players I'm coaching didn't ruck. I know it's going to happen, but I don't want my players to ruck unless they have to. Rucks don't move nowadays – it's all just standing still and gives the opposition time to organise their defence. I'd like to see players trying to pass out the tackle more, but guys are now drilled to think of safety first. If you watch rugby league, when a player gets tackled the first thing he wants to do is get on his feet and get the ball away, so what does the tackler do? He holds onto him for as long as possible so that his team-mates can get back and get organised. It's the same in union with rucks, and that's what kills the game for me – guys coming over the top, slowing you down and stopping you getting the ball away.

Good players are players who are in control when they go into the tackle so that they can get quick ball – now that might mean passing out of contact, or posting the ball early, but it means taking a bit of a risk and trusting yourself and the guys around you to get it right.

In rugby what you're trying to do is create an extra man, but I sometimes think we don't concentrate enough on doing that. And the way rucks are handled at the moment you're always going to struggle to create an overlap as long as you are looking to ruck. A ruck should only happen when all else fails.

Don't get me wrong, you still get some great rugby, but it's not great all the time. And even though the ball is in play a lot longer than it was in my day a lot of the time it is just hitting up and hitting up, which is very predictable.

The Lions

Jim Renwick was a very important part of the Lions tour of South Africa in 1980. He was a skilful player and a very good travelling companion. I had good craic with Jim and I valued knowing him. Coming from Ballymena I could understand him alright, but for some people it was quite difficult – although not as difficult as understanding Bruce Hay, who was also on the trip. Jim was almost as good a rugby player as he was a singer – he used to sing The Comencheros *if I remember correctly. He was a very lively member of the party and you need guys like him because they keep the thing buzzing.*

Syd Millar, Manager, 1980 Lions tour of South Africa

Having been overlooked for both the 1974 trip to South Africa and the 1977 expedition to New Zealand, Renwick could be forgiven for doubting whether it would be third time lucky when the selectors sat down to pick the British and Irish Lions squad to tour South Africa during the summer of 1980.

Struggling with a niggly back injury during the early stages of the 1979–80 season his form had, by his own high standards, been pretty poor. He had played in Scotland's 20–6 defeat to New Zealand at Murrayfield in November 1979, but with the Scottish forwards being totally outplayed at the breakdown, he had little opportunity to impress with the ball in hand. He had recovered sufficiently from his back problem to play all four games of the 1980 Five Nations Championship, but it was yet another period of transition for Scotland, with five players making their international debuts against Ireland at the start of that season: Steve Munro, Roy Laidlaw, Jim Burnett, Bill Cuthbertson and John Beattie. With 31 caps to his name Renwick was one of the few senior players in the squad, but he couldn't resist causing mischief with his sharp native wit.

Roy Laidlaw:

I stayed pretty close to Jim in Dublin because he was very experienced. I remember going out to check the pitch when we arrived at Lansdowne Road then walking back up the tunnel. David Irwin, the Irish centre, was in-front of us and I said to Jim: 'Hell, he's a big boy for a centre!'

And Jim replied: 'Aye, you know what they say: 'The bigger they come, the harder they hit you.'

That put me on edge a wee bit, but it was typical of Jim. He was always looking for an opportunity to get a bit of craic and a bit of a laugh.

Scotland lost that match 22–15, despite racing into a 9–0 lead through an Irvine penalty within 60 seconds of kick-off and a converted David Johnston try in the seventh minute. It was a very promising start, but the Irish forwards soon found their rhythm and before long were dominating at the breakdown. Then two key moments played pivotal roles in the ultimate outcome of the match.

Just after Campbell had kicked his first penalty of the afternoon Renwick sent a diagonal grubber towards the right wing and Munro hacked the ball on into the in-goal area. A try which would have established a formidable 13–3 lead looked certain but then the ball seemed to stick in the soggy surface of the rain-soaked Lansdowne Road pitch and the young winger over ran it.

Not long after Campbell added a second penalty, then Colin Patterson, the Irish scrum-half, slipped through three Scottish tackles and ran 70 yards from his own 25 to just short of the Scottish line, providing the field position from which Moss Keane was able to squeeze over in the corner. Scotland's commanding position had been reduced to a 10–9 half-time deficit.

In the second half Terry Kennedy added a second Irish try, which Campbell converted, before adding a penalty and a drop-goal to establish a 22–9 lead. Four minutes into injury time Rutherford created a try for Johnston which Irvine converted, but it was too little too late.

If the Irish game had provided the sort of frustration that Scottish rugby supporters had become used to during that spell of thirteen international matches without a win, the events at Murrayfield when France came to play two weeks later must have made all the heart-ache seem worthwhile.

Trailing 14–4 with thirteen minutes to go the Scots staged a spectacular comeback. Not surprisingly it was Andy Irvine who led the charge – more than compensating for a miserable first half performance, during which time he missed seven kicks at goal, including one from in front of the posts just before half-time. Irvine's kicking performance was so bad that the Murrayfield crowd even began to jeer the player who had so often delighted them in the past. Eventually Renwick was given a chance but his first attempt also missed.

With this sort of wastefulness it must have seemed like this was yet another lost cause – except the Scots were not actually playing that badly, and once they started to get a bit of momentum going they became almost unstoppable, with Irvine to the fore. He scored the first of his two tries after overlapping Hay on the left wing and charging into French territory, linking with Johnston and Hay again, who carried the movement on, and when the latter's pass was knocked-down just short of the line it was Irvine who swooped on the loose ball and propelled himself over for a score that revived Scottish hopes.

Seven minutes later Scotland took the lead. Hay dislodged the ball as he flattened French full back Serge Gabernet with a thumping tackle, Renwick countered, and after some slick inter-passing it was Irvine who broke clear and darted between the posts. Renwick converted and before the end Irvine added two penalties to polish off a remarkable turnaround in fortunes for both the individual player and his team. It was Scotland's first win since before the last Lions tour had set off for New Zealand in 1977.

JMR:
It was a big relief. Andy was the hero in the end but he had a nightmare up until half time. He couldn't kick his erse. Nowadays he would have been taken off at half-time and I remember him saying he felt like going home there and then. I said: 'I'll get you a taxi.' But in the second half he scored two tries, kicked a conversion and kicked a couple of penalties and Scotland won 22–14.

That's just the way Andy played. He would make mistakes and it didn't really effect him; he'd just come back and make up for it with a moment of brilliance.

Irvine's magic was not as evident in Scotland's next match against Wales at Cardiff Arms Park, which they were lucky to lose by only eleven points (17–6), despite a Renwick try, scored at the end of a fine handling move involving Gossman, Beattie, Irvine and Robertson.

Scotland's final match of the 1980 Five Nations season brought England to Murrayfield for the final leg of their Grand Slam campaign. The visitors raced into a 19–3 lead at half-time with John Carleton scoring twice and Mike Slemen also touching down. At the start of the second half Steve Smith got try number four for the visitors, but the Scots fought on bravely and in a thrilling final 30 minutes played some wonderful running rugby. Tomes picked up and barged over for a try after Renwick was tackled just short of the line; and before the end Rutherford added a second touchdown, but only after Carleton had kept the Scots out of range with his third try of the match. The final score was 30–18 to England, which meant they had registered their biggest score against Scotland in 96 matches, and had scored five tries in a Test match for the first time in 27 years, but those naked stats do not do justice to the valuable role Scotland played in an exhilarating exhibition of rugby.

They might not have won too many games during the last three seasons, but Scotland had played some attractive rugby, and that was enough to persuade the Lions selectors to name five Scots in the squad – Renwick, John Beattie, Bruce Hay, Andy Irvine and Alan Tomes.

This was a controversial expedition. Apartheid was a burning issue at the time. Resolutions had recently been passed by both the United Nations and the Commonwealth heads of state condemning the regime and discouraging sporting contact with South Africa.

South Africa had not appeared at the Olympic Games since 1960 and was barred from competing internationally at athletics, cricket or soccer. All South African teams were barred from Australia, and a proposed Springboks tour of France had recently been blocked at the last moment when the French government refused to grant the squad visas.

In 1979 the Home Unions, encouraged by promises from the South African Rugby Board to break down the barriers of racial segregation in the sport, had sanctioned a tour of Britain by a South African Barbarians side. This prompted considerable opposition from anti-apartheid lobbyists and the government, with the Irish Rugby Union eventually acceding to the considerable pressure exerted on them by various organisations and withdrawing their support for the invitation.

When the Home Unions said at the start of 1980 that they were still intent on a Lions tour of South Africa later that year, the anti-apartheid movement became even more active in its opposition. Hector Munro, the Minister for Sport, who had managed Scotland's tour of Australia in 1970 and had been President of the SRU in 1976, made overtures to the Tours Committee of the Four Home Unions on behalf of the government.

The USA's decision to boycott the 1980 Olympics in Moscow took some heat off the Lions, but it was still thought wise to keep the details of the squad's departure secret in order to avoid any unwanted attention. This trip attracted the largest press corps in Lions history – which soon became known as the 'rat pack' by the players.

Syd Millar:
In those days apartheid was a raging subject and we got a lot of abuse, but I had a very simple philosophy. Rightly or wrongly I felt that politicians should not interfere with sport. We asked the South Africans to play mixed teams, which they did. We asked for mixed crowds, which we got. So we thought that was a step forward and more than the politicians were achieving. I remember one press report at the time which said the UK had improved their trading position with South Africa by tens of millions and thinking, why isn't that causing as much fuss?

You could argue for hours about the rights and wrongs of going on that trip, but my point of view is that we did achieve various things and I along with others spent a lot of time speaking to blacks and coloureds and finding out how we might help them in rugby terms, so it was a positive experience and I have no regrets.

That is a sentiment echoed by Renwick.

I was only there to play rugby, but you can't help notice what's going on around you. If I really thought we could change it by not going to play rugby there then I might have had a different attitude. But I felt, if you stop dealing with them, is that the solution? Does that make the situation better or worse? Maybe if you can see how bad it is then that helps the situation because it's in your face. I always think that if there's a problem you speak about it – that's what I was taught to do. When we stopped trading with South Africa it was like we were doing our bit and we didn't have to think about it anymore – out of sight out of mind.

Millar had been capped 37 times for Ireland at prop, had been on three Lions tours as a player, and moreover had coached the victorious 1974 Lions in South Africa. He is now President of the IRB. The coach was Noel Murphy, who had been Ireland's most capped flanker until Fergus

Slattery had overtaken him earlier that year. He had toured with the Lions in 1959 and 1966 and had coached Ireland to two Test victories in Australia the previous summer. Bill Beaumont was named as captain – he had just led England to their first Grand Slam since 1957, and was a well-liked and well-respected individual who led from the front. All three were popular choices, but they were all forwards, and this would prove significant as the tour progressed.

With players such as Peter Wheeler, Fran Cotton and Beaumont in the tight five the Lions felt they would be able to take the Springboks on up front. The loss of Stuart Lane, the only back-rower in the squad with pace to burn, who tore ligaments in his right knee after only 51 seconds of the first game of the tour against Eastern Province, could only have reinforced the management team's commitment to keeping it tight and grinding out a Test series victory that way.

JMR:
There's no doubt in my mind that they wanted to play ten-man rugby, they wanted to take the Boks on up front then bring big men down the middle – and to be fair I think we did beat them up front, but we didn't win the series.

Some people might say the backs let us down and I wouldn't argue with that. But they didn't put anyone in charge of the backs, we were more or less left to do it ourselves, and we had a lot of injuries to key players.

This was the first Lions tour in which there was an official doctor – Jack Matthews, who had played in the centre for Wales during the 1950s. As events unfolded the appointment proved to be a wise move. The original squad consisted of 30 players – twelve from Wales, eight from England and five each from Scotland and Ireland – but by the end of the tour an unprecedented eight replacements had been called out due to a horrendous catalogue of injuries.

Before the tour had even got under way the injury problems began, with Irvine being forced to withdraw from the squad in London on the day of departure, just hours after waving good-bye to family and friends at Edinburgh Airport. He had torn a hamstring whilst playing for the Scottish Co-optimists against New Zealand in the semi-finals of the Hong Kong Sevens six weeks earlier and it had failed to mend in time. He was replaced by Elgan Rees from Wales, but was soon back involved when he was flown out after the first Test as a replacement for Mike Slemen, who had to fly home for family reasons.

As well as Lane, the Lions lost Gareth Davies with a dislocated shoulder after half an hour of that first match against Eastern Province. Renwick was on the bench but was caught unawares by Davies's injury.

JMR:
Syd said: 'You're on.' But I had been watching the game and sunbathing at the same time and I couldn't find my boots. So they had a meeting about it and decided from then on boots had to be worn at all times by the subs and you had to be ready to get on as soon as anybody goes down. I maybe didn't make a very good first impression.

Despite this inauspicious introduction Renwick kicked a penalty and a conversion during the Lions' 26–18 victory. It was a rusty start to the tour – but at least it was a victorious one.

The injury jinx continued into the next match against the multi-racial South African Rugby Association Invitation XV, when Phil Blakeway, the English tight-head prop, left the field clutching his ribs. He would soon be replaced on tour by Ian Stevens from Wales. Renwick, along with Tomes, played in this 28–6 victory, but the Lions were still unable to find any rhythm.

Renwick missed the next match, when the Lions left it late before defeating Natal 21–15, but was back for their 22–19 victory over a South African Invitation XV. Having pulled his calf muscle, Ollie Campbell was sidelined for a month, which meant Dai Richards, the Welsh centre, had to deputise at stand-off.

During that match Renwick played a crucial role in what was described as a 'wonder try' – which saved the Lions' unbeaten record and raised spirits after a rather subdued start to the tour. With the Lions trailing by three points heading into the final five minutes of the match, David Richards shook himself free of the conservatism which seemed to have settled on the team to break from his own 25 and straight through the opposition defence. That triggered a sequence of play which lasted two minutes and 46 seconds, involved three rucks and 33 passes, and in which Renwick played a crucial role – running the ball back at the South Africans with irresistible zest after collecting a desperate clearance kick. Eventually it was Mike Slemen who scored, after the English winger worked a scissors pass with Bruce Hay, but it was a team effort and one of the few occasions on the whole tour when the Lions demonstrated how tantalising they could be in open play if they would only give themselves the chance.

In *The Scotsman* the following day Chris Rea wrote that: "There were times when it seemed impossible that anything good would come of the multitude of switches and turns that the Lions tried. On each occasion the Select defence held firm and even managed once to drive the tourists back over the halfway line, but back there was Jim Renwick to start yet another series of attacks. In the end, with players laid out on the field in various stages of exhaustion, Hay came up on the left and, as he had done in the first half, provided Slemen with a winning pass."

"A fabulous try, the like of which will be remembered in South Africa as long as the game is played," wrote another pundit.

It was a glittering moment in an otherwise turgid affair. The game plan had already become apparent.

"Like Saturday, the Lions concentrated most of their efforts on keeping the game tight, a doubtful tactic in view of the strength of the opposition forwards," noted Rea.

Against Orange Free State three days later, the Lions looked ragged in the first half before scoring two tries within six minutes at the start of the second half to set up a 21–17 victory. Renwick contributed a conversion and a penalty. It was yet another victory achieved at considerable cost with Terry Holmes injuring his shoulder, meaning that he would be out of action for two and a half weeks.

While in Bloemfontein for that match Renwick accompanied Tomes as the big lock forward fulfilled a lifelong ambition.

Alan Tomes:
I was speaking to our liaison officer and he was asking what we fancied doing. I said that I had always wanted to drive a train, so he told me to meet him in the hotel foyer at half-eight the next morning. I kept it quiet and I only told Jim. The next day this guy took us along to the depot and we got to drive a train. And this wasn't any Mickey Mouse train – this was a proper piece of machinery. It was a steam engine so we had to pull these big levers to get the thing going, and the power of it was unbelievable. It was a great experience.

Tomes was known as Casey Jones for the remainder of the tour.

Another excursion which was just as memorable although for very different reasons was the squad's trip to Sharpeville, a huge township near Johannesburg.

Alan Tomes
They had us in a back of a truck and one of the guys threw a pocketful of change. All the kids were crawling around the street after the coins, so we all started throwing cash. Thinking about it now I'm a bit embarrassed – big shots throwing scraps to the kids – but at least they got the money I suppose.

On the Wednesday of the week leading up to the first Test, Fran Cotton retired from the bad-tempered match against the South African Federation XV clutching his chest. He was later diagnosed as suffering from pericarditis – which in layman's terms meant he had inflammation of the covering of the heart.

This meant that by the time the first Test came around on 31 May, the Lions had lost seven players, all of whom were serious Test contenders. They were still unbeaten, but were yet to show the form which would be necessary if they were to win the series. Renwick was the only Scot named in the Test side. Only five of the team had played in a Lions Test match before and they were all forwards.

The team for that first Test was:

R.C. O'Connell (Ireland); J. Carleton (England), D.S. Richards (Wales), J.M. Renwick (Scotland), M.A.C. Slemen (England); A. Ward (Ireland), C.S. Patterson (Ireland); C. Williams (Wales), P. Wheeler (England), G. Price (Wales), W.B. Beaumont (England, captain), M.J. Colclough (England), J Squire (Wales), J.B. O'Driscoll (Ireland), D Quinnell (Wales).

The South Africans were pre-match favourites, partly because the Lions had not been particularly convincing in their early matches, but also because Naas Botha, the most prolific goalkicker on the planet at that time, was playing for them. In the event the accuracy of Botha's boot was academic. The difference between the two teams was the try count, which was 5–1 in the home team's favour.

As the Lions management team had anticipated, the touring pack was more than a match for the Springboks. They won the scrums, held their own at the line-out and dominated the loose play – but it still wasn't enough, disproving the frequently voiced theory that forwards decide who wins rugby matches and the backs decide by how much.

The tourists rarely moved the ball past stand-off; and such was the influence on this match of Rob Louw, the insuppressible Springbok break-away, that on those rare occasions when possession did go wide the three-quarter line found themselves out-numbered with nowhere to go.

Rodney O'Donnell was a popular member of the squad and a reliable player at full back, but he lacked the attacking flair which Irvine would have brought to the party had he recovered from his hamstring problem in time for the first Test. This meant Botha was able to kick for territory with abandon, safe in the knowledge that any miscalculation was unlikely to be severely punished.

Having arrived in South Africa as a replacement only a week earlier, Tony Ward's haul of eighteen points, through five penalties and a drop-goal, broke Tom Kiernan's 1968 record for a Lion in a Test match. But he was also culpable for two Springboks tries, when his loose clearances were punished by the sort of inventive counter-attacking which the Lions appeared to be totally incapable of. But to make Ward a scapegoat would be grossly unfair. He played with a badly bruised thigh, and the frailties shown by the visiting backline had a much more fundamental cause than just the inconsistencies in his performance at stand-off.

By the time the referee had blown for half-time South Africa had scored three tries, through Rob Louw, Willie Du Plessis and Moaner Van Heerden. Botha kicked two conversions but Ward kept the Lions in touch with three penalties. After the break Ward kicked a fourth penalty to reduce the gap to four points, before Graham Price drove over at a line-out to make it 16–16. Then, with the Springboks beginning to show some signs of wear and tear up-front, Ward collected a laboured pass from Patterson and with remarkable agility jinked inside Louw before chipping a left-footed drop-goal over the bar and through the posts. At 19–16 it looked as if the Lions might steal the victory, despite the limitations of their game plan.

All the Lions needed now was control, but it wasn't to be. Gerry Germishuys collected Ward's poorly angled clearance from inside his own 25, and with the aid of Gysie Pienaar, Louw and Ray Mordt, the Springbok winger finished what he had started at the other end, to make it 22–19 to the hosts.

The Lions pack dug deep and managed one final push. They won a scrum and at the base of a rock-solid set-piece Derek Quinnell showed control and composure in tempting Divan Serfontein into stepping off-side, which meant Ward was able to kick a 45-metre penalty to tie the score once again. But in injury time David Smith, the dashing South African centre, broke a number of tackles before setting up a ruck just short of the line which was furiously contested. When the ball was recycled by the Springboks Serfontein atoned for his earlier misdeamour by lunging over the line for the winning try. It finished 26–22 to the hosts.

Renwick played again on the Wednesday after the first Test, scoring a try in a 27–7 victory over South African Country XV – the fourth of the five multi-racial invitational sides the Lions met on that tour. Gareth Davies scored three penalties and a conversion in his first game since dislocating his shoulder at the start of the trip. That game was also Irvine's first since rejoining the tour, after his false start more than a month earlier.

Dai Richards was the next tour casualty, suffering a dislocated shoulder during the 32–12 victory over Transvaal the following Saturday. Renwick played for half an hour in that match as his replacement, but from then on he became primarily a midweek player, while a combination of Clive Woodward, Ray Gravell and Paul Dodge were preferred in the centre for the Saturday side.

> JMR:
> When Ollie Campbell and Gareth Davies got injured they put Dai Richards at stand-off, and I was in the centre. Dai was more of a runner than a kicker so I would do a lot of the kicking for him. That meant I was getting quite a lot of ball and I was pretty heavily involved in the decision making, and that's a big part of the reason why I got in for the first Test. But by the Wednesday after the first Test Gareth was fit again, and two weeks later Ollie was back, and they did their own kicking, which meant I wasn't used as much, and that was it as far as my chances of making the Test team were concerned. They went back to the way they wanted to play – which was taking them on up-front and bringing big boys like Ray Gravell down the middle.

On the Tuesday before the second Test the Lions faced an Eastern Transvaal side intent on playing a spoiling game. The Lions won 21–15 but Renwick did not have a great game. Chris Rea reported that: "Jim Renwick missed too many tackles to be certain of winning a Test place."

Sure enough, when the Test team was named later that week, Renwick could only make it onto the bench. Scotland was represented by Andy Irvine at full back and Bruce Hay on the wing. While the pack remained the same, there was a total of five changes in the backline to the one which played in the first Test, with Irvine, Hay, Gravell, Woodward and Davies, replacing O'Donnell, Slemen, Richards, Renwick and Ward respectively.

There might have been plenty of new faces, but the same old shortcomings were exhibited once the match kicked off. The Lions showed plenty of spirit, but were too fragile against the strong running Springbok backs. Despite this they were still in the hunt with ten minutes to go – trailing 16–15 they were beginning to pile some serious pressure on their opponents, and two minutes after replacing the hapless Davies, whose miserable tour finally came to an end with a nasty knee ligament injury, Campbell failed with a penalty which would have given the tourists a two-point lead. Then, for neither the first nor the last time on that tour, the Lions were sucker punched by a sweeping South African counter-attack. It started with a typical rush of boots, knees and elbows by the Springbok pack before the ball was moved left to full back Gysie Pienaar, whose deft chip over the line was latched onto by Germishuys.

Naas Botha missed the conversion, but any hope of a Lions fight back were brushed aside when the home forwards charged straight back up field from the kick-off and Pienaar touched down. This time Botha had no problems converting, which meant that Gravell's late try was nothing more than a consolation score. The tourists had lost again: 26–19.

Renwick contributed a drop-goal to the Lions 17–6 victory over a rugged Junior Springboks side the following Tuesday, but the match was overshadowed by a nasty injury to Rodney O'Donnell, who broke his neck in a head-on collision with Danie Gerber, a young centre destined for great things. Fortunately O'Donnell made a complete recovery, although he never played rugby again.

With Renwick watching from the sidelines the Lions registered a confidence boosting 16–9 victory over Northern Transvaal the following Saturday, in a game which had been labelled beforehand as the fifth Test. The match was played in front of the biggest ever crowd for a provincial match of any sort, with 68,000 spectators packed into the magnificent Loftus Versfeld.

The series could not be won, but a draw could still be salvaged and after this performance the Lions approached the final three weeks of the tour with a renewed sense of confidence. With no midweek game to negotiate they enjoyed a well-earned rest in Durban, where those of the squad who were still fit to play could relax and recuperate, before heading to

Port Elizabeth for the third Test. Highlights of that short break included Ollie Campbell landing a 26lb barracuda, and the squad taking part in a parade of vintage cars for which 100,000 people lined the streets. Renwick shared a 1931 Rolls Royce with John Carleton, Andy Irvine and a posse of beautiful women.

However, the story which has provided Renwick with most mileage over the years relates to his run-in with a superstar of the music world. It is told with a fair dose of artistic licence.

> We were staying in a hotel in a place called Umhlanga Rocks near Durban and Matt Munro was performing in the hotel across the road from ours. I didn't think much about it until late one night when I was heading off to bed. I got in the lift and there's this guy next to me who I'm sure is Matt Munro. I'd had a few drinks, so I sang: 'Born Free.'
>
> Sure enough, he sang back: 'As free as the wind blows.'
>
> So we had a sing-along in the lift, but when it got to our floor the lift stopped six inches short and when the doors opened Matt fell out and jarred his shoulder. I took him along to the team doctor and he sorted it out. Matt gave me four tickets to his concert as way of a thank you.
>
> So the next night I took along some of the guys – Bill Beaumont, Ollie Campbell and Gareth Davies – and at half-time I got a note requesting my presence backstage. I went to his dressing room and he thanked me again and asked if there was anything else he could do for me.
>
> I told him that I was close to getting in the Test team, that I wanted to impress these senior players I was with, and that it would make me look good if he came round and said hello. He said he was happy to help out and promised to come over to our table after the show.
>
> I went back out and sat down with the boys and sure enough after the show Matt appeared.
>
> 'Jim! How are you?' he said, with a broad smile.
>
> 'Shove off Matt, I'm with my friends!'

The third Test was another game the Lions could and should have won. They dominated possession but were unable to convert that into points. Leading 10–6 with fifteen minutes to go Colin Patterson broke down the narrow side from a ruck but scorned a three on two, opting to go himself instead, and being smothered by the covering defence. Then Clive Woodward, who was playing on the wing instead of in the centre, showed his naivety in that position. He was turned on his heels by a low diagonal from Botha and instead of booting the ball into the back row of the stand he tapped it over the touchline. His opposite number Gerry Germishuys couldn't believe his luck. He quickly got hold of the ball and took a quick throw-in to number eight Theuns Stoffberg, who returned the pass to give Germishuys his third try in as many Test matches against the Lions. With two minutes to go the Lions were presented with one final opportunity to keep themselves in contention for a tied series, when they were awarded a penalty near the left touchline just outside the Springbok 25. However Campbell's effort sailed wide of the far upright, meaning the score line would remain 12–10 in South Africa's favour until the final whistle. The series had been lost in the most frustrating of ways.

Four days later the midweek team kept up their unbeaten record with a 25–14 victory over a South African Barbarians XV featuring Hugo Porta, the Argentine stand-off. Tomes and Irvine both touched down, while Ward kicked two conversions, three penalties and scored a try of his own.

There followed a 37–6 victory over Western Province and a 23–9 win over Griqualand West – after which Renwick and Tomes, inspired by John Lennon and Yoko Ono, decided to conduct their own bed marathon.

Alan Tomes:
I think we'd just had enough by then. The Griqualand West game had been a really dirty match. We were knackered after two months of tough touring. We were sick of eating steak all the time. We weren't going to get in the Test side. It was wind down time for us really, so we decided to stay in bed for two days, and all we ate was beans on toast. Word got round the hotel that we were doing a bed marathon so guys kept coming up to see what the chat was. It was good fun.

The pair eventually had to drag themselves out of bed for the Final Test. Tomes, contrary to his own expectations, was named on the bench for the Lions, while Renwick had agreed to play for the South African Barbarians against the emerging Springboks in a warm-up match for the main event.

JMR:
They were looking for guys to make up the team so I said I would play. They got five or six Lions players – John Beattie, Alan Martin, Peter Morgan and a few others – and Hugo Porta, the Argentinean, was in the side as well. We got a doing. They were young guys wanting to impress and we had all been out on the sauce the night before. But it

was good fun, and we got blazers, ties and jerseys to keep. I remember
Toomba was a bit jealous of that – I just told him that it served him
right for worming his way onto the bench.

In the Test match the Lions managed to avoid the ignominy of a whitewash
with a victory built on a dominant performance by the visiting forwards.
Given the amount of possession the Lions enjoyed the margin of victory
could easily have been more, but Ollie Campbell managed to kick only two
out of eight attempts at goal. The Irish stand-off's running, however, was
more effective, and he played an important role in the first try, acting as
linkman between Andy Irvine and John O'Driscoll, after the Scottish full
back ran the ball from his own half. O'Driscoll, who was the outstanding
performer for the Lions, drove tantalisingly close to the line before being
tackled just short, but from the pile-up of bodies Clive Williams rolled over
for the try. With Campbell having already missed four kicks out of five,
Irvine was given the chance to have a shot at goal, but he also missed.

The Springboks had hardly been in the game, but a Naas Botha penalty
had kept the score line fairly tight at 7–3, and when Willie du Plessis
cruised past a couple of defenders and over the line the home side drew
level. For the next few minutes the home side enjoyed their one and only
period of dominance in the match with Gysie Pienaar kicking two penalties
to establish a six point cushion.

But the Lions forwards refused to yield, and at last the backs began to
put something towards the cause. Hay broke down the left and then fed
Irvine for a try in the corner, which meant he had equalled Phil Bennet's
world record of 210 for points in international matches.

Then O'Driscoll thundered over the line, dragging a collection of
Springbok tacklers with him. Campbell's conversion from almost directly
in front of the posts made the final score 17–13. It was the first time the
Lions had ever won the last game in a four Test series in South Africa.

Having lost the Test series 3–1, the 1980 Lions tour of South Africa can
hardly be considered a success, even though they won all their provincial
games. Injuries played a crucial role, but Renwick believes that the tourists
might have done better if they had approached the trip with a different
outlook.

We had a plan to play ten-man rugby, and that is what we were going
to do. But if you arrive with two or three different ways you can play
then it makes life easier for you when plan A doesn't work. On a tour

like that plan A is not going to work all the time. You are coming up against different teams every three days and sometimes it might take something a wee bit different to get the result you need. Remember they are getting to see plenty of how you are playing so you have got to have something else tucked away to keep them on their toes. I'm not saying we didn't have another plan, but we didn't have it prepared like we should have.

They had been waiting six years for us and when we got out there they were ready. I didn't think we were as ready as they were. I don't think for a minute that I would have got in for the first Test if we hadn't picked up injuries, because I didn't fit into the way they were playing. And I wasn't playing as well as I maybe could have. I wasn't playing badly but I wasn't doing anything exceptional. Having said that, the Wednesday side never lost a game and we were up against good sides, and I don't think many touring teams will ever do that in South Africa.

I knew pretty early in the tour I wasn't going to get in because of the type of game they were wanting to play. They were always going to be better off with Gravell and Dodge crashing through the middle, but I never stopped trying because we wanted to keep the Wednesday team going – we didn't want to lose a game. I ended up playing in eleven games, and only Graham Price and Clive Williams played in more matches, so I got plenty of rugby and did my bit for the squad.

Maybe I should have said more, but it's difficult when you are fighting for your place. Some people might think you're trying to take over, some people might think you are trying to undermine them, so you try to do what's best for the team and then you end up saying nothing. I suppose it's just not my style, I wouldn't impose myself on folk.

It was a good tour, a good experience and a good set of guys – but I suppose when I look back I wish I'd been more organised. It's the chance of a lifetime, and I suppose it rankles in the back of my mind that maybe I should have taken it more seriously and maybe I should have said more. But I didn't at the time because I didn't know what was in front of me. It's like playing a game of rugby, you assume that your going to get the ball at the line-out, but its not always that cut and dried and if what you've got planned doesn't happen then you have to adapt and make the most of the situation.

Clive Woodward played in the centre in the second Test and got in on the wing for the final Test. He was probably a bit like me from the point of view in that he wasn't happy with the way the back play was going, and I think he felt there should have been a backs coach. At

Leicester, where he was playing, Chalkie White was the backs coach, and he was actually in South Africa at the time, so there was some chat amongst the players about trying to get him involved, but it never came to anything. Most teams had two coaches. Scotland would have had Nairn McEwan in charge and Colin Telfer helping with the backs, but the Lions only had one and it was maybe time to think about changing that.

But having said that, we had good fun and I enjoyed it all. I used to get stick because of my accent – nobody could understand what I was saying. My number was 22, so I used to shout 'twinty-twae' and they all used to take the mickey. Bruce Hay got it as well because he kept on saying 'ken' – everybody wanted to know who Ken was.

The first night I shared with Peter Morgan, he could speak Welsh but he didn't have a clue what I was on about. So I had to try and speak a bit properly but I soon got sick of that, I wasn't going to change and neither were they, but they soon got used to it. They used to send guys out to schools to speak to the kids. So I got sent along to this one school and they couldn't understand a word I was saying. So I didn't get to do that anymore – which was a shame because I liked that part of it.

Quite often we'd be asked to go and open a local shop or something like that - get our photo in the local press and things like that. I used to volunteer because it meant you got to go out and meet folk and have a blether with them and just see what was going on.

We trained in the morning, had a bit of light lunch, then played a bit of golf or did different things depending where we were in the afternoon. Then it would be onto the beers depending on whether you were playing the next day or not. And when we went drinking we did it in style. Some boys didn't drink or didn't drink much, but some boys drank a lot – and I think I was in that second category. We always had big nights after the games – basically it was back to the hotel where we'd have a bar organised and we'd take it from there.

Some of the boys like John O'Driscoll and Maurice Colclough were wild with drink. They'd get hell of a drunk at the after-match functions and throw food about. I remember at one dinner Syd was speaking and Colclough poured a tub of beans over the top of him. It was schoolboy stuff that you wouldn't get away with in Scotland, where it was always far more disciplined. It was quite a laid back tour, I suppose.

Then there was the Sunday School which was basically going out for a couple of beers and having a bit of fun after our lunch on Sunday. Beaumont was the leader, and you had to be invited in. I was in it,

Toomba was in it, so was Bruce Hay, John Carleton, Pricey, Jeff Squires, Colclough, John O'Driscoll and a few other guys. We ended up getting t-shirts made.

Andy Irvine:
I got the impression that Noel Murphy didn't really take Jim seriously. To me Jim was a better centre than the centres that played in the Tests, but he got associated with the Wednesday team, going out for a few beers and all that sort of thing, so I don't think they took him all that seriously – which to me was wrong. He enjoyed the fun side of rugby, but deep down Jim was a pretty serious player. There were some guys who went to seed on that tour, and there were some guys whose hearts weren't in it, but Jim stuck in all the way through. He only missed one session when his back was playing up, and I think if he had been managed properly he would have been in my Test side.

Over the piece Jim was very unlucky not getting more from the Lions. In some ways Scotland were a wee bit short changed in the seventies because guys like David Leslie should have been selected – he was a phenomenal player and far better than some of the guys that got to go on Lions tours in his place. And Jim, although he made it eventually in 1980, was unlucky as well, which was a great shame because he was a tremendous tourist. As far as company is concerned, I don't think I've ever met anyone who has got a bad word to say against Jim, he's such a nice guy and he's got that cocky sense of humour.

He became a bit of a cult figure in South Africa, partly because of his accent – nobody could understand what he was saying - but mainly because he was always so laid back and cool about things that I think guys liked being around him.

It had been an enjoyable trip, but by the end Renwick was glad to get home – even if it took a while to readjust.

JMR:
From a playing point of view you were sad because you know you'll never be as fit as that again. Peter Morgan was a bit of a fitness guy and he used to take over at the end of sessions and put us through our paces. We did a lot of press-ups and a lot of circuits and I lost a lot of fat and put on a bit of muscle. Before I left my fighting weight had been twelve and a half stone, when I came back I was fourteen stone and bum fit, and from then on I was playing at around thirteen and a half, which is a big difference. I think I played a lot of my best rugby after I came back from South Africa, and a big part of that was because I built myself up over there.

I was glad to be back but it took me a while to settle. I found it hard to just sit and watch the telly, I wanted to be up and away because that's all I'd been doing for two months. So I couldn't settle, every spare moment I felt I had to go out for a walk or a pint or do something. I soon came back to earth but for a while it was difficult to adjust because it was a habit I had got into.

My only real regret about the whole thing is that we've never met up again since. You wonder what they are all up to. Which ones are still alive? How many are still involved with rugby?

On the day Renwick returned from the Lions tour Terence and Bobby Froud, along with a couple of friends, were golfing.

Terence Froud:
We were coming down the fifteenth at the Vertish when we saw this head popping up from behind the fifteenth green. It was Renwick; he'd got back from South Africa that afternoon, dropped his bags, and headed up to the Vertish. He was just lying there looking out over Hawick. So we played the last three holes and headed down to the golf club for a couple of pints and to catch up.

New Zealand 1981

Before embarking on Scotland's month long tour of New Zealand in the summer of 1981, Ken Smith, the tour manager and a former British Lion himself, said: "This will be the best prepared squad to ever leave Scotland for an overseas tour."

Renwick does not take issue with that, but he feels that in his drive to attain a supreme level of fitness Jim Telfer, who had taken over as Scotland coach the previous year, undermined some of the other considerations essential to a successful tour – particularly in terms of morale and maintaining the freshness necessary to take New Zealand on in their own back yard.

Since Telfer had taken over as Scotland coach the team had shown definite signs of progress. Their international record in the 1981 season of two home wins and two away defeats was hardly earth shattering, but it was the first time Scotland had managed a 50 percent return in the Five Nations championship since 1976.

The campaign started in a less than promising fashion when France and Scotland offered a sharp contrast to the excitement the two teams had conjured up at Murrayfield the previous year. While neither side played well, the Scots deserved to trail 16–3 at the break after some slip-shod forward play and truly abysmal tackling. All the same it might have been closer had Renwick not been penalised by Welsh referee Ken Rowland early on, after he was brought down just short of the line but returned to his feet and dived over. Renwick said at the time that he was convinced that he hadn't been held by his tackler, but the score was chalked off and the home team awarded the penalty. In the second half Scotland tightened things up and a Rutherford try, which was converted by Renwick, added respectability to the final outcome.

It was perhaps a disappointing day for Scotland, but it was a memorable occasion for at least one player. Irvine's early penalty lifted his tally in international matches to 213, meaning that he had overtaken the previous record of 210 held by Phil Bennett of Wales.

Three weeks later Scotland put in a performance against Wales at Murrayfield which was almost unrecognisable to their showing in Paris. Tomes had, what was by common consent at the time, his best game in a Scotland jersey, dominating the middle of the line-out and proving an abrasive menace all round the park. David Leslie and Bill Cuthbertson had been brought into the pack in place of David Gray and George Dickson, and the Scottish forwards dominated the loose exchanges to the extent that the ball often arrived back too quickly for the backs to utilise it properly. Wales perhaps had a touch more in terms of quantity when it came to possession, but as far as quality was concerned the Scots won hands down.

After 25 minutes it was still 3–3, with Renwick and Steve Fenwick exchanging penalties – but then Keith Robertson broke a tackle in midfield, Deans and Calder carried the move on, and when the latter was stopped just short Tomes charged into the fray to score. Renwick converted but a second Fenwick penalty made it 9–6 at half-time.

That lead remained until eight minutes before the end, when Irvine was first of all pulled back by Gareth Davies as the pair chased a hack ahead by Hay, then obstructed by the same player, leaving referee David Burnett with no choice but to award a penalty try. Renwick converted to give Scotland a surprising but well-deserved 15–6 victory.

Scotland carried on their new found form when they faced England at Twickenham in their next match, though they were not quite able to topple the reigning Five Nations champions, despite leading four times and matching their opponents in scoring three tries. This was a quiet game for Renwick although he did set up the first of Munro's two tries with a neat grubber kick. That score came just after Clive Woodward had scored the try of the match, ghosting past a gaggle of Scottish tacklers and over the line. Scotland's other try was scored by Calder with six minutes to go and gave the visitors a 17–16 lead, but a famous victory was denied when Huw Davies skipped through the Scottish defence and over the line to make it 20–17 to the home team, with Dusty Hare adding his third penalty of the match and before the end to confirm a 23–17 victory for England.

The season finished on a high for Scotland with a 10–9 victory over Ireland at Murrayfield. They came out on top in this encounter because they made a brighter start, scoring all ten of their points before the conditions really deteriorated in the second half. Much of the match was played in driving rain, on a soggy pitch, with a soapy ball – which added to the size of the task facing Ireland as they tried to claw back the points which would avert a Five Nations whitewash. In the end David Irwin's try, and a conversion and penalty by Ollie Campbell, was not quite enough.

Scotland's try in that match was scored by Bruce Hay, who by his own admission was never the speediest of wingers but still managed to intercept David Irwin's floated pass and outpace Tony Ward to score in the corner. As Hay trundled back into position he passed Renwick, who mischievously noted that Hay's score had been the first try he had seen in slow motion watching it for the first time.

Telfer was clearly keen to use that summer's trip to New Zealand to build upon this promising start to his time as an international coach, and he set the tone before the tour party had even left Scotland with some heavy squad sessions at Murrayfield. It was at one of the sessions that John Beattie became the tour's first casualty, when he cracked his knee-cap in a collision with Iain Milne – universally known as 'The Bear' – three weeks before the trip was due to commence. Iain Paxton, the Selkirk number eight, was called up in his place.

The first match of the tour was against King Country, who were coached by Colin Meads, the legendary All Blacks lock of the 1960s. In the week leading up to this match anti-apartheid demonstrators, protesting against South Africa's tour of New Zealand later in the summer, threatened sabotage, so as a precaution the Scotland squad was shadowed by two detectives from the New Zealand Police force and the pitch in Taumarunui was guarded night and day by volunteers from the 30 clubs in the province.

In the event, the day went off without a hitch and Scotland were able to start the tour with a convincing 39–13 win over a side which had been hit hard by injuries during the build-up to the match. Andy Irvine clocked up 24 points with a try, four conversions and four penalties, on the same field as he had scored five tries for the Lions against King Country-Wanganui in 1977. Scotland's other points came from a drop-goal by London Scottish stand-off Ron Wilson, and tries by David Leslie, Gerry McGuiness and Gordon Hunter.

Renwick was selected in the centre alongside Alistair Cranston, and the Hawick pair had a busy afternoon keeping Murray Kidd, an All Blacks trialist, subdued. However Renwick did find time to make a long break down the right wing before passing inside for Leslie's try.

It had looked certain to be a baptism of fire for Roger Baird, the 21-year-old former boarding school pupil who played for Kelso and was making his first appearance in a Scotland jersey. During the build-up to the match the local newspapers reported that his opposite number was making a comeback after a spell in prison. Naturally the rest of the squad took great delight in using this to wind up the young winger, who could not conceal his trepidation. In the end Baird proved his mettle with a solid performance.

Next stop was Wellington where the Scotland squad were invited to a state reception at the parliament buildings.

> JMR:
> I was just keeping out the road, hanging about at the buffet stand, dipping my prawns in the sauce, when this old boy comes across: 'How are you enjoying our beautiful country?' he asks.
>
> 'Aye, its fine,' I said. I couldn't really be bothered with this but I thought I better make some small talk, so I said: 'And what do you do?'
>
> 'I'm Robert Muldoon, the Prime Minister of New Zealand,' he says.
>
> 'Aye, and I'm the provost of Gala,' I said back at him.
>
> So off he went his own way and a bit later, when it was time for the speeches, up this guy gets and he was exactly who he had said he was. I was saying to the rest of the boys that we better get ready to do a runner because he might want the Provost of Gala to speak next and I hadn't prepared anything.

Renwick played again in the Wellington match and this time he was alongside Richard Breakey of Gosforth in the centre. Scotland were up against a pretty formidable Wellington side, with the All Black back three of Stu Wilson, Allan Hewson and Bernie Fraser all in the side, although Wilson was playing in the centre on this occasion. In the pack Murray Mexted, the All Black number eight, was sure to be a handful. So it was a surprise, but not a major shock, that the tourists lost this match 19–15. Fraser scored two tries for the home team, to go with a Brendan Gardner try, and a penalty and two conversions from Hewson. The Scottish points came from a Bill Cuthbertson try, a John Rutherford drop-goal, and a conversion and two penalties by Peter Dodds – who was named man-of-the-match after being called into the side as a late replacement for Andy Irvine, the Scotland captain, who was struggling with a groin injury.

"The Wellington game served notice that Scotland will have to improve immensely on their midfield play. There is a lack of devil and penetration with only Jim Renwick looking the part," reported *The Scotsman* the following Monday.

The Scottish cause had not been helped by the loss of scrum-half Gordon Hunter early in the second half with a cracked cheek-bone. This meant Roy Laidlaw had to come on as a replacement, but like his captain, the Jed-Forest player was struggling with a groin injury so was not his usual all-action self. With only two scrum-halves in the 24-man tour party it was clear that a replacement would have to be flown out. Alan Lawson got the call on Sunday morning and was happy to oblige, but could only do so after an important business meeting in London on Wednesday morning. That meant he would only make it to New Zealand just in time for Scotland's match against Canterbury the following Saturday. As a precaution Bruce Hay and Roger Baird, who both had some experience of playing scrum-half, trained in that position during the build-up to Scotland's midweek match against Wairapa Bush.

Fortunately Laidlaw was declared fit to play against Wairapa Bush and he came through the challenge unscathed, although he was still clearly protecting his groin and did not risk going flat-out. As a near certainty for the Test team Renwick was rested, which gave Cranston and Breakey the opportunity to go head-to-head in the race for the other midfield slot.

The Scots won 32–9 in a bad tempered affair in which there was fighting both on the pitch and in the crowd. For the second time on tour Irvine scored 24 points with three penalties, one drop-goal, two tries, and two conversions. Hay and Breakey also scored tries.

Scotland's next match against Canterbury promised to be a more challenging encounter. The Scots had lost to the province in 1975, when they had not won a single ruck and had also fared pretty badly in the line-out. On this occasion Scotland named the team they hoped would play in the first Test, with Renwick alongside Cranston in the centre, and despite the withdrawal from the side of Irvine before kick-off, the Scots were able to run out fairly comfortable 23–12 winners in miserable weather conditions.

Peter Dodds, who took Irvine's place in the side, had a torrid start to the match – missing each of his first four attempts at goal. But the Gala player showed real strength of character to turn his kicking game around and scored two penalties just before half-time, then added another two in the second half. Laidlaw and Steve Munro scored tries and Rutherford slotted a penalty.

Sensibly Irvine was rested for the next match against Mid-Canterbury, which finished with an identical score line to the previous match. Scotland scored four tries with Breakey, Munro, Leslie and Lawson all touching down, while Dodds added two conversions and Wilson chipped in with a drop-goal. It was, however, a bad afternoon for number eight Derek White, who ruptured ligaments in his knee.

There was a mood of quiet optimism in the Scotland camp as they headed into the first of their two Test matches the following Saturday.

An early try by Steve Munro had been chalked-off by Dick Byres, the Australian referee who was the first neutral to officiate in a Test match in New Zealand. Byres ruled that momentum had not carried the winger over the line and that a second movement had occurred after the tackle had been made. Replays the next day suggested that the referee had got it wrong, though the Scots had plenty more golden opportunities to put themselves in a commanding position.

Cuthbertson dived over the line from a line-out, but that score was disallowed because Leslie was in an offside position. Then a dazzling run by Renwick spread-eagled the All Blacks' defence and brought the 35,000 spectators at Carisbrook to their feet, but somehow Irvine fumbled Renwick's pass as a certain six points beckoned. And another try-scoring opportunity was missed when Munro – having out-paced Bruce Robertson, Eddie Dunn, Fraser and Loveridge to be first to his own kick ahead – knocked the ball forward as he tried to pick-up. Had he opted to hack on it is more than likely he would have scored.

In the end New Zealand were to scramble an 11–0 lead through tries by Loveridge and Wilson to add to Hewson's early penalty. Colin Deans managed a late consolation score.

Scotland had come close to achieving their first ever victory over the All Blacks, which would also have been their first victory in the southern hemisphere, but in the end they lacked the composure and cutting edge to convert a winnable match into a match that had been won.

JMR:
I thought we had a chance because the Blacks maybe weren't as strong as they had been in the past. If we had taken a few chances earlier in the match then we might have done it. We had a good scrum and we kicked well. The difference was that when we had them under the cosh

they held on, then at the start of the second half they were putting a bit of pressure on us and we gave away an easy try when the ball came out the side of a scrum and Dave Loveridge pounced on it. That wrapped it up for them and that was maybe the difference between them and us – they did the damage when they got the chance.

After a 38–9 defeat of Marlborough the following Tuesday, it was a bumped, bruised and weary Scotland squad which travelled to Auckland for the second Test. However their close shave in Dunedin had given them confidence and there was a genuine feeling of anticipation that this was a real opportunity for Scotland to beat their southern hemisphere duck. It was to be Renwick's 41st cap, which would take him past Hugh McLeod to become Hawick and the Borders' most capped player.

It proved to be one match too many for the tourists. It started off positively enough and at half-time the All Blacks were only ahead by four points. Renwick had slotted a drop-goal to go with Irvine's earlier penalty, while Wilson and Hewson had touched down for the hosts, with Hewson also kicking one conversion .

Then, even when both Graham Mourie and Wilson scored after the break, the All Blacks still could not quite finish the Scots off. They clawed their way back to 22–15 with a Bruce Hay try and a conversion and a try by Irvine, but eventually the All Blacks cranked it up another gear and in the final quarter they added eighteen unanswered points. The 40–15 score-line maybe flattered the home team, but it was telling that having kept in touch with the All Blacks for the first hour, Scotland collapsed in the final quarter, allowing the All Blacks to chalk up 40 points in a Test match for the first time in their long and distinguished history.

JMR:
We trained hard for the second Test right up to the day before the match and I felt we were just a wee bit burned out by the time we got there. We were in the game until the last twenty minutes, then they started moving the ball and we just didn't have enough gas left in the tank to cope with it.

If I'm being honest then I think we trained too hard on that trip. Boys were picking up injuries, pulling muscles and that sort of thing. We trained in the morning and afternoon, and then watched videos at night. Sometimes the videos were two or three years old so they weren't even relevant to what we were trying to do. But I suppose Jim [Telfer] just wanted us to be together and watching rugby and thinking about the game. That was his way of doing it and I'm not saying he was wrong, I'm just saying that it's not the way I would have done it. A lot of boys had taken time off their work so there should have been more of a balance between work and play.

He wanted to put up a good show – there's nothing wrong with that – and to be fair we didn't play too badly. We only just lost the first Test in Carisbrook, which was a good effort, so maybe he was right in some ways. But they put 40 points on us in the second Test, and I thought we did too much work in the week before that match. We were in the game right up until half-time, and it was only in the last twenty minutes that they ran away with it, and I think a lot of that was down to boys being dead on their feet.

I could see a lot of differences between that tour and the '75 one. The players didn't get out to see the country and meet folk. Things were changing, they were taking fat content measurements, and maybe it was the right idea because that was the way the game was going, but I don't think it had been properly thought through yet. At the end of the day you have to make sure the boys are ready to play on match days but we seemed to be carrying a lot of guys with knocks and pulled muscles. You've got to remember we were amateurs, and our bodies weren't used to that level of work.

I remember there was training on the Sunday morning after the Wellington game. It was optional, but me and Bruce Hay were the only two that didn't go. Everybody else went along but I felt I needed a rest. We trained pretty hard in that first week and played two tough games so there comes a point when you have to look after number one. I don't suppose Jim was too impressed with that.

It was the hardest tour I had been on. With the Lions we trained hard but it wasn't as intense as that tour. The day we got to New Zealand we arrived and trained for two and a half hours in the morning and then went back out for an hour in the afternoon. In fact we even trained in Singapore in the heat when we stopped on the way over. Some of the boys really struggled with that – Tom Smith from Gala collapsed with exhaustion.

Now I'm not saying that Derrick Grant didn't train us hard as well, but for me Jim didn't know when to stop. He didn't know how to put it away fresh. Too often he would go over the top.

Telfer and Grant were fairly similar. But I think Derrick was more sympathetic to what was going on throughout the team, while Jim was very much a forwards man. Derrick had more rugby flair; Jim was more about hard-work, discipline and long training sessions.

I also felt that Derrick liked a good time once in a while which made him easier to approach, but I never saw Jim Telfer let himself go. Maybe it was because I knew Derrick better than I knew Jim, but I just always got the impression that Derrick was more interested in what the players had to say.

The following summer Scotland toured Australia. Renwick made himself unavailable.

Captain

Renwick didn't ever captain Scotland, despite an international career spanning twelve years during which time he earned 52 caps – a record at that time – and toured New Zealand twice, the Far East and Romania. "I muck about too much to be captain," he says.

However, he was elected by his team-mates to captain Hawick in four separate seasons. Renwick's explanation is frank: "It's more important at Hawick."

Renwick is being slightly mischievous – it would be ridiculous to suggest that a player who gave so much to the cause was anything other than fully committed to his international career. What he really means is that it was more important to Hawick than it was to Scotland that he fulfilled that function. At international level Renwick was only one of several highly experienced players in the set-up, and his naturally cautious approach towards taking on responsibility meant that players such as Ian McLauchlan, Ian McGeechan and Andy Irvine were much more suited to the task. At Hawick his experience set him apart from most players, which meant it had to be put to full use.

The difference in intensity between club and international rugby is also significant. Renwick is a laid-back, affable character who is ideally suited to maintaining a happy ambience in the squad over the prolonged course of a club season. International rugby takes place in short, sharp bursts meaning that a player willing and able to dominate proceedings is a better candidate for this job.

JMR:
At international level what you want is a player who will lead from the front and set the tone, and then let the key men play their game. That's maybe why guys like Finlay Calder and David Sole were so successful when they did the job. At club level it's a wee bit different because you

have to keep it going over the whole season, so you maybe want someone with a different approach to these guys.

I'm not a fire and brimstone talker, it's just not my style. And I used to joke about too much for some people's liking. It's not that I wasn't serious about it – it's just that I'm not as intense as some folk. I think you can still have a laugh before the game and then switch on, but some guys can't do that.

I would never shove myself forward like some other folk did. I captained the South a few times, but it wasn't anything I aspired to. If it needed to be done I could do it, but I didn't go looking for it.

To be honest I don't think captaincy is that big a deal. You can make it a big deal if you want but I don't think that makes you the best captain. The best captains are the guys that do it with as little fuss as possible. When guys speak all the time the important stuff they say sometimes gets lost in amongst the rest of it. With guys like Billy Murray and Norman Suddon, when they spoke folk listened, because you knew they wouldn't open their mouths unless they had something important to say. Mind you Colin Deans used to speak a lot, but that was okay because he could back it up. Different guys can put different emphasis on different things. Heg was a fitness guy, he led by example at training. That was his thing.

Renwick first captained Hawick for the 1974–75 season, and he insists that he was not ready for the role.

The first few years you're in the Hawick side you don't say anything. You just shut up, listen to what the senior players say and do the training. Then, gradually, it becomes your turn. Norman Suddon was the captain the year before me and he was a good captain – probably the best I played under at Hawick. He was a sensible head, he didn't complicate things, he just looked at the situation and knew what needed to be done and what could be left alone. But he hurt his back halfway through the season and I was vice-captain so I had to take over, so I suppose I was the obvious choice for the next season, but I think it was a bit early for me. I had a bit of experience because I'd played for Scotland, but I was only 22 so I was quite young and I wasn't a very good captain. I think they were wanting to take it off me at one point. I was a better captain when I did it again later.

We won the league but it wasn't so much my captaincy as experienced players in key positions calling the shots. In they days Colin Telfer was still running the show, you just had to toss up – you were really just the figurehead.

By the time Renwick captained the club again, during the 1978–79 season, the circumstances had changed. Telfer was no longer the puppet-master pulling the strings from the stand-off position, and several of the forwards who had been so important to the style of play championed by Derrick Grant during the glory days of the mid-seventies had either hung up their boots or were well into the twilight years of their career. It was a tough campaign for Hawick and they finished fourth in the Division One table, behind Heriots, Gala and Stewart's Melville. That season they lost four matches in the league, which was as many as they had lost during the previous five seasons put together. It was the first time since the official championship had been set up in 1973 that Hawick had not finished at the top of the table.

JMR:
That was disappointing but there was a funny sort of relief there as well. When you're on top for so long it begins to take its toll. You know that it's going to have to end at some point, but until it happens the idea of coming second seems like a nightmare. It gave us a chance to catch our breath, regroup and get ready to get the championship back the next season.

But before that I went on tour to South Africa with Surrey. They had a fairly tough itinerary lined up against strong provincial teams like Orange Free State, and I think they wanted to bolster the side with a few internationalists. They'd got Alan Martin, Alan Phillips and a few other Welsh internationalists to go, I was the only Scot, and they had a few English boys who actually played their rugby for clubs like Rosslyn Park which were based in Surrey.

I met up with the squad at the airport and I was the last there. All the other boys had picked up their kit already and I had to take what was left. Little did I know that they wore a maroon blazer, and my one was about eight sizes too big – it was hanging doon to my knees. But I just rolled up the sleeves and got on with it. It got us into the tour a wee bit because I didn't know anybody but they were all taking the mick out of me.

It was a good trip. They took us all over the country and I met some good folk. We trained hard in the morning, but if you wanted a few Bacardi and cokes around the pool in the afternoon then that's what you did. I think we won three and lost three in the end, but even if we had trained every day and taken it really seriously we weren't going to win any more.

Then on the way back we were all in our shirts and blazers coming through customs at Heathrow and the boy on the gate recognises me and is delighted he's caught me with a maroon blazer on.

'I was reading Rugby World the other day and it said you'd rather be a lamp-post in Hawick than the provost of Gala,' he says. 'Well I'm frae Gala, so you better gie us your bags.'

I had two diamonds that I shouldn't have had, but I got away with it.

Colin Deans took over the captaincy at Hawick for the 1979–80 season and things improved slightly, with the club finishing third in the league behind Gala and Heriots although this was still well below the expectation level set by previous successes. Hawick's three defeats in the league that season were against Boroughmuir at Meggetland on the opening Saturday of the competition, Heriots at Mansfield three weeks later, and Melrose at the Greenyards on the final day of the competition.

With Renwick back in the role of captain, Hawick repeated that third place finish in the 1980–81 season. Their title challenge had spun off course before it was under way, with an away defeat to newly promoted Gordonians on the opening weekend of the season, then a loss at home to Boroughmuir the next week, followed by a draw with West of Scotland at Burnbrae the week after that. They rallied sufficiently, however, to defeat Melrose (18–3 at home), Kelso (30–7 at home) a and Langholm (24–6 at Milntown), before their famous match against Gala at Mansfield on 14 February.

Going into injury time Gala were leading 6–4, thanks to a drop-goal and a penalty from Arthur Brown, against a try from an overlap by Alistair Taylor. But then Renwick ran a penalty from inside his own half and Keith Murray, Taylor and John Hogg all played their part before Keith Mitchell touched down in the corner. The conversion would have made it 10–6, but Renwick's effort from wide on the left never looked like going over. It seemed, however, that the 8–6 score line would be enough. Especially as Hawick were awarded a penalty from the restart and Renwick sent the ball into the corner, where he hoped play would remain until the final whistle. However, Peter Dodds sent a 60-metre clearance kick back into Hawick territory and the visitors were then awarded a penalty after Tomes was found guilty of preventing release at a ruck. The visitors appeared to have secured a last gasp chance to grab the victory – only for Dodds to push his effort to the right of the posts.

But Gala weren't finished yet and from a scrum on Hawick's ten metre line Arthur Brown, at stand-off, threw a miss pass to Ivor Roy in the centre, who fed Peter Dodds coming into the line off his shoulder. The Gala full back went outside Renwick, inside Taylor, outpaced Donald Whillans, and sent Hogg the wrong way to score a fine try. The same player hit the post with his conversion effort, but he had already done enough to secure a dramatic victory for his club. That result helped Gala become only the second team, after Hawick in 1975–76, to win all eleven of their league matches in one season.

The experience prompted Henry Douglas, a local farmer and well-known Borders entertainer, to vent his frustration in verse.

The referee made history that day at Mansfield Park,
For hei played that long in the second half that it started to get dark.
When Hoojie Mitchell scored yon try A thought oo'd won the match,
But damn, yon stupid referee had went and lost his watch.
Hei didnae ken how long oo'd played, 'Time up' the crowd did roar,
But hei kept on adding extra time till Gala got a score.

Hawick's sense of injustice was not, however, enough to disguise the club's failings over the last three seasons – and especially that season when they lost fourteen and drew two of their 31 games.

Derrick Grant:
By that time a lot of the guys had reached the end of the road and that meant we had to build a new side. We took a lot of stick then because we had been so successful for so long and people expected us to continue like that forever – but it was always going to take us a while to find the right combination.

It should be noted that there was still the sort of experience there that other clubs could only dream of. Renwick, Deans, Alan Tomes and Alastair Cranston all played in Scotland's two Test matches in New Zealand that summer, while Brian Hegarty had been capped in 1978. And there was no shortage of emerging talent in the squad either, with four future internationalists (Alister Campbell, Sean McGaughey, Keith 'Slugger' Murray and Derek Turnbull) all appearing at various points during the season. Add to that Colin Gass, Paul Hogarth, Billy Murray and Ronnie Nichol, who were all future Scotland B internationalists, and it is clear that this was a squad with potential to become a major force in Scottish club rugby sooner rather than later.

So it proved during the 1981–82 season when, with Renwick doing his second year on the trot as captain, Hawick once again reached the summit of the club game in Scotland – winning their first championship title since their run of five consecutive triumphs came to an end four years earlier. It is clearly an achievement which gives Renwick a lot of satisfaction.

> We played a different style of rugby that year. We didn't have the dominance that we used to have up front. We were getting shoved around in the scrum, so we had to move their forwards about and it was more important that the backs did the business. In the seventies it wouldn't have mattered most of the time whether I was in the middle or not, we would still have won because we were getting all the ball we wanted. It was pretty easy being a Hawick back in the seventies because you can waste a bit of possession if you're getting plenty – but in '81 it was different, there were no foregone conclusions, every game was a battle and I enjoyed that. It was a satisfying way to win the league.

The title was decided in what was effectively a winner-takes-all game against Gala at Netherdale on the penultimate Saturday of the season. Keith Murray was injured early on and, in these days before replacements were permitted, Hawick had to play most of the game with fourteen men. With two minutes to go Jim Maitland dropped a goal to put Gala two points in front, then in injury time Hawick were awarded a penalty.

The ball sailed over and the Hawick section of the crowd went wild, followed by the players when the referee blew for full-time a few seconds later. It was the sweetest of revenges after Gala's controversial victory at Mansfield the season before.

> JMR:
> I looked over to Colin Gass to see if he fancied it, but in the end I just decided to take it myself. I'd been practising during the week, and I just kept my head down and hit it.
> That's the only time I've seen Hawick get like that. Even Derrick was jumping up and down, and I think it was because we had the game won then Gala dropped a goal to put themselves in front and we had to win it again. So I suppose it was a bit like that time when Andy scored the winning penalty against England in 1974 – it had been tense and the relief meant that you lost sight of yourself a wee bit.

Hawick went on to win the championship by a point from Heriots, after defeating Watsonians at Mansfield in their final match of the campaign. Gala had to settle for third place after losing their last three games to Heriots, Hawick and Kelso. Hawick also won the Border League that year for the first time since 1979.

By the end of that season Renwick had played in 95 of Hawick's 97 league matches since the official championship had been introduced in 1973, during which time he had scored 911 points.

1982, And All That

Renwick played probably the best rugby of his career in the two years following his return from the 1980 Lions tour. He was in his late twenties, he had the experience of eight years of international rugby behind him, during which time he had played with and against the best in the world, and as Terence Froud points out: "He was a mean looking specimen after going to South Africa, he really was. He always kept himself in good nick, but that was the fittest I ever saw him."

That level of fitness was built upon the following summer in New Zealand with Scotland, when the squad were worked incredibly hard by Jim Telfer. And with players such as John Rutherford, Roy Laidlaw, David Johnston, Colin Deans, Iain Milne and Iain Paxton all emerging as genuine world class players, Scotland were beginning to show glimpses of the potential which would be realised with a Grand Slam victory in 1984. However the inconsistency of their results proved that this team was still very much a work in progress.

In December 1981 Scotland defeated Australia 24–15 at Murrayfield. The Australians had come to Britain with an outstanding reputation. They had recently achieved Test series victories over both New Zealand and France, playing some exhilarating rugby, and there was a high level of expectation that they would enliven the British winter with some similar performances.

Instead there was anti-climax from the start of the tour as the visitors struggled to come to terms with the unfamiliar conditions of a British winter, and cracks in their forward play were exposed by regional opposition. In their first four games they lost to Midland Counties and Bridgend, drew with the Northern Counties and managed only one win over Oxford University.

But they eventually found their feet and lost only one more provincial match on tour, to Munster during the week leading into their Test match against Ireland. Even still, this was not the magical Wallaby side which had been expected, and they relied heavily on an uncompromising defence which conceded only nine tries in their 23 matches.

In Test matches they struggled. By the time they came to Scotland they had scraped a victory over Ireland but had lost to Wales, and two weeks later they would lose again to England. This Scottish victory, therefore, was a highly commendable achievement but not the momentous occasion it would have been had the Australians lived up to their billing.

The game itself represented a triumph of the boot over enterprising rugby. On a gusty afternoon the Australians scored three very good first half tries through Simon Poidevin, Brendan Moon and Andrew Slack, but Paul McLean managed to kick only one of his seven attempts at goal. This allowed Scotland to stay in touch through five penalties. Then a Rutherford drop-goal put the home side 18–15 ahead. And the killer blow came when Roger Gould, the usually flawless Australian full back, completely misjudged a towering kick from Rutherford and the ball bounced into Renwick's arms for a score under the posts. Irvine's conversion was a formality and there was no time for the Australians to stage a comeback.

JMR:
Gould had caught me with his boot as he made a mark and I'd had to go off so that Donald McLeod, the team doctor, could put some stitches in my cheek. I was just back on the park and Rudd put a high kick up which David Johnston chased. I should have done the same, but I was still a wee bit groggy. Anyway Gould and Johnston both missed it and the ball bounced over everyone's head into my hands and I scored under the posts. That's what they call good vision. I call it being lucky. It shows you that rugby isn't always a fair game, I didn't deserve to score, I was in the wrong place, but that's why it's called the luck of the bounce.

Some days it goes against you. I remember charging a kick down in Paris and they scored at the other end. Now, what do you do? Stop trying to charge down kicks? It was just a lucky bounce and good play by them and that's what happens. That's why there's no point getting all worked up if you lose – what's going to happen is going to happen, and you can't change that. If you've done the best you can, then you've done enough to enjoy a pint and a bit of chat with the boys after the game. Folk might make the wrong decision, but they don't try to do that, it's just the way they see it at the time. What they were trying might have worked, or maybe it was never going to work, but you can't change what they've done, you've just got to hope they've learned from the experience.

A month later Scotland started their Five Nations campaign with a 9–9 draw with England at home. They then played poorly when losing 21–12 away to Ireland, but turned things round with a 16–7 victory over France in Edinburgh which was based on a dominant performance up front, although Chris Rea noted that: "Renwick's astuteness in attack and anticipation in defence were invaluable."

The final match of the championship was away to Wales, and would go down in history as one of the greatest ever performances by a Scottish rugby team. Wales were undefeated in Cardiff in 27 matches going back to 1968. During that time Scotland had managed only three victories on the road and had not won in Cardiff since 1962.

The Welsh had been the team of the 1970s, but their powers were on the wane. The midfield flair that had been their trademark during the previous decade was almost entirely absent and despite dominating possession they could not contain Scotland's lively backs – who counter-attacked with audacity and flair, and were keenly supported by a forward unit which, despite struggling in the tight, played a marvellous supporting role. At the end of the match the try-count read 5–1 in Scotland's favour and the scoreboard showed that Wales had conceded more points than ever before on their own patch. The final score was 34–18.

"The seeds of a famous victory were sown in the stifling speed of our offensive-defence with the two centres, Johnston and Jim Renwick, utterly superb," said Norman Mair, in the *Sunday Standard*, on the day after the match. "The Hawick captain was in scintillating form," he added.

Chris Rea agreed. "With Johnston and Renwick playing the game of their lives, the Welsh inadequacies in midfield were embarrassingly exposed," he wrote. "Renwick's display was the most influential I have seen from an international centre. His dropped goal, which came from a line-out ball won by Cuthbertson, was every bit as important to Scotland as the one he dropped against France two weeks ago."

Renwick's try originated from a Welsh mistake in midfield. Ackerman lost possession to Rutherford who passed to Calder. Calder accelerated up field, slowed, held back the pass until Renwick was in full flight, and from inside his own half the Hawick centre showed the pace and power to shrug of a challenge from Ackerman and charge over beneath the sticks for his third try in as many matches against Wales at Cardiff Arms Park.

Scotland's other points came from tries by Jim Calder, Jim Pollock,

Derek White and David Johnston, with four conversions from Andy Irvine and a drop-goal by John Rutherford. The pick of the scores was Calder's, which came about after Roger Baird swept up Gareth Davies' kick ahead and, rather than kick for touch, opted to launch a counter-attack from deep inside his own 25. He darted up the left touchline before feeding Iain Paxton who carried on the momentum, and Alan Tomes acted as the link man to Calder who tumbled over the line.

The teams that day were:

Wales: G. Evans (Maestag); R.A. Ackerman (Newport), R.W.R. Gravell (Llanelli), A.J. Donavon (Swansea), C.F.W. Rees (London Welsh); W.G. Davies (Cardiff), G.W. Williams (Bridgend); G. Price (Pontypool), A.J. Phillips (Cardiff), I Stephens (Bridgend), R.C. Burgess (Ebbw Vale), R.L. Norster (Cardiff), R.D. Moriarty (Swansea), J.R. Lewis (Cardiff), E.T. Butler (Pontypool).

Scotland: A.R. Irvine (Heriots); J. Pollock (Gosforth), J.M. Renwick (Hawick), D.I. Johnston (Watsonians), G.R.T. Baird (Kelso); J.Y. Rutherford (Selkirk), R.J. Laidlaw (Jed-Forest); I.G. Milne (Heriots), C.T. Deans (Hawick), J. Aitken (Gala), D.B. White (Gala), W. Cuthbertson (Kilmarnock), A.J. Tomes (Hawick), J.H. Calder (Stewart's Melville), I.A.M. Paxton (Selkirk).

JMR:
Keith Robertson went down with the flu and they brought Jim Pollock in. It was a bit of a surprise because most of the boys didn't know him that well. He'd maybe been at a couple of training sessions but he was a new face I remember he was a wee bit nervous when he came in, which I can understand, but he did well. He scored a try and we won that game and then every time he was called he always did well and we always seemed to win. He achieved more in his first couple of games than some boys managed in their whole careers so we started calling him Lucky Jim. He ended up playing in a losing side for Scotland a few times, but he had a good run at it for a while.

I remember Telfer wanted us to go to bed on a Friday afternoon, but if I'd done that I wouldn't have slept at night so Rudd, Andy, myself and Gordon Hunter, who was on the bench, played a few holes on the golf course. I think Jim Telfer found out about that and Andy got a row, but we won the next day and we all played well, so it couldn't have done that much harm.

The big turning point in that game was happened a week before kick-off when Jeff Squire and Terry Holmes called off. That gave us a wee bit of a boost I remember. They brought Gerald Williams in at scrum-half and he hadn't played with Gareth Davies before so I think there was a wee problem at half-back. And they brought Eddie Butler into the back row who was a good player, but he wasn't Jeff Squires.

Renwick was picking up his 47th cap that day, which makes it astonishing that this was his first away win in a Scotland jersey, and he might have added his second away win that summer had he not declared himself unavailable for Scotland's tour of Australia.

I think I'd had enough of touring by then. New Zealand in '81 was the final straw for me – it was getting too much like hard work. It had been exceptionally hard over there, and I was coming to the end of my career and I couldn't be bothered going through that again.

But the boys did well over there. They beat Australia 12–7 in the first Test and that was the first time they had won an international match in the southern hemisphere. I remember watching the game on the telly, and Toomba was shouting to the pack: 'Come on boys, Scotland have never won a Test in the southern hemisphere.' So he must have been pretty geared up, because Toomba wasn't the type of guy that did a lot of talking unless he had something important to say.

Australia came back and gave us a bit of a doing the next week, but a win over there is some achievement so they did well.

He might have ruled himself out of Scotland's trip to Australia, but Renwick had no intention of handing back his ticket to ride quite yet.

Almost straight from the Welsh victory he headed off with the Scottish Borderers to compete in the Hong Kong sevens. They reached the final, where they were slightly unlucky to lose 18–14 to an Australian side containing both Mark and Glen Ella. The Borderers squad was: Eric Paxton, Gary Callander, Paul Hogarth, Derek White, Bob Hogarth, Rutherford, Renwick, Robertson and Baird.

JMR:
The rugby was hard because it was so warm but I enjoyed it. We all had to walk round the ground at the beginning with a flag held out in front of us, and we had a big dinner at the end with each team having to do a party piece. I think we sang *Flower of Scotland*. We spent a good day

on a boat out in the harbour playing Trivial Pursuit. If you got a question wrong then somebody kicked the ball and you had to swim and get it. That was probably pretty dangerous because there's all sorts of animals swimming round in there, and Rudd could kick the ball a long way.

While Scotland were in Australia, Renwick travelled to South Africa to play for a Five Nations XV against a South African President's XV in a match to celebrate the reopening after renovation of the magnificent Ellis Park.

Syd Millar was the manager, Willie John McBride was the coach and Fergus Slattery was the captain. I only played a half in the big one at Ellis Park, but I got a fortnight's holiday out of it, and we played a couple of other games while we were over there, so I was happy. We trained in the morning, but it wasn't over the top, and we had a good time. I shared a room with Serge Blanco for a couple of nights. He didn't speak much English and even less Hawick, and my French isn't too hot either. So all he said to me during the time we spent together was 'Good morning Jim' and 'Good night Jim'. And all I said to him was 'Bonjour Serge' and 'Bonne nuit Serge'.

The Beginning of the End

The 1981–82 season had ended on a high for Renwick. He'd captained Hawick to their first league victory in four years, played a crucial role in Scotland's historic triumph over Wales in Cardiff, and was by common consent playing some of the best rugby of his career. By comparison the 1982–83 season was a bit of a disappointment.

Hawick could only manage second place in the league behind Gala, which was particularly frustrating given that they defeated their local rivals 13–9 at Mansfield in their second match of the new season. Ultimately, it was their 25–10 defeat by Heriots on 16 October which had cost them the title. If they'd beaten West of Scotland by 109 points in a rearranged fixture at the end of the season Hawick could still have won the title, but both teams agreed not to play the match when a suitable date could not be agreed.

That year the wisdom of raising the number of teams in each league to fourteen was brought into question by the plight of Gordonians, who lost all their games by an average margin of over 30 points. Their two worst results were a 102–4 drubbing by Hawick on 12 March, and an even more embarrassing 112–4 hammering by Gala the following week.

Hawick retained the Border League and their only other defeat in the 32 matches they played that season came in a friendly during December – away to Bill Beaumont's Flyde. Not a bad record – but the big prize had slipped through their fingers.

It was a similar sort of story at international level, where Renwick's old friend Colin Telfer had taken over as Scotland's head coach while his namesake Jim Telfer concentrated on preparing for the up-coming Lions tour of New Zealand.

Rather than build on the potential they had shown at the end of the previous season, and during their tour of Australia in the summer, Scotland managed only two wins in the six matches they played – over Fiji in a non-cap international during September and over a demoralised, wooden spoon winning England the following March.

Against a Fijian team which had already been thrashed by Edinburgh, and well beaten by the South and the Anglos, Scotland fielded their strongest available team. The final score was 32–12, but given the superiority of the Scottish pack it probably should have been much more. Three weeks later England took 60 points off the hapless tourists at Twickenham, which put Scotland's result in context. The Pacific Islanders lost all ten of their matches in Britain that autumn.

With Andy Irvine out for the season with an ankle injury and John Rutherford missing the first three games of the championship after undergoing shoulder operation the previous November Scotland seemed to lack direction during the 1983 Five Nations competition.

In their first match the Scottish forwards were out-thought and out-fought by an experienced and committed Irish pack, which had been branded as a Dad's Army before kick-off. Playing with the wind in the first half the Irish raced into a 15–4 lead at half-time, with Ollie Campbell mastering the gusty conditions to kick three penalties and convert Michael Kiernan's try. Scotland's only score during that 40-minute period came via a Roy Laidlaw try, when the scrum-half scampered down the blindside at a scrum close to the Irish line and hurled himself over the line. In the second half Scotland slowly but surely chipped away at Ireland's lead, with Renwick dropping a goal and Dodds slotting two penalties, which meant that despite losing out in the forward exchanges Scotland were, in the end, only one score away from reversing the result. The 13–15 score line maybe did not do justice to Ireland's superiority, but even so the visitors could count themselves lucky to escape with a win after a late onslaught by the Scots. It took a spectacular leap by Fergus Slattery in the closing seconds to block a last-ditch drop-goal effort by Renwick, which looked certain to go over.

The Scottish forwards made up for their ineffectual performance against Ireland with a ferocious display when they travelled to France for their next match. They raced into a 12–3 lead thanks to a try from Keith Robertson, a penalty and conversion from Peter Dodds and a drop-goal by Bryan Gossman, who had taken over from Ron Wilson at stand-off. However, inspired by the great Serge Blanco, France clawed their way back into the contest. With the scores tied at 15–15, Dodds missed a penalty from in front of the posts – and a few moments later Patrick Esteve went over for the decisive try.

It was one of Renwick's less impressive performances in a Scotland jersey, with Chris Rea commenting that: "The Scottish midfield looked flustered and seldom can Renwick have made so many handling errors in the course of one game."

By the time Wales arrived at Murrayfield in mid February, their selectors had discarded several of the old guard who had played in their shock defeat to Scotland the previous year – including Gareth Davies, Alan Phillips, Graham Price and Ray Gravell. However many doubted whether those who had come in were up to the job, and the selection for this match had been heavily criticised in the press. Scotland bore the brunt of the backlash, as a fired-up Welsh team set out to prove their doubters wrong. After Mark Wyatt's early penalty they never looked like losing. Once again Scotland finished strongly, with Renwick, leading the charge in his 50th international match – but just as with Ireland, it was too little too late.

Scotland needed to take something from their final match of the championship against England at Twickenham if they were to avoid a whitewash, while England had only one draw against Wales to buffer them from the bottom of the table. This was, therefore, a wooden spoon decider.

On the day England played poorly, as they had done for most of the season, and Scotland took full advantage. With Jim Aitken having taken over from Roy Laidlaw as captain, John Rutherford back in the number ten jersey, the back-row in rousing form, and the whole pack's rucking game finally coming together, Scotland started to show glimpses of the ability and sense of purpose which would bring them the Grand Slam the following season.

England drew first blood with a John Horton drop-goal, but with Paxton, Deans and Beattie all making significant in-roads with the ball in hand it seemed to be only a matter of time before Scotland's dominance would be reflected on the score board. Sure enough the visitors should have taken the lead when Keith Robertson broke clear and Renwick was tackled by Steve Smith before being able to collect his fellow centre's pass. Scotland could easily have been awarded a penalty try, but the referee decided a straight penalty would be enough – much to the chagrin of the visiting team. Dodds took the points and had kicked two more penalties by half-time, which was matched by the boot of his opposite number Dusty Hare.

In the second half Scotland were able to put daylight between themselves and their hosts. In the 47th minute Laidlaw took advantage of a quick heel at a scrum close to the English try-line. He swerved outside Nick Jeavons, then straightened the angle of his run to slip past Huw Davies and Hare, before riding John Scott's despairing tackle as he stretched over the line. Hare kept the English in touch with his third penalty of the afternoon, but that was soon cancelled out by a Robertson drop-goal. And in injury time Tom Smith collected the ball at the front of the line-out and flopped over the English line to make it 22–12 which ensured that the Calcutta Cup would spend the next 12 months north of the border for the first time since 1976.

JMR:
I tried a drop-goal and it just about hit the corner flag, then Keith Robertson put one over and as he ran back into position the cheeky bastard says: 'That's the way you do it, Jim.' The other thing I remember about that match was two lassies streaking at half-time and Jim Aitken trying to get our attention – as if we were going to listen to what he was saying while they were running about.

That was only the fourth time we had ever won down there, and the first time we had won there since 1971, so we had a good night afterwards. The guy who used to play the piano at the Scottish rugby dinners was there, so we nabbed him and brought him back to the hotel and we had a sing-song which went on pretty much all night. We've not won there since.

Renwick won his 51st cap in this match, which brought him equal with Andy Irvine's Scottish record, and there was speculation in the press that this would be his swansong at international level, but the player himself was happy to carry on for the time being.

Scotland's last match of the season was against the Barbarians at Murrayfield to celebrate the official opening of the new East Stand, which had been constructed the previous summer at a cost of £3.1 million.

JMR:
The Baa Baas played well that day. They had a strong side out with Jean-Baptiste Lafond, Danie Gerber and Terry Holmes the star performers. Holmesy was causing a hell of a trouble at scrum-half.

But we didn't play well at all – the problem was that a lot of the boys were going with the Lions and they didn't want injured – they wanted to be right, so they didn't push it, which was fair enough really. We ended up well beaten [26–13].

Eight Scots were named in the Lions squad for that tour, but Renwick was not one of them, having declared himself unavailable for selection.

I'd had my shot at the Lions in 1980 and I'd enjoyed it, but it was a long time away from home. Jim Telfer was the coach and I'd toured with him in New Zealand, so I knew it was going to be too much like hard work at that stage of my career.

Besides, Hawick were organising their first ever overseas tour to Boston at the same time, and he was keen to go on that.

Terence Froud:
We put a lot of work into getting the money together for that trip to Boston. We collected lemonade bottles three Sundays on the trot, we organised dances, we did all that sort of stuff – and we ran the London Marathon.

The marathon was on the weekend of the Hawick club dinner, so we went to that on the Friday night and travelled down to London in mini-buses on Saturday morning. That afternoon we went to the Twickenham Sevens. Stew Mel had won it the year before and they were back this year, so Jim and I managed to sneak our way into their changing room where we had a bit of a blether and got some sponsorship money. They said that if they won the sports then we had to win the marathon or they wouldn't pay us – but they got knocked out in the quarter-finals so Jim and I decided to take it easy the next day.

We had a few pints that night and off we went and ran the marathon the next morning. Jim had done a little bit of running, so had I – but we'd done ten miles at the most. Very few of the boys had done anything like the sort of running we should have done. I remember getting to the Isle of Dogs and saying: 'Well, we're in unchartered territory now.' And that was us after thirteen miles or something like that.

We all started as a group but soon got split up, although Jim and I stuck together. He was really struggling after twenty miles and he was ready to chuck it in. I wasn't feeling great either, so we agreed to have a break at the next water stop. But when we came round the corner there was a whole load of Hawick boys – Jock Rae, Colin Gass and Derek Turnbull – having a breather. So Jim wouldn't stop – in fact he picked up the pace because they were standing there. We got round the next corner and he was about dead.

We got over the finishing line at exactly the same time as each other. Jim's story is that he carried me for the last three miles – but if he had done that then he would have still been out there yet.

When you get to the finish they put those tinfoil blankets over you,
Jim said at the beginning that he wasn't putting that on because it was
soft – but that was the first thing he grabbed when he got over that line.

Three weeks before setting off for Boston, Renwick was playing for Hawick
against Edinburgh Academicals in the second round at Langholm sports
when he was tackled fractionally late. He felt his knee jar and knew
straight away that it was serious.

He was replaced by Robbie Douglas, and Hawick battled on to the
semi-finals where they were defeated by Jed. Renwick had ruptured the
cruciate ligament in his left knee and would miss the first three months
of the following season, and Scotland's first Grand Slam since 1925.

The Rust Sets In

The extent of Renwick's knee injury wasn't fully apparent when he hobbled onto the plane which would take Hawick RFC on their first major overseas tour to Boston in mid May 1983. Having had a major role in organising the trip he was determined to travel no matter what, and he even harboured hopes that he might be able to play. It quickly became obvious to everyone on the trip that this was a pipe dream.

JMR:
Along with Robin Charters, I was one of the key guys in getting the thing going. There was a bit of a rift in the club, some folk thought the money should be used for other things, but we went anyway and I think the success we had in the years that followed proves that it was the right thing for the club to do.

It was a funny set up they had in that tournament. Winning the games didn't win you the tournament – you were rated on how you played and how you toured, so I suppose really it was the best all-round club that won, which isn't a bad way of doing it. It was a good standard of rugby with clubs like Orrell, from England, and Lansdowne, from Ireland, there. But Hawick won all three of their matches, played really well, and had a good time – so they couldn't really give it to anyone else.

I'd hoped my knee would be alright, but when I got there it was obvious that there was no way I was going to be able to play. So I had to be Hawick's representative on the judging panel and rate the other teams. It was a pain in the arse because the rest of the boys were already away enjoying themselves, but it was the least I could do given that I wasn't able to play. And you got to meet a lot of interesting folk, so it wasn't too bad.

It was a good trip and the boys enjoyed themselves, and it set the tone for the next couple of years at Hawick. That was beginning of the new guard coming in, and they won the league for the next four years.

I would think a lot of that was down to that trip to Boston. It was a
good way of pulling it all together.

Back on home soil Hawick embarked upon perhaps their most successful
season ever. By the end of the campaign they had won all thirteen of their
league matches, lost only once whilst retaining the Border League, and
in all matches scored more than 1000 points for the first time in the
club's history.

Renwick was back in action for Hawick by mid November, making his
first appearance of the season in a 27–12 victory over Kelso on 19 November
– one week after Scotland's 25–25 draw with Stu Wilson's All Blacks at
Murrayfield.

The previous summer the Lions had endured a torrid tour of New
Zealand. But this All Blacks team was a shadow of the side which had
dismantled Jim Telfer's squad four months earlier. The tour had been
organised at short notice after the situation in the Falklands caused
Argentina's visit to be cancelled, and several key players were unable to
travel. The whole front-five from the Lions whitewash – John Ashworth,
skipper Andy Dalton, Gary Knight, Andy Haden and Gary Whetton –
were missing; as was scrum-half Dave Loveridge, who had been the man
of the series. With 13 new All Blacks in the 26 man tour party this New
Zealand squad was a shadow of the force it would normally be. They lost
to both Midland Counties and England on that trip. Under the circumstances the draw was less than Scotland had hoped for.

After the New Year Scotland defeated Wales in Cardiff (15–9), England
at Murrayfield (18–6) and Ireland in Dublin (32–9) before meeting France
at home in a winner-takes-all Grand Slam decider. In a tense and hard-
fought match Scotland seemed to cling on for dear life in the first half,
before French indiscipline played a key role as the Scots slowly but surely
wrestled the initiative away from the visitors. Then, with scores tied at
12–12, Jim Calder latched onto a deflected ball at a line-out close to the
French line and bundled himself over the chalk, to give Scotland their
first Grand Slam since 1925.

JMR:
Obviously I was disappointed to miss out on the Grand Slam season
but I didn't lose any sleep over it. I'd been injured and there was nothing
I could do about that. And maybe we wouldn't have done so well if I
had been playing.

I was playing for Hawick all the way through the Grand Slam but I wasn't right. I actually played for the Blues in the National Trial after Euan Kennedy dropped out with a viral infection, but we got a bit of a doing off the Whites and when Euan was fit again they went with him, which was the right decision. He did well for them that season until he injured his knee.

When that happened they decided to go with Keith Robertson in the centre, but I almost managed to squeeze my way into the squad for the Ireland game. Ian McGregor, the chairman of selectors, phoned me and said that one of the boys was struggling and asked if I would be available to come into the squad if they needed a late replacement. I don't know who it was that was in doubt, but it never came to anything anyway – which was maybe just as well because I was far from at my best. In fact I don't think my knee was ever right again – it still bothers me yet.

Renwick was able to salvage something from the international season when he was selected for Scotland's three-match mini-tour of Romania in May – giving him the opportunity to step ahead of Andy Irvine to become Scotland's most capped player with 52 appearances to his name.

At the end of the season I came into a bit of form and then I played well when we won the Hawick sevens, and I think that must have been what got me in. I think it helped that Robin Charters was the manager and Colin Telfer was the coach. I'm not sure if Euan Kennedy, whose place I got, was so pleased. Mind you he'd been out for a while with a knee injury so he wasn't fully fit either.

Romania wasn't a great place to tour. It was before the revolution and there was nothing in the shops, there was no food, you couldn't get a cup of coffee, and folk were feared to speak to you. When I went on tour I always tried to bring something back, and the only thing I could find to buy in Romania was a mandolin, so that was what I brought back from there.

We'd brought our own supplies with us, so the boys were queuing up for rations of one Cuppa Soup and one chocolate bar a day. I remember one day giving a kid a Mars Bar at training and the next day there was about a hundred kids there. I think Norrie Rowan brought his own camping stove and a whole load of tins of beans. I'm pretty sure we phoned Bill McLaren in Hawick and asked him to bring some supplies when he flew out to do the commentary.

I remember Sean McGaughey doing pull-ups over the side of a balcony in the hotel – there was nothing to do so we were just making our own fun, killing time before the Test match that afternoon. We both got our last caps on that trip – it's just a shame it was also McGaughey's first. He had played well and deserved his chance, it's just a shame he didn't go on from there because he was some player when he put his mind to it, and he could have been a big performer for Scotland for years.

But he was a wild man. I remember playing for the South down in England somewhere and we were staying at this hotel on the Friday night. There was a wedding going on down the stairs and I got speaking to one of the guests.

'You come from Scotland?' he says.

'Aye.'

'So what do Scottish folk do at weddings?'

'Well let us in and we'll show you.'

So we get in, have a few pints, and the next thing one of the boys is slow dancing with the bride, and he slips his hands doon onto her arse in the middle of the dance floor. The groom clocks them, goes over and pulls them apart – but before you can say jack-mouse Sean's right across the table and banjos the groom. There's blood all over her wedding dress. What a carry-on: the groom's lying in the corner and Sean's got the mad-dog in him. We manage to pull him away and get out the road and it all calms down, but we probably ruined their wedding.

Anyway, we played Romania on a scorching hot day and in the second half we just ran out of steam. Romania were a good outfit then, they had some good players and they used to beat France fairly regularly. They'd beaten Wales earlier in the year. So it was disappointing that we got beat but it wasn't the end of the world. We'd taken quite a young squad and we weren't expecting to set the world alight.

Jim Telfer couldn't travel so Colin Telfer was head coach on that tour, and I think he found it tough. He tried to be hard but he couldn't pull it off. He'd tell us it was time to go to bed and we'd say: 'Aye right Telfer, is that what you'd do?' I took on board what he said at training and all that – but I knew, and he knew, that he wouldn't have gone to bed if it was the other way round. He'd have had another vodka fresh. Maybe I should have toed the line with him more and that might have made things easier for him, but that wasn't the way it worked between us.

The following season Australia toured Britain. Unlike their predecessors in 1981 this squad had no problems adapting to the weather conditions of a northern hemisphere winter, and had the power up front to allow their scintillating backs to shine. With Mark Ella the commander-in-chief at stand-off they strode to their first ever Grand Slam over the four home unions.

Scotland were in the unfortunate position of being Australia's final hurdle in their Grand Slam run, and the tourists were in irresistible form in that match at Murrayfield on 8 December 1984. David Leslie and John Rutherford were both unavailable through injury, while Renwick was named on the bench. Australia won 37–12, with tries coming from David Campese twice, Ella and Nick Farr-Jones. All Scotland's points came from the boot of Peter Dodds.

JMR:
I didn't want on that day. They played with this flat alignment and would come at you with four of five players coming off the stand-off at pace. Even if you picked the right man it was tough to defend because they were running at great angles and comfortable off-loading out the tackle. It took a high skill level and a lot of pace but they had it sussed and it was very, very hard to defend. They were a good side – I don't think they were as good as the All Blacks up front but I like the way they attacked. They beat all four countries playing good rugby.

The South beat them 9–6 in the rain at Mansfield the week before and I had played in that match, but it was a different story when they got to Murrayfield. They had a few Test team players in the side that played against the South, but you could tell they weren't that bothered about grinding out the win. They were there to win the big matches.

The teams for the Test match were:

Scotland: P.W. Dodds (Gala); P.D. Steven (Heriots), A.E. Kennedy (Watsonians), K.W. Robertson (Melrose), G.R.T. Baird (Kelso); D.S. Wyllie (Stewart's Melville), R.J. Laidlaw (Jed-Forest); A.D.G. McKenzie (Selkirk), C.T. Deans (Hawick), I.G. Milne (Harlequins), A.J. Tomes (Hawick), W. Cuthbertson (Harlequins), J.H. Calder (Stewart's Melville), J.R. Beattie (Glasgow Academicals), J. Jeffrey (Kelso).

Australia: R. Gould; F. Grigg, A. Slack, M. Lynagh, D. Campese; M. Ella, N. Farr-Jones; E. Rodriguez, T. Lawton, A. McIntyre, S. Cutler, S. Williams, D. Codey, S Tuyman, S Poidevin.

That match was to be Renwick's last involvement with the national team. By the time the Five Nations championship kicked off with an 18–15 home defeat to Ireland on 2 February 1985, he'd stepped aside and Keith Murray was wearing the number thirteen jersey for Scotland. Murray was team-mate of Renwick's at club level, and his promotion was a vivid demonstration of the changing face of the national side at that time. By the end of the season Renwick had decided that this would be his last as a Hawick player as well.

JMR:
All the older guys like Cranny and Heg were finishing up, and young guys like Keith Murray were coming through, so it was time to move on. I suppose it was like 1970, when I first came into the side. There were a lot of good players around who had done a great job for Hawick over the years, but if the club stood still it was in danger of getting left behind. It was time for the next generation to take things forward.

Playing For Fun

You can watch rugby, you can coach rugby, you can talk about rugby, you can write about rugby and you can read about rugby. But nothing can beat playing rugby. My advice to anyone who enjoys the game is to play it as long as you can, because you're a long time retired and you don't appreciate how good it is until you can't do it anymore.

Jim Renwick

It might have been time to move on from Hawick, but Renwick wasn't ready to hang up his boots quite yet. He went back to play for the Quins which was a bit of a culture shock at first.

JMR:
I remember my first game back there. I went into the dressing room and there was a stink of beer – some of the boys must have been out on the sauce the night before. It was very different to what I was used to. Guys were missing training, putting their work before their rugby, and things like that. But what do you do? Do you shoot your mouth off and try to change everything at once? Or do you let it go and hope that the guys see what you're trying to do and buy into it?

Well . . . I wasn't going to come in and tell them how to do it. I was there as a player, I was happy to help out with some coaching if they needed me, but it wasn't my place to call the shots. And I'm a laid back guy, I wouldn't want to push folk into doing things they don't want to do. I suppose I became a wee bit like the rest of the players – if I didn't fancy it I wouldn't go. But to be honest that only happened the once, and I was disappointed with myself so I didn't do it again.

In the end we tightened it up, but it took a while and we made sure we didn't get too serious, because the boys still wanted to enjoy themselves. We won the Border Junior League in 1986 and we had a bit of success on the junior sevens circuit. I think it was a good time to be at the club.

Gary Murdie, who played at the club at that time recalls:

> He was still really fit, and he was the catalyst for a couple of good seasons for the Quins. We didn't have a great team and he basically held everybody together.
>
> He was a big influence both on and off the pitch. There's not many coaches that all the boys want to sit next to on the bus after the game, but that was what it was like with Jim.
>
> I remember one Saturday we stopped in Gala for a late night. Jim and a few other players went to one pub and came back with this huge vodka bottle which they said they had won in a raffle. They wouldn't let us open it until we got back to the clubrooms and all the chat on the bus was about the drinking games we were going to play and that sort of stuff – it got the boys on a bit of a high. It was only when we got back to Hawick and opened it that we found out it was only water. He was always playing little tricks like that, which kept the thing going.

Renwick played three years at the Quins but was finding it harder and harder physically. Then he agreed to help his friend Hector Barnfather by coaching the backs at Langholm for half a season, and he ended up playing a few games for the club at stand-off.

> JMR:
> I didn't really want to, but it was the usual story – you go along to help and you end up doing more and more.
>
> It's a fair old drive to Langholm, and I remember going down there to train one night and the weather was really bad and I only just managed to make it through. When I got there I found there'd been a power-cut so there was no lights and the pitch was covered in snow. I was all for turning round and heading straight back to Hawick, but they had a big game coming up and they were desperate to get something out of the night. So we had the car head lights shining over the pitch and we worked hard for an hour and when we came off we were all soaked. But the showers were cold so I just jumped straight back in the car and drove home. I'd just got back ower Mosspaul and I thought: 'Why am I putting myself through all this hassle?' I suppose it was just that Hector asked me and because I had a soft spot for Langholm I said I'd help out.
>
> I've always liked and admired Langholm. For a town of 2000 folk they've produced a lot of good players over the years. The club has gone through a tough time recently but they're starting to turn it around again, and I'm pretty sure that it will always survive at some level. Rugby suits

the way Langholm folk are brought up – hard working boys from the mills and the farms.

During the seventies they were always a good, hard side and you were always pretty happy to come away from there with a result. A lot of teams met the sword at Langholm. On the far side of the pitch they had a moving crowd – they called them the 'waterside crowd' – and although there was only a few hundred of them at most, it seemed like there were thousands because they followed the play up and down the touch-line all the way through the game. And it didn't matter if you had 52 caps or you were a schoolboy playing your first game: they gave you nothing. They'd be over the fence shouting at you and giving you dog's abuse. The only thing you could do was ignore them and concentrate on the game, which wasn't easy to do with all that abuse ringing in your ears.

When you got on the pitch at Langholm the first thing you would do was count how many players they had on their side. When you played Langholm they were always right in your faces and it sometimes seemed like there was a hundred of them out there – and I'm pretty sure there would be that many if they thought they could get away with it.

Langholm always wanted Hawick to move the ball so that they could get in amongst us, but we always kept it tight and the crowd never liked that. Their ball skills were maybe not as good as they should have been, and they sometimes lacked a bit of pace, but they made up for it in other ways. They were committed guys and they were masters of gamesmanship. They would try and get one over you in any way they could.

We used to always play them on Boxing Day, but 1971 was their centenary year and for some reason we ended up playing them on Christmas Day. Hector Munro was the Langholm President at the time and he came into the changing room before the match and said he wanted us to stand outside and sing 'We Wish You a Merry Christmas' when Langholm ran onto the pitch. Derrick Grant looked at Norman Suddon and they both said at the same time: 'You must be joking.' We were there to get our arses kicked and they wanted us to wish them a Merry Christmas and a Happy New Year before they did it. Eventually we agreed to give them three cheers when they ran on the pitch.

Derrick [Grant] tells a story about going to Langholm one night with Hawick for a Border League match. He was captain and when he went to toss-up he could see in their changing room all the match balls floating in the bath. Of course Langholm always wanted it wet so that it would level the skills, but it was a nice night and they must have decided to take matters into their own hands. Derrick told them to take a hike and eventually they found a new set of balls to play with, but after the first line-out the wet balls were back again. That was sort of things they would do.

I remember playing for the Quins there when I was just coming through. We were on their seconds pitch up at the Castleholm and Norrie Leadbetter made a break. He was running up the wing, clear of everyone and a certainty to score, but this Langholm boy whose been lying on the touchline injured for the last ten minutes jumps up and tackles him from behind. Norrie didn't know what had hit him – how can you expect that? I think it was in the same game that I put a kick into touch which hit a tree at the side of the pitch and came back down into play. Their full back just collected the ball and kept on going.

Langholm is always the last sports of the season so we always used to have a late night there. We used to have sing-songs in all the pubs and it was just a great atmosphere. I got knocked out the first time I played there in 1970 and I injured my knee there in 1983, so it's not always been a happy hunting ground for me but I've got a few Langholm medals too and I just like it there. It's not the biggest tournament but you go up there, have a bit of banter and it's always a good day out. They've also got the second best Common Riding in the Borders. So when Hector asked me to come down and take the backs I was happy to help out.

Coaching

After his brief stint at Langholm, Renwick spent a couple of seasons when he was not officially attached to any club. But despite previous promises that he would quit rugby altogether when his playing days were over, he could not resist wandering along to watch either Hawick or the Quins train – "just to see what was going on and get a bit of banter with the boys". The game had been too big a part of his life for too long to go cold turkey. He even answered a couple of SOS calls – turning out for both clubs at various points.

Derrick Grant had stopped coaching at Hawick in 1983 but came back for a season and a half in the early nineties when the club were going through a sticky patch. At this point Renwick agreed to coach the backs, and his standing at the club allied with his knowledge and enthusiasm for the game proved invaluable.

Tony Stanger, who came through the Hawick system, was capped 52 times on the wing for Scotland, and is now speed and skills coach at London Irish.

> He had been finished playing for a couple of years before I got into the Hawick side, but he used to come down to watch training and he'd always be happy to give you advice. You could tell that Jim thought about the game a lot more than he let on. I remember after one match he gave me a critique of my performance, he'd written down all his thoughts, and this was before he was officially involved as a coach at the club.
>
> Jim was someone you could go to and ask for an opinion and be confident of getting a straight answer without any bullshit attached. It was a few years before he actually began to coach us on an official basis but when that did happen he really did do a great job. He was only there for two seasons while I was there but during that time it was great to have a coach who was prepared to tell you, good or bad, what he thought of your performance on the pitch.

He had some great ideas and regularly came up with some really original stuff. We had a mixed bag as a back division, we were quite often cobbled together, but he always made the most out of what he had.

And to have someone as highly regarded as Jim there . . . well . . . you want to please him, you want to show him that you're a good player and I think that's what he also brought to it. He's so well known and so well liked that you want to be good for him.

Coming back from the Scotland set-up, I think it's always useful to have the opinion of someone from outside that environment who you respect and trust. I could have a more open conversation with Jim about my international performance than if I was speaking to my national coach, and I'm certain that helped me a lot as a player.

You learn lessons from every coach you play with – sometimes it is something you would want to use yourself and other times its things that you don't think work – from Jim I would say I learned a lot about enthusiasm, being passionate about what you are doing and genuinely wanting to make a difference. He just loves the game, and even if you are a full-time professional you've got to enjoy it – otherwise, what's the point? There are other ways to make a living.

What sticks in my mind is that he had the knowledge and he had the willingness to work with anyone – whether they were a seasoned internationalist or a junior player in the side for a one-off game.

Since then Renwick has had two more spells coaching at Hawick – between 1994 and 1996 when the club won the inaugural Scottish Cup, and between 1998 and 2000. On each occasion he was an assistant to a friend who was prepared to take the lead in terms of managing and co-ordinating the team, insisting that he was not comfortable with the idea of being the driving force but would much rather be the side-kick.

JMR:
I've always said that I only coach what I know, but it's becoming harder to do that because the game is far more integrated now with backs and forwards doing each others' job.

In the old days you could ask someone, when does back play start? And the answer was easy: when the scrum-half gets the ball after a scrum, a line-out, a ruck, or a maul. But that's not the case anymore, because backs and forwards are so integrated.

As for getting satisfaction from coaching, I'm not sure I've ever had that. Maybe I've not had enough success. I'm not an ambitious guy but even still I've never really achieved what I wanted to achieve in coaching. Having said that I don't think I ever had a clear idea of what I wanted to achieve, I just helped out where I wanted to and did the best I could at the time. I don't think I ever wanted to become a professional coach.

But I do like coaching. I don't like the sheep that just do what they're told, I like when guys ask questions and if they disagree with me then I don't have a problem with that.

Renwick's philosophy towards coaching is simple.

I think I've got the same attitude as Pierre Villepreux, the French full back in the seventies. He was a classy player who went on to be a good French coach. He was very open-minded – the type of guy who would say: 'Right, I want four defenders in the line there, and I want four attackers in the line there – now I'm away for a cup of tea and while I'm away I want the attackers to try and score and I want the defenders to try and stop them. I want you to have ten goes each.' He'd go for his cup of tea, come back and say: 'Right, what have you found out?'

It's about learning to read what you see – rather than learning to do what you're told. It's no good the coaches having all the answers, it's the players that have to have all the answers. And that's the art of creative coaching – it's getting over to the players the basics of what the team are trying to do, without stifling their individuality.

Mind you, coaches need to put the players through their paces as well. You need to have done the hard graft first, because that's the base on top of which you can do all the nice stuff. So it's about finding a balance between getting players thinking about the game and expressing themselves, and getting them ready to do the dirty work. I don't know how many coaches can do both, that's maybe why you need a couple of coaches working together.

Renwick continued to play for various invitational sides and in veteran matches until he was well into his forties. Fergus Slattery, the great Irish flanker of the seventies, recalls playing against Renwick in a charity match in Dublin.

"At one point I grabbed him and smacked him off the ground," he says. "It took him two minutes to catch me up and do the same thing back. So, even in a charity game for old crocks, the competitive instinct was there."

Since 2003 Renwick has coached at Edinburgh Academicals.

JMR

I finished coaching at Hawick and then out of the blue I got early retirement from the electricity board so I was at a bit of a loose end. By that time Barney was coaching at Edinburgh Accies and he asked me to come up and help out. Terence was team manager at the time and Crab [Kenny McCartney] said he'd do the backs with me, so it was just like old times.

It's different from coaching at Hawick because afterwards I can get in the car, come back down the road, and escape all the hassle. But I enjoy it and there are some good boys at the club. I don't think rugby is as important to them as it is to Hawick boys, but there's a few guys there with potential, and if we can start getting them thinking about it a bit more then who knows? They might surprise themselves.

At the start of the 2004–05 season Edinburgh Accies played their first pre-season friendly away to Livingston. It was a sunny day and Renwick was in shorts and a t-shirt. The pitch was rock solid and a succession of Accies players picked up injuries. At one stage they were down to thirteen men so Renwick decided to come on at stand-off. "Are you not a bit old to be playing this game you little fat bastard," shouted his opposite number. A few moments later the same player tried to step inside Renwick and was flattened by a forearm smash – his legs were still going when his body hit the ground.

A Contented Man

Having retired from the electricity board in 2003, Jim Renwick now works two days a week for a local company called Border Safeguard – helping his friend Jake Whillans install burglar alarms.

JMR:
It gets me out the house. When I'm 60 I might feel that I don't want to do anything at all, but I'm still only 54 and if I wasn't doing any work I'd be pretty bored.

It gives me a wee bit extra pocket money so that we can afford to go on holiday or splash out on a treat for ourselves once in a while. I usually work with Jake on Mondays and Tuesdays. I try to do something positive on Wednesdays – a bit of DIY around the house or something like that – then the rest of the week I behave like a retired man. If it's a nice morning I might pack a sandwich and go out for a walk over the hills. I spent a lot of my working life in the countryside – checking power lines, installing new lines and all that sort of stuff. Quite a lot of the time it was about getting your head down and grafting. It was a fair wage for a fair day's work and I always enjoyed being out and about. Sometimes we were just walking through field and along country lanes checking that everything was in order and that was great. Old habits must die hard because I still enjoy getting out and seeing a bit of the countryside. I'd like it better if there was a few guys with me, but most of my pals are still working, which means that there's usually nobody around, so I just go myself.

During the winter I'm up training at Edinburgh Accies every Tuesday and Thursday night. I'll carry on helping out there until it becomes too much of a hassle. I know I'm one of the last of the old-style guys, as there won't be many coaches still around who made their senior debut in 1970, but I think I still have something to offer. And I've always been the kind of guy who is happy to take on advice from boys that have a different point of view, so hopefully I'm not too out of touch. At the start of the season I phoned John Thorburn and he arranged for me to watch the Reivers team train – just to see how the professional boys are doing it and to get some new ideas.

A lot of guys of my generation think the game has changed for the worse but I wouldn't want to say that. All I know is that my boys play rugby now and they think it's great – and who am I to tell them it was better in my day. You can only play in your own time and I enjoyed my time – we had good fun on an off the pitch. But I think the boys that play now do as well. I know I still enjoy being involved. You'll always get good boys playing rugby – it's that sort of sport.

If I wasn't still involved in coaching I might go along and watch the Reivers play on a Friday night, but to be honest I think I would rather go to Mansfield to watch Hawick on a Saturday, even if the standard isn't as good. I'm not interested in doing both and I don't think many people are, that's just too much rugby. I'm not against the Reivers but I was a Hawick man long before the Reivers came along, and you can't just change overnight, no matter how much the SRU want that to happen. So the club game is always going to encroach on the pro game, at least as far as crowds are concerned, which is a problem, but to be honest I don't see any way around that.

I suppose what they should be doing is targeting people like my son Neil. He's playing on Saturdays so he's looking for something to do on a Friday night that doesn't involve going to the pub, and it would do him good to watch the professionals in action. But they have to make it attractive and make it into something that boys can relate to. They'll have to start winning a few games to do that.

I'll always try to get a round of golf in with Harry Whitaker on a Friday afternoon. Harry was a great scrum-half for Hawick in the sixties and would have got caps if he hadn't gone to play rugby league. He's been back in Hawick for about twenty years now and I've got pretty friendly with him. We play golf together on Fridays and sometimes during the week, then on Saturdays we'll go for a few drinks at the High Level and then maybe take the wives out for a meal.

As two of Hawick's most gifted sons, the pair are often asked if they ever played rugby together. Whitaker's answer is always the same. "No – and if we had they would have needed two balls," he says.

As a whisky drinker Whitaker usually reaches the bottom of his glass before his beer drinking friends, and if it is Renwick's turn to buy the next round he will invariably comment that: "Harry's got a speech impediment – he can't say no."

JMR:

I don't drink that often these days – only at the weekend. I'll drink on a Saturday night, on a Sunday afternoon, and that's about it – unless there's something going on during the week. But most of the time I'm quite happy sitting in the house watching an old movie or the football on the telly.

I enjoy going to the High Level because it's all familiar faces. Harry and Terence will be there, a few of the older guys like Jock Edgar and Billy Hunter still come along, and Addie occasionally makes it down – but he's had a few problems with his hips recently so we've missed him a bit.

I go to the gym three times a week. Not so much to lose weight but just to keep the heart beating – because a fat man who's fit has less chance of dying than a skinny man who isn't.

I enjoy a bet on the horses, but nothing major. I'm happy putting a couple of quid on just to have an interest. There are quite a lot of serious gamblers at the High Level, but I'm not one of them.

Renwick was divorced from Shelagh in the mid 1980s and now lives with his partner Jane Gilligan and their three children Neil (born on 3 April 1988), Stuart (16 November 1990) and Alex (9 May 1993), in a flat on Buccleuch Street in Hawick – not quite in the West End but only the punt of a rugby ball away.

It's the perfect place for me to be living. I've never been interested in having a fancy house with a great big garden – this place has got everything I need. Jane's hairdressing shop is down the stair, we're just round the corner from the West End, and just along the road from Hawick High Street. That's perfect as far as I'm concerned. I can't see myself ever needing to move.

On the evening of 31 December 1999 Renwick and his family climbed to the top of the Moat to greet the arrival of the year 2000. They then rushed down to Mansfield Park, switched on the floodlights and got out a rugby ball. That night James Menzies Renwick kicked the first penalty of the new millennium at the famous ground where he had enjoyed fourteen great years as a player. Then Neil Renwick kicked the first drop-goal of the 21st century, Stuart punted the ball through the posts, and Alex scored the first try. "I couldn't think of a better way of starting the new millennium," says Renwick.

I'm quite a contented man really. I'm retired now and I'm never going to be a millionaire, but I've got enough to get by. I've never been ambitious and I've always been quite happy with life. I've seen the world and made a lot of friends playing rugby. I suppose I've always been a pretty lucky boy.

Index